CHALLENGING THE MYTH OF GENDER EQUALITY IN SWEDEN

Edited by
Lena Martinsson, Gabriele Griffin
and Katarina Giritli Nygren

First published in Great Britain in 2016 by

Policy Press
University of Bristol
1-9 Old Park Hill
Bristol
BS2 8BB
UK
t: +44 (0)117 954 5940
pp-info@bristol.ac.uk
www.policypress.co.uk

North America office:
Policy Press
c/o The University of Chicago Press
1427 East 60th Street
Chicago, IL 60637, USA
t: +1 773 702 7700
f: +1 773-702-9756
sales@press.uchicago.edu
www.press.uchicago.edu

© Policy Press 2016

British Library Cataloguing in Publication Data
A catalogue record for this book is available from the British Library

Library of Congress Cataloging-in-Publication Data
A catalog record for this book has been requested

ISBN 978-1-4473-2596-3 hardcover

Cover design by Soapbox Design
Printed and bound in Great Britain by Marston Book Services Ltd, Oxfordshire
Policy Press uses environmentally responsible print partners

For Siv Fahlgren,
Professor of Gender Studies extraordinaire

Contents

List of figures and tables

Figures

Table

Notes on contributors

Siv Fahlgren is Professor Emerita in Gender Studies at Mid Sweden University. Fahlgren's research has focused on criticism of scientific theory and methodological issues from a gender perspective. In her current research she uses normalisation as a central analytical tool in order to analyse the processes that define and produce what is considered 'normal' and thus privileged, *at the same time* as it produces 'the other'.

Katarina Giritli Nygren is Associate Professor in Sociology, and the Director of the Forum for Gender Studies, Mid Sweden University. Her current research deals with normalisation in different contexts.

Gabriele Griffin is Professor of Gender Research at Uppsala University Sweden. She was previously Professor of Women's Studies at the University of York, UK. Her research interests centre on Women's Studies as a discipline and on women's cultural production, in particular theatre. She is editor of the Research Methods for the Arts and Humanities series (Edinburgh University Press), and was co-founding and managing editor of *Feminist Theory* (1999–2009). Recent publications include *Cross-cultural interviewing: feminist experiences and reflections* (editor, Routledge 2016) and *Research methods for reading digital data in the humanities* (co-editor with Matt Hayler, Edinburgh University Press, 2016).

Anders Johansson is a lecturer in Literary Studies at Mid Sweden University. He is currently working on a book concerned with poetry and materiality as well as analysing how normalisation works in contemporary Swedish society.

Nina Lykke is Professor of Gender and Culture at the Unit of Gender Studies, Linköping University, Sweden. She is Co-Director of the international research centre GEXcel Collegium for Advanced Transdisciplinary Gender Studies, LiU-ÖU-KaU, and Director of the Swedish-International Gender Research School, InterGender. She has published extensively within the fields of feminist cultural studies, including studies of technoscience and feminist theory, among others, in *Feminist Studies* (2010). Her current research focuses on patienthood, from feminist materialist and intersectional perspectives.

Lena Martinsson is Professor in Gender Studies at the University of Gothenburg. Her research interests focus on intersectional, queer and postcolonial studies in relation to norms on gender equality and diversity. She has co-edited several books, including *Skola I normer* [School in norms] (2008); *Norm-struggles* (2010); and *Norms at work* (2007).

Diana Mulinari is Professor at the Centre of Gender Studies at the University of Lund. She has published extensively on racism and the extreme Right in Sweden, including a co-edited volume on *Complying with colonialism: Gender, race and ethnicity in the Nordic region* (Ashgate, 2009).

Gunilla Olofsdotter is a Lecturer in Sociology at Mid Sweden University. She has done extensive research on the flexibilisation of Swedish work life and its gendered patterns. Her recent publications include "'The other woman": Construction needs in a training project for disabled women and immigrant women', in *Normalization and 'outsiderhood': feminist readings of a neoliberal welfare state* (eds S. Fahlgren, A. Johansson and D. Mulinari).

Paulina de los Reyes is Professor of Economic History at Stockholm University. She has conducted research on gender, ethnicity and intersectionality, with a special emphasis on working life. Her research interests also include feminist theory, postcolonial feminism and globalisation.

Angelika Sjöstedt Landén is a lecturer in Gender Studies at Mid Sweden University and a PhD student in ethnology at the Department for Culture and Media Studies at Umeå University in Sweden. Her research interests include studies of work life, ethnographic methods and poststructuralist and feminist theory. She has published in *Qualitative Research* and in the *Nordic Journal of Feminist and Gender Research* (NORA).

Kajsa Widegren is Senior Lecturer in Gender Studies at the University of Gothenburg, Sweden. She published her PhD in 2010 in which she explore discourses on sexualisation and constructions of girlhood in Swedish contemporary art. Since 2012 she has been involved in a research programme with a case study on Japanese environmental movements after the crisis in Fukushima 2011.

Acknowledgements

In the course of our work we benefited from the support of several other institutions: Mid Sweden University, Sundsvall and the Forum for Gender Studies, which hosted a number of workshops, where Katarina Giritli Nygren works as Associate Professor, and where Gabriele Griffin was visiting professor and guest researcher; the Centre for Gender Research at Uppsala University, where Gabriele Griffin was visiting professor in 2015. Professor Lena Martinsson had the support of the Centre for Interdisciplinary Gender Research, University of Gothenburg, and of the Beatrice Bain Research Group at Berkeley University, USA, where she was a guest researcher in 2015. The editors also benefitted from discussion and exchanges with many colleagues, whom we'd like to thank – you know who you are.

Finally, we'd like to thank Policy Press for responding enthusiastically to this project, Victoria Pittman for being such a supportive editor, and the production team for making it all possible.

Introduction: challenging the myth of gender equality in Sweden

Lena Martinsson, Gabriele Griffin, Katarina Giritli Nygren

> Sweden ranks as one of the world's most gender-egalitarian countries, based on a firm belief that men and women should share power and influence equally. An extensive welfare system makes it easier for both sexes to balance work and family life. However, the Government recognises that there is still room for improvement in many areas. (Sweden.se, Official source for facts about Sweden)[1]

The Nordic model of gender equality has been constructed as very successful in both national and international discourses (Esping-Andersen, 1990; Melby et al, 2009). One of these Nordic countries, Sweden, has a strong and well-documented self-image as the most modern and gender-equal country in the world, an image described by many as 'Swedish exceptionalism' (de los Reyes et al, 2002; Andersson, 2009; Shierup and Åhlund, 2011; Habel, 2012; Fahlgren, 2013).

Feminist, queer, anti-racist and postcolonial scholars in Sweden argue that while gender equality as a mythical Swedish success story has become a mantra nationally as well as internationally, this cherishing of the gender-equality norm is also highly problematic. This mantra, as the opening quote indicates, makes gender equality a national trait, which belies the actuality of equality in Sweden, not least in an age when the welfare state is in retrenchment and neoliberal politics rule. It also ignores that this gender-equality model (re)produces a whole range of problematic norms. Our aim in this volume is to explore the Swedish gender-equality model and ask what norms, emotions, challenges and fantasies are produced through, as well as iterated by, this mantra. Drawing on extensive research (de los Reyes, 2001, 2002; Molina and Mulinari, 2002; Martinsson, 2006; Dahl, 2005; Mattsson, 2010; Listerborn, 2011; Lundahl, 2010; Mulinari and Selberg, 2013; Mulinari and Neergaard, 2014), we suggest that the hegemonic norm of gender equality in Sweden builds upon and produces naturalised, nationalist, hetero- and cisnormative and racialised positions in a postcolonial and neoliberal time and space. We will analyse the actuality of equality politics and policies in Sweden in relation to their enactment and argue that the gender-equality norm is strongly performative (Butler, 1990) in ways that are not always predictable. In the Afterword, the possibility of rethinking the Swedish gender-equality model will be discussed.

Although we critique the model of Swedish gender equality in this volume, we also want to differentiate ourselves clearly from other critical voices that challenge this model. The notion that Sweden is the most gender-equal country in the world, and that the Swedish people are therefore the most gender equal, is a problem also for conservative forces. Since the mid-2000s a highly vocal anti-feminist movement[2] called 'jämställdisterna' (Ström, 2007) has challenged the gender-equality project, and the culturally racist right-wing party the Sweden Democrats (*Sverigedemokraterna*), now represented in the Swedish Parliament, wants to change laws and education curricula in order to get rid of gender-equality goals in schools and society at large.[3] For us, it is therefore important to take a stand in support of the gender-equality project, even as we argue that this project needs to be significantly transformed in order to have radical potential.

In much of the literature on welfare states and gender equality the Nordic states are held up as a unified model for gender-equality policies (see, for example, Gornick and Meyers, 2009). In this volume, however, we do not use the 'Nordic countries' or the 'Nordic model' as our starting point. There are three main reasons for this: the first is that the concept of the 'Nordic model' involves a regionalised notion, not tied to nationally specific feelings and self-understandings. Talking about the 'Nordic model' or the 'Nordic countries' therefore conceals the effects of the ongoing co-articulations of nationalism and the gender-equality norm we want to problematise. Second, while national feelings in relation to the gender-equality norm are also significant in the other Nordic countries (see Chapter Five in this volume), there are some differences between Sweden, Denmark, Iceland, Finland and Norway that make Sweden an especially important case. Sweden has been described as having the most institutionalised model of gender equality. This is partly because feminist issues have never gained the same ground in political parties in the other Nordic countries as they have done in Sweden. Swedes continue to be reminded of this, since the majority of the Swedish political parties call themselves feminist[4] (Borchorst and Siim, 2008). This is not the case elsewhere, and it is hard to imagine in relation to almost any political party in most other western countries. The third reason to focus on Sweden is that it is famous for its former social-democratic welfare system, in which gender equality played an integral part. Sweden's transformation into a neoliberal society has therefore had a powerful impact on the gender-equality norm (Tollin, 2011).

The literature on Swedish gender equality is very extensive but much of it is written in Swedish and other Nordic languages. However, the ongoing emergence of Sweden as the most gender-equal nation in the world is of international as well as national interest, since that notion has had such significance in international deliberations about equality. Since the late 1990s there has been an increasing recognition that globalisation and the retrenchment of welfare states across Europe and globally have led to shifts in the gender-equality agenda (Gornick and Meyers, 2009; Lombardo, Meier and Verloo, 2009). Sweden, with its strong welfare-state background, is an interesting example of these global processes. One of our main concerns, the establishment of gender equality as a nationalist trait, is also an important issue in a time when culturally racist movements are growing in Europe, as the rising numbers of people voting for extreme right-wing parties show.

Much of the Swedish literature on gender equality is concerned with how policies on gender equality are successfully implemented or not, and, if so, why (e.g. Callerstig, 2014; Lundqvist, 2011). There is also research that problematises the rhetorical construction of gender equality as not matched in practice and not evident in everyday life (see Melby et al, 2009; Svensson et al, 2011). Finally, the rather narrow way in which gender equality is conceptualised in Swedish policies has left many issues of gender equality related to the so-called private sphere outside the scope of political reforms (Gunnarsson, 2013). We shall discuss these further in this volume.

The emergence of a mythical mantra

The mythical mantra of gender equality as a Swedish national trait has emerged through a range of different discourses, including research reports, statistics, political rhetoric and popular culture. It began in the 1970s, when special efforts were made to change the condition for women to take part in working life on more equal terms as men. A law on parental leave was first introduced in 1974; its subsequent iterations are still talked about in Sweden 'as the most generous parental leave insurances in the world'[5] (Hernes, 1987; Lewis and Åström, 1992; Hellgren and Hobson, 2008).

Sweden has featured prominently as one of the most gender-equal countries in the world in a range of gender-equality ranking lists that have been iteratively produced since the mid-1990s. One of the first such indexes was the gender-related development index, produced by the United Nations Development Program. Already in its first report of 1995, the Nordic countries were at the top, and Sweden was listed as the number one (Human Development Report 1995). Since then, this way of measuring and comparing gender equality has been reproduced in diverse contexts. The World Economic Forum (WEF),[6] for example, has produced specific figures on gender equality around the world since 2006. Similar figures are also produced by the World Bank and the European Union.[7] In all of these lists Sweden stands out as the leading country. These figures, presented over and over again, are part of (re)producing Sweden as a certain kind of imagined national community (Anderson, 1983). They are performative in the ongoing construction of Sweden as a specific territory, distinct from others. In this context, to be a Swede is to be gender equal. The same figures also construct Sweden as a nation, as a heterosexual couple, a kind of national marriage. 'He' and 'she' are constantly constructed as essential categories in statistics and policies and are always related to each other in a heteronormative way. The law on parental leave, mentioned above, interpellates a 'he' and a 'she' as parents. This connects them and produces not only equality but also an expectation of the two together as the optimal parents. Indeed, when it comes to figures, the most common way to define gender equality in Sweden is to do it quantitatively: if there are as many men as women, or a mix of perhaps 60%–40%, this is considered gender equal and 'in balance'.[8]

Critiquing the Swedish model of gender equality: key issues

There are six issues regarding the gender-equality norm that we want to highlight in this volume. The *first* concerns the production of nationalism and a nationalised space through the gender-equality project. The official website for Sweden (sweden.se) describes gender equality as a 'cornerstone of the modern Swedish society'. The use of this phrase on an official state website is indicative of the ways in which Swedish gender-equality discourses are closely connected to the state and the nation. The state treats gender-equality rights as consensual and free of controversy and, moreover, gradually achievable as a natural linear process of evolvement undertaken by Swedes. The lists and figures produced by the WEF and others, referred to above, also produce an image of Sweden as the most gender-equal country and one where consensus seems to reign.

Although gender equality is often treated as an unequivocal and supposedly well-understood concept, it has multiple meanings, emerges out of different contexts and is critiqued from different positions. We are interested in this messiness and how it relates to Swedish nationalism. This is explored in most of the chapters in this volume. For instance, In Chapter Seven Angelika Sjöstedt Landén and Gunilla Olofsdotter analyse how the idea of Sweden as 'being better than' other countries is iterated in gender mainstreaming. Diana Mulinari, in Chapter Six, examines how the culturally racist right-wing party Sverigedemokraterna reproduces gender equality as typically Swedish in a paradoxical and very conservative, nationalistic way. In Chapter Three Kajsa Widegren problematises how the white Swedish male is constructed as gender equal in images from the Swedish social insurance agency. Lena Martinsson, on the other hand, focuses in Chapter Eight on how feminist, queer, anti-racist and transactivists struggle against nationalistic and other problematic iterations in the gender-equality practices. In Chapter Four Gabriele Griffin discusses the problematisation of the gender-equality mantra in Swedish popular culture with an international reach, namely in the work of author Henning Mankell. In Chapter Five, Nina Lykke shows how Sweden and the *Swedish* gender-equality model are understood, critiqued and ridiculed by journalists, politicians and others in Denmark. Even in this Danish critique of the gender-equality model, however, the latter is constructed as *Swedish*, in contrast to the *Danish* way of handling gender equality. The nation is thereby, again, merged with the notion of gender equality.

The *second* issue we address in this volume concerns the fantasies and temporalities that are produced through notions of the gender-equality norm and its many paradoxes. The gender-equality norm is part of a modernist assemblage of discourses, technologies and ideals of rational organisation that promise progress and a particular fantasy about the future. It has a linear temporality, produced through a certain visionary language of gender equality (see Halberstam, 2005). However, despite the mantra about Sweden as the most gender-equal country in the world, there is also another, darker description: those who identify themselves as women and men remain profoundly unequal 'even in Sweden' (Pred, 2000). Reports from 2014, ordered by the Swedish government, show that both family and working life as well as the system of social insurance remain unequal in many respects (Abrahamsson and Gonäs, 2014; Boye and Nermo, 2014; Sjögren Lindquist and Wadensjö, 2014). The need to improve gender equality in Sweden – at the same time as there is a rhetoric about the excellence of Swedish gender equality – is repeated in the Swedish media, schools, working life, trade unions, in research and among politicians and activists. These two contradictory narratives make it obvious that it is possible to describe and understand the gender-equality situation in Sweden in quite different ways. This is politically significant. The two descriptions create different notions and fantasies as well as political strategies for the future. However, the two often merge into one story, suggesting that even if Sweden is one of the most gender-equal countries, it struggles for more gender equality. The underlying assumption is that 'women and men have been really unequal before, it is better now, but still not good, but in the future it will be even better'. As Sjöstedt Landén and Olofsdotter show in their chapter, that narrative produces specific fantasies about the future.

The *third* concern in this volume is that the equality mantra not only creates a particular idea of the Swedish nation and fantasies about a great and gender-equal future, but also recreates a hierarchical order between an imagined modern, highly developed 'we' and a less developed 'other' that lacks those attributes, an imaginary map of a Swedish modern territory and 'the rest'. That 'rest', people born abroad and living in Sweden, or countries outside Scandinavia and Europe, is often stereotypically understood as less equal and therefore as less modern and less developed. 'They' are in need of help, or at least guidance, from 'us' (Mohanty, 2003; Lundahl, 2010; Habel, 2012). When the 'Swedish people' are described as struggling to become gender equal, the 'rest' are viewed as slower, stagnant or even reactionary (Mattsson, 2010). This rhetoric has also become part of certain racialising processes (Puar, 2007). Being a Swede is not only connected to being equal and anti-racist, it is also related to whiteness, as Paulina de los Reyes and Diana Mulinari (2005) have shown. Some researchers even claim that being an anti-racist in Sweden today is a way of 'doing' whiteness, of inhabiting a white position (Hübinette and Lundström, 2011).

Since the gender-equality norm produces particular notions of place, time, racialisation and subjectivity, it has been mobilised in nationalist discourses. Right-wing, culturally racist parties, arguing for keeping Sweden Swedish and limiting immigration, are drawing on gender equality as a norm. However, these same parties also threaten the gender-equality norm, as Mulinari shows in Chapter Six, in a see-saw motion between asserting the pre-eminence of equality as part of Swedish culture and insisting on Swedishness as a special status, not open to non-Swedes.

Another paradox, and the *fourth* issue we want to emphasise, is that the gender-equality norm rematerialises the genders in hetero- and cisnormative ways (Butler, 1993, Martinsson, 2001; Dahl, 2005; Bremer, 2011; Reimers, 2014). Gender equality expressed as a relation between a he and a she is a strong repetitive and performative discourse around how to understand oneself – to identify oneself as a woman or as a man. It carries the expectation of an inevitable relation to the other sex. In this account the genders seem stable and binary. 'He' and 'she' in Swedish national discourse have a past, a present and a joint future. Such heteronormative iterations are commonly found in workplace gender-equality strategies that construct the workplace in terms of human resources as a heterosexual family, where the work will be done better and more creatively if both women and men participate. The two genders are supposed to have different perspectives, to be like two halves, and together they will form a united whole. Education and school policies, for example, proceed from the notion that children need male and female role models (Nordberg, 2005; Bengtsson, 2013). In Chapter Two of this volume Katarina Giritli Nygren, Siv Fahlgren and Anders Johansson argue that to justify the importance and value of having both women and men as role models, gender differences are normalised as gender complementarity. However, they suggest that the notion of gender equality as complementarities of gender differences does not deal with the complicated and messy relations of power that inform social relations. Instead, this simply panders to a heteronormative ideal.

Our *fifth* concern is the role that neoliberalism plays in how gender equality is (re)articulated. Neoliberalism is often described as a discourse that reshapes, destabilises or restricts welfare policies (Harvey, 2006; Ball, 2012). We are particularly interested in the transformed understanding of the state that comes with neoliberal normativity and the effects of the merger of neoliberal ideals with the gender-equality norm (Lindborn, 2001; Hartman, 2005; Banting and Kymlicka, 2006; Kus, 2006; MacLeavy and Peoples, 2009; Schierup and Ålund, 2011; Bergqvist and Njberg, 2013). The notion of neoliberalism as a discourse that curtails the welfare state is of course relevant only in those parts of the world where there has been a welfare state. Neoliberalism is also emerging in countries without this background, and there are certain global neoliberal traits. One of these traits is the expectation that the market will solve everything, even poverty, inequalities and lack of education, and the expectation that the state should support the market (Rofel, 2007; Ball, 2012; Martinsson, 2014). The global hope that the market will solve everything makes political struggle or political visions less important (Mouffe, 2005).

In the first chapter in this volume Paulina de los Reyes' historical analysis of the political arenas in which anti-racism and gender equality have been negotiated and (re)formulated illustrates how new representations of racialised gender differences have been articulated within the framework of neoliberal citizenship. Mulinari, in Chapter Six, raises the question of the impact that the decline of the welfare state and neoliberal interventions have had on the rise of racist right-wing parties in Sweden. In Chapter Two, Giritli Nygren, Fahlgren and Johnsson discuss how concepts such as equal rights and gender equality have become important dimensions of neoliberal discourses, and have therefore also been subjected to the possibilities and restrictions inherent in the kinds of freedom these policy discourses produce.

The *sixth* issue we address in this volume is the complicated relation between gender equalities and feminism and the role of the emotions involved; what does the story of Sweden as the most gender-equal country do to future possibilities of feminism? As Fahlgren and Sjöstedt Landén (2014) have argued, separating research on gender equality that fits gender-mainstreaming frameworks from feminist research on gender in terms of power relations makes feminist critiques of those frameworks impossible (see, for example, Pereira, 2012). Several chapters in this volume deal with affects and emotions related to gender-equality work, or how it has been critiqued. In Chapter Seven Sjöstedt Landén and Olofsdotter discuss their struggle with their feeling that gender mainstreaming work 'stuck' to them in a way that made them want 'to rub it off', while Giritli Nygren et al in Chapter Two worry that feminist researchers could be caught in a political depression. Mulinari's Chapter Six describes a situation when she met racism in a waiting room at a hospital, and in Chapter Eight Martinsson discusses how the insight of being part of exclusionary practices affects the activists she meets as well as herself. In all these chapters the issue on how the gender-equality norm affects feelings and emotions is evident.

Altogether, then, in this volume we scrutinise the paradoxical emergences of gender-equality claims in different settings. We do this to interrupt the meta-narrative of the Swedish gender-equality mantra. The six issues raised above serve as examples of how the hegemonic normative reiterations of gender equality in the national Swedish imaginary and beyond are stabilised and challenged by the actualities of the everyday life of people in Sweden. We argue that while the equality mantra in Sweden has, without doubt, produced opportunities for some, related to work–life balance, childcare provision and so on, Sweden's 'equality situation', as we call it, is 'messy'. Notions of gender equality are shifting (see Lewis, 2006; Krook and True, 2012; Van der Vleuten, 2013) in Sweden, and potentially elsewhere. By discussing these shifts in this volume we explore not only how different norms and their unequal effects are repeated as part of the mythical gender-equality mantra, but also how different sorts of gender equalities emerge when they are repeated in different contexts and articulated through different discourses. We therefore also ask: what new sorts of gender equalities can we discern? What do fantasies about the future for gender equality do and how can we understand them? As a part of this we investigate new possible figurations, produced for the possible re-composition of subjects for change (Braidotti, 2006).

Structure of the volume

To disrupt the story of Swedish exceptionalism, the volume begins with a genealogical view: in Chapter One de los Reyes examines how social mobilisation around feminist politics and anti-racism became state policy. She investigates how discourses of gender equality have become intertwined with neoliberal discourses and policies in Sweden today. The neoliberal reforms during the 1990s are often described as a paradigmatic shift in Swedish public discourses and policies (see Hedin et al, 2012; Peters, 2012; Bergqvist and Njberg, 2013; Harlow et al, 2013; Hedlund, 2013), not least because of these reforms' negative impact on social and economic equality. Paradoxically, as de los Reyes shows, it was also during this period that policies that aimed at achieving gender equality and the integration of immigrants were formulated and put into practice. While many researchers have focused on the remaking of gender-equality issues within a neoliberal framework (see Verloo and van der Vlauten, 2009), there are few studies dealing specifically with the transformation of anti-racist struggle for change into diversity management. Researchers in Sweden have traditionally studied gender and the ethnic/race divides separately. The intersectional approach, however, here understood as the theoretical move towards analysing phenomena such as inequality in terms of multiple intersecting discourses (for example, Crenshaw, 1991; de los Reyes and Mulinari, 2005; Martinsson, 2006; McCall, 2005; Yuval-Davis, 2006; Brah and Phoenix, 2013), has opened up the possibility for new insights and perspectives in relation to the articulations of gender equality and antiracism. De los Reyes' analysis of the political arenas in which anti-racism and gender equality have been negotiated and (re)formulated, illustrates how new representations of ethnic and gender differences have been articulated within neoliberal citizenship.

In Chapter Two, Giritli Nygren, Fahlgren and Johansson analyse how the intertwining of different interpretations of gender equality with neoliberalism is 'done' in current welfare institutions and policy discourses, and what this 'does' to the (im)possibility of feminist theory and agency. They argue that neoliberal policy and governmentality have today penetrated the Swedish welfare state to the extent that they have made Sweden a highly marketised country. In spite of that, many researchers in Sweden and elsewhere are unaccustomed to discussing neoliberalism in relation to the Swedish case, still regarding it as a good example of the so-called 'third way' (e.g. Edenheim and Rönnblom, 2012). An important aspect of this image of Sweden is the assigning of equality rights to women and other marginalised groups. Against the background of the national self-image of Sweden as gender equal and tolerant, they argue that concepts such as equal rights and gender equality have also been made important dimensions of neoliberal discourses. Drawing on their empirical research within the Swedish welfare state (Fahlgren et al, 2011; Johansson, 2011; Giritli Nygren et al, 2015), they explore how discourses of gender equality have become entwined with processes of normalisation and thus reassembled and reinterpreted in new ways in the neoliberal Swedish welfare state.

One kind of discourse through which gender equality is articulated and normalised in the Swedish context is the visual material through which one of the flagship reforms of the Swedish welfare state, the move to parental = paternal leave on the birth of a child, is articulated. In Chapter Three, 'Emotionally charged: parental leave and gender equality, at the surface of the skin', Widegren explores such 'visualisations of gender equality'. In official, state-mandated information and campaign materials designed to increase Swedish fathers' use of parental leave, visual material is almost always included. This kind of material has been produced since 1974, when the parental leave insurance changed its name from 'maternity leave' to 'parental leave'. Widegren shows that the images, with meanings that go beyond the intention to 'inform' the viewer, are reproducing Sweden and Swedish fathers as modern, heterosexual and white. At the same time as the images strive to articulate the message that 'dads should get pregnant', that is, become bodies capable of taking care of infants, many of the images in the material analysed show little or no closeness between fathers and children, either emotional or corporeal. The chapter suggests that these images are part of the 'messiness' of the ongoing struggle for gender equality.

Taken together, the first three chapters show how different policies contribute to the 'messiness' of this ongoing struggle. They are followed by a discussion of Swedish gender equality from two views from outside of Sweden. In Chapter Four, 'Rethinking gender equality and the Swedish welfare state: a view from outside', Griffin critically interrogates the persistent hold that the equation of Sweden with equality has in certain public imaginaries, by investigating the gendered constructions of racism in Swedish internationalised popular culture, in particular the works of Henning Mankell (2011; 2013). Mankell's writings serve as a cultural barometer of changing Swedish attitudes towards the socioeconomic realities of immigration. These writings challenge Sweden's image as a model culture in terms of equality. In her analysis, Griffin draws on the theoretical elaborations of Arjun Appadurai's work *Fear of small numbers* (2006; 2009) to suggest that the fears Appadurai diagnoses as central to neoliberal regimes are also present in Sweden, and that the discussion of these fears throws light on the inequalities that govern that country. Griffin argues that the weakening of the Swedish nation-state, due to certain forces of globalisation, in particular the flows of people, capital and information, has led to the construction of Sweden as an embattled territory with strongly delineated, gendered contours.

Nina Lykke also applies an outside gaze in her discussion in Chapter Five of how the myth of Swedish gender equality is viewed outside of Sweden. Lykke uses mainstream public discourses about Sweden from the neighbouring Scandinavian country of Denmark as a lens for her discussion. Even though neoliberalist ways of breaking down the welfare state and producing new inequalities and racisms have also swept across Denmark in recent decades, in much the same way as they have done in Sweden, Danish mainstream public discourses, too, construct Denmark as one of the most gender-equal countries in the world. In this sense, Danish mainstream national self-understanding has many similarities with the Swedish one. In this, just like in Sweden, racist and orientalist constructions of a modern, nationalist Danish 'we' versus 'backwards others out there' who lack the highly-prized gender equality 'we' seem to have in 'our' national(istic) genes are also very much present in Denmark. At the same time, paradoxically perhaps, the Swedish gender-equality model is generally not viewed very positively in mainstream Denmark, and certainly not seen as a model to adopt. On the contrary, the Swedish model is strongly ridiculed in mainstream public discourses in Denmark. It is considered old fashioned, and as a form of negatively connoted political correctness. Lykke analyses these negative images of Swedish gender equality with reference to two relevant public media debates. The first concerns a kindergarten in Stockholm, Egalia, that is run in accordance with a policy of treating children in a 'gender-neutral' manner. The second is about an argument in Danish and Swedish literary circles over whether people from ethnic minorities should 'wash their dirty linen in public', that is, disclose negative intra-communal experiences in public texts. Lykke uses this and other recent media cases to discuss the discursive mechanisms by which the myth of Swedish gender equality and tolerance is upheld and nourished outside of Sweden, even when it is not celebrated or adopted as a model.

The next three chapters of the book return to the gaze from inside Sweden and the unpredictable future of gender equality. They investigate what is happening to gender equality norms now and what sort of new figurations or possibilities are produced when those norms are challenged and co-articulated with other norms and other political figurations such as neoliberal normativity, racism, the religious/secular divide or anti-racist and transgender activism. In Chapter Six, in critical dialogue with feminist and postcolonial scholars, Mulinari explores how the culturally racist Sweden Democrats act upon notions of gender equality at the cross-roads between their criticism of feminism and their defence of gender equality as a Swedish national trait. One might argue that they have hijacked the gender-equality agenda for non-equality purposes. Sweden's social structures, its welfare and migration regimes, are undergoing substantial changes as neoliberal restructuring (Boréus, 1997) has rapidly increased inequalities (although from a quite low starting point), and multicultural policies are in retreat while neo-assimilationist policies are growing (Schierup and Ålund, 2010; Hübinette and Lundström, 2011). In this context, controversies over nation and belonging have been at the core of Swedish public debate. Representations of the Swedish Muslim population as a problem and a threat to Swedish gender equality follow a very similar discursive repertoire: Swedish culture is constructed as secular, women friendly and respectful of individuality. Muslims, in contrast, are viewed as religious, patriarchal and living in collectivist cultures (Razack, 2004; Gardell, 2010). At a certain level, these controversies are a response to the neo-Nazi movements of the 1990s and to the successful establishment of a culturally racist party – the Sweden Democrats – in national parliamentary politics since 2010 (Norocel, 2013). While the scholarship on this and similar parties has expanded, the role of gender in general and gender equality in particular for the racist articulation of their agenda has remained unexplored. Central to that analysis is the reading of party documents in dialogue with narratives collected from women representatives of the party. Mulinari reflects on the many communities that are threatened by these types of parties. From the perspective of the migrant communities, she argues that the debates about gender equality must be radically transformed.

In Chapter Seven, '"What should we do instead?" Gender-equality projects and feminist critique', Sjöstedt Landén and Olofsdotter view gender mainstreaming as another situation where the equality agenda is co-opted as a fantasy that actually is intended to close off critiques of institutionalised practices. To counteract this fantasy, they suggest that we should think about gender mainstreaming as something that could give feminists hope – not out of a misguided utopianism that posits that gender mainstreaming is going to offer solutions for a better world, but as a site for offering feminist critiques in a field of politics that has been described as depoliticised. Sjöstedt Landén and Olofsdotter draw on their experiences of ethnographic research in gender-mainstreaming projects in the public sector in order to discuss the conditions for feminist critique in gender-equality projects. They show that feminists who insist on criticising current orders are faced with the question: what do you think we should do instead, then? For feminist researchers, this raises the question of what the conditions for feminist critique of gender equality, as well as the role of gender-equality projects, are in Sweden today. Sjöstedt Landén and Olofsdotter seek to address this question. Drawing on their empirical research on how to change gender relations in large public-sector organisations, they have previously argued that, although much energy has been spent on acquiring the latest research and developing (organisational) knowledge about gender relations, this seems to have occurred without really questioning the organising principles that construct women as the problem in the first place (Sjöstedt Landén and Olofsdotter, 2013). In this, they are in good company (see for example Abrahamsson and Johansson, 2013; Bacchi and Eveline, 2010). Sjöstedt Landén and Olofsdotter utilise the notion of ideological fantasy (Glynos, 2008) to explore what kind of work bears the promise of fulfilling certain ideal images of the gender-equal nation that are thought to be legitimate and desirable. The concept of fantasy also draws attention to how certain ideologies exert their hold over us (Glynos, 2001). Researching the ways in which Swedish state policy becomes practice and vice versa, they combine the concept of fantasy with Sara Ahmed's (2004) queer phenomenological approach to the notion of affect. For example, if gender mainstreaming is seen as an empty concept, open to signification, gender-mainstreaming practices could (in theory) be constructed in a myriad of ways, but instead the concept tends to 'stick' to or attach itself to certain ways of doing and being.

The question of how one produces a feminist critique is also raised in Martinsson's chapter on 'Frictions and figurations: gender-equality norms meet activism' (Chapter Eight). Martinsson focuses on how modernist and radical feminism and gender-equality norms are criticised by researchers as well as activists for reiterating exclusionary norms. Martinsson shows that for some decades now, Swedish activists and researchers have strongly criticised Sweden's welfare state policies and its gender-equality politics (de los Reyes, 2001, 2011, 2013, 2014; Martinsson, 2001, 2014; Dahl, 2005; Mattsson, 2010; Rönnblom, 2011; Wottle and Blomberg, 2011; Wasshede, 2010; Bremer, 2011). Gender-equality policies, from their perspective, have not been a success: they have been criticised for being neoliberal, postcolonial, nationalistic, heteronormative, incapable of problematising transsexual issues, racism and class differences or of relating to global inequalities. Nonetheless, the gender-equality norm remains a powerful force, even if it is challenged in multiple ways. Drawing on the work of de los Reyes, Molina and Mulinari (2002), Butler (2004, 2009), Mouffe (2005) and Braidotti (2006), and interviews with feminist, queer and trans-activists, as well as auto-ethnography, participant observations and text analyses of material produced by activists, Martinsson explores some of the critical activists' work in order to understand the role of the body, emotions and frictions and the emergences of possible new political spaces, and political subjectivities.

In the Afterword to this volume, 'Rethinking gender equality', Martinsson, Griffin and Giritli Nygren problematise the emergence of the Swedish gender-equality model as a single nationalist story. To rethink gender equality is about turning it into a site of political controversies, different models, movements and actions. Such contestations are essential for rethinking gender equality.

Notes

[1] https://sweden.se/society/gender-equality-in-sweden/.

[2] See, for example https://genusnytt.wordpress.com/programforklaring-for-jamstalldismen/.

[3] http://www.riksdagen.se/sv/Dokument-Lagar/Forslag/Motioner/ndringar-i-Lpfo-98-reviderad_H2022937/?text=true.

[4] www.folkpartiet.se/politiker/.../tina.../liberal-feminism, https://www.centerpartiet.se/var-politik/alla-fragor/jamstalldhet-och-diskriminering/jamstalldhet-och-

feminism/, http://www.socialdemokraterna.se/Var-politik/Var-politik-A-till-O/ Feminism/, http://www.mp.se/politik/jamstalldhet.

[5] See, for example, http://www.moderat.se/debatt/en-av-varldens-mest-generosa-foraldraforsakringar, http://www.goteborgsfria.se/artikel/113126._

[6] http://datatopics.worldbank.org/gender/.

[7] See http://eige.europa.eu/apps/gei/content/Gender-Equality-Index-Report.pdf.

[8] All of these ranking lists build on these national statistics, which have been collected since 1984. This allows one to follow the development of gender equality figures from that date onwards (Statistics Sweden, 2014).

References

Abrahamsson, L. and Gonäs, L. (2014) *Jämställt arbete?* [Equal work?], Stockholm: Fritzes förlag.

Abrahamsson, L. and Johansson, J. (2013) 'One hundred years of inertia: an exposé of the concept of the psychosocial work environment in Swedish policy and research', *Nordic Journal of Working Life Studies*, vol 3, no 1, pp 5–29.

Ahmed, S. (2004) *The cultural politics of emotion*, Edinburgh: Edinburgh University Press.

Anderson, B. (1983) *Imagined communities: Reflections on the origin and spread of nationalism*, London: Verso.

Andersson, J. (2009) 'Nordic nostalgia and Nordic light: the Swedish model as Utopia 1930–2007', *Scandinavian Journal of History*, vol 34, no 3, 229–45.

Appadurai, A. (2006) *Fear of small numbers: An essay on the geography of anger*, Durham, NC: Duke University Press.

Appadurai, A. (2009) 'Fear of small numbers' in J. Harding and E.D. Pribram (eds) *Emotions: A cultural studies reader*, London: Routledge, pp 235–50.

Bacchi, C. and Eveline, J. (2010) 'Mainstreaming and neoliberalism: A contested relationship', in C. Bacchi and E. Joan (eds) *Mainstreaming politics: Gendering practices and feminist theory*, Adelaide: University of Adelaide Press, pp 39–60.

Ball, S.J. (2012) *Foucault, power, and education*, London: Routledge.

Banting, K. and Kymlicka, W. (eds) (2006) *Multiculturalism and the welfare state: Recognition and redistribution in contemporary democracies*, Oxford: Oxford University Press.

Bengtsson, J. (2013) 'Jag sa att jag älskade han men jag har redan sagt förlåt för det' [I told him I loved him but I have already said sorry for that]. PhD thesis, Linköping: Department of Social and Welfare Studies.

Bergqvist, C. and Njberg, A, (2013) 'Welfare state restructuring and child care in Sweden', in S. Michel and R. Mahon (eds) *Child care policy at the crossroads: Gender and welfare state restructuring*, London: Routledge, pp 287–308.

Boréus, K. (1997) 'The shift to the right: neoliberalism in argumentation and language in the Swedish public debate since 1969', *European Journal of Political Research*, vol 31, pp 257–86.

Borchorst, A. and Siim, B. (2008) 'Woman-friendly policies and state feminism: theorizing Scandinavian gender equality', *Feminist Theory*, vol 9, no 2, pp 207–24.

Boye, K. and Nermo, M. (2014) *Lönsamt arbete?* [*Profitable work?*], Stockholm: Fritzes förlag.

Brah, A. and Phoenix, A. (2013) 'Ain't I a woman? Revisiting intersectionality', *Journal of International Women's Studies*, vol 5, no 3, pp 75–86.

Braidotti, R. (2006) *Transpositions*, Cambridge: Polity Press.

Bremer, S. (2011) *Kroppslinjer: kön, transsexualism och kropp i berättelser om könskorrigering.* [*Body lines: Gender, transsexualism and body in narratives on sex reassignment*], Göteborg: Makadam.

Butler, J. (1990) *Gender trouble: Feminism and the subversion of identity*, New York: Routledge.

Butler, J. (1993) *Bodies that matter: On the discursive limits of 'sex'*, New York: Routledge.

Butler, J. (2004) *Undoing gender*, New York: Routledge.

Butler, J. (2009) *Frames of war: When is life grievable?* London: Verso.

Callerstig, A.-C. (2014) 'Making equality work: ambiguities, conflicts and change agents in the implementation of equality policies in public sector organizations', PhD-thesis, Linköping University.

Crenshaw, K. (1991) 'Mapping the margins: intersectionality, identity politics, and violence against women of color', *Stanford Law Review*, vol 43, pp 1241–99.

Dahl, U. (2005) 'Scener ur ett äktenskap' [Scenes from a marriage], in D. Kulick (ed) *Queersverige* [QueerSweden], Stockholm: Natur och Kultur, pp 48–71.

de los Reyes, P. (2001) *Diversity and differentiation*, Stockholm: SALTSA, Arbetslivsinstitutet.

de los Reyes, P. (2002) 'Det problematiska systerskapet' [The problematic sisterhood], in P. de los Reyes, I. Molina and D. Mulinari (eds) *Maktens (o)lika förklädnader: Kön, klass och etnicitet i det postkoloniala Sverige* [*The different disguises of power: Gender, class and ethnicity in postcolonial Sweden*], Stockholm: Bokförlaget Atlas, pp 31–48.

de los Reyes, P. (2011) 'Structural discrimination and causalised work: an intersectional approach to (un)equal conditions in Swedish working life', in A. Thörnquist and Å.-K. Engstrand (eds) *Precarious employment in perspective: old and new challenges to working conditions in Sweden*, Brussels: Peter Lang, pp 249–61.

de los Reyes, P. (2013) 'Bortom nationen?' [Beyond nation?], in P. de los Reyes, M. Eduards, F. Sundevall (eds) *Internationella relationer. Könskritiska perspektiv* [*International relations, Gender critical perspectives*], Stockholm: Liber, pp 67–83.

de los Reyes, P. (ed) (2014) *Inte bara jämställdhet* [*Not gender equality only*], Stockholm: Fritzes förlag.

de los Reyes, P. and Mulinari, D. (2005) *Intersektionalitet - Kritiska reflektioner över (o)jämlikhetens landskap* [*Intersectionality – critical reflections on unequality*], Malmö: Liber.

de los Reyes, P., Molina, I. and Mulinari, D. (2002) *Maktens (o)lika förklädnader: Kön, klass och etnicitet i det postkoloniala Sverige.* [*The different disguises of power: Gender, class and ethnicity in postcolonial Sweden*], Stockholm: Bokförlaget Atlas.

Edenheim, S. and Rönnblom, M. (2012) 'Tracking down politics and power in neoliberal society', *NORA*, vol 20, no 4, pp 227–9.

Esping-Andersen, G. (1990). *The three worlds of welfare capitalism*, Princeton, NJ: Princeton University Press.

Fahlgren, S., Johansson, A. and Mulinari, D. (2011) *Normalization and 'outsiderhood': Feminist readings of a neoliberal welfare state*, UAE: Bentham eBooks.

Fahlgren, S. (2013) 'The paradox of a gender-balanced work-force: the discursive construction of gender among Swedish social workers', *Affilia*, vol 28, no 1, pp 19–31.

Fahlgren, S. and Sjöstedt Landén, A. (2014) 'När genusforskningen blir ett hot mot jämställdheten: en diskursanalys av en debattartikel' [When gender research becomes a threat to gender equality: a discourse analysis of an article], *Tidskrift för Genusvetenskap*, vol 1, pp 7–26.

Gardell, M. (2010) *Islamofobi* [Islamophobia], Stockholm: Leopard.

Giritli Nygren, K., Fahlgren, S. and Johansson, A. (2015) '(Re)assembling the "normal" in neoliberal policy discourses: tracing gender regimes in the age of risk', *Nordic Journal of Social Research*, vol 6, pp 24–43

Glynos, J. (2001) 'The grip of ideology: a Lacanian approach to the theory of ideology', *Journal of Political Ideologies*, vol 6, no 2, pp 191–214.

Glynos, J. (2008) 'Ideological fantasy at work', *Journal of Political Ideologies*, vol 13, no 3, pp 275–96.

Gornick, J. and Meyers, M. (2009) *Gender equality*, London: Verso.

Gunnarsson, Å. (ed) (2013) *Tracing the women-friendly welfare state: Gendered politics of everyday life in Sweden*, Göteborg, Stockholm: Makadam Förlag.

Habel, Y. (2012) 'Challenging Swedish exceptionalism? Teaching while black', in K. Freeman and E. Johnson (eds) *Education in the black diaspora: Perspectives, challenges and prospects*, London: Routledge, pp 109–22.

Halberstam, J. (2005) *In a queer time and place: Transgender bodies, subcultural live*, New York: New York University Press.

Harlow, E., Berg, E., Barry, J. and Chandler, J. (2013) 'Neoliberalism, managerialism and the reconfiguring of social work in Sweden and the United Kingdom', *Organization*, vol 20, no 4, pp 534–50.

Hartman, Y. (2005) 'In bed with the enemy: some ideas on the connections between neoliberalism and the welfare state', *Current Sociology*, vol 53, no 1, pp 57–73.

Harvey, D. (2006) *Spaces of global capitalism*, London: Verso.

Hedin, K., Clark, E., Lundholm, E. and Malmberg, G. (2012) 'Neoliberalization of housing in Sweden: gentrification, filtering, and social polarization', *Annals of the Association of American Geographers*, vol 102, no 2, pp 443–63.

Hedlund, G. (2013) 'New public management and gender in Swedish local government', *Women and Representation in Local Government: International Case Studies*, vol 39, pp 193.

Hellgren, Z. and Hobson, B. (2008) 'Cultural dialogues in the good society: the case of honour killings in Sweden', *Ethnicities*, vol 8, no 3, pp 385–404.

Hernes, H. (1987) *Welfare state and women power: Essays in state feminism*, Oslo: Norwegian University Press.

Human Development Report (1995) *Human Development Report 1995*, Oxford: Oxford University Press, at: http://hdr.undp.org/sites/default/files/reports/256/hdr_1995_en_complete_nostats.pdf, accessed 24 November 2015.

Hübinette, T. and Lundström, C. (2011) 'Sweden after the recent election: the double-binding power of Swedish whiteness through the mourning of the loss of "old Sweden" and the passing of "good Sweden"', *NORA, Nordic Journal of Feminist and Gender Research*, vol 19, no 1, pp 42–52.

Johansson, A. (2011) 'Democratic values as normal values: on normalization as a social process', in S. Fahlgren, A. Johansson and D. Mulinari (eds) *Normalization and 'outsiderhood': Feminist readings of a neoliberal welfare state*, UAE: Bentham ebooks, pp 80–90.

Krook, M.L. and True, J. (2012) 'Rethinking the life cycles of international norms: the United Nations and the global promotion of gender equality', *European Journal of International Relations*, vol 18, no 1, pp 103–27.

Kus, B. (2006) 'Neoliberalism, institutional change and the welfare state: the case of Britain and France', *International Journal of Comparative Sociology*, vol 47, no 6, pp 488–525.

Lewis, J. (2006) 'Work/family reconciliation, equal opportunities and social policies: the interpretation of policy trajectories at the EU level and the meaning of gender equality', *Journal of European Public Policy*, vol 13, no 3, pp 420–37.

Lewis, J. and Åström, G. (1992) 'Equality difference, and state welfare', *Feminist Studies*, vol 18, no 1, pp 25–40.

Lindborn, A. (2001) 'Dismantling the social democratic welfare model? Has the Swedish welfare state lost its defining characteristics?', *Scandinavian Political Studies*, vol 24, no 3, pp 171–93.

Listerborn, C. (2011) 'Våldets topografi', [The topography of violence], in C. Listerborn et al (eds) *Våldets topografi [The topography of violence]*, Stockholm: Atlas, pp 9–23.

Lombardo, E., Meier, P. and Verloo, M. (2009) *The discursive politics of gender*, London: Routledge.

Lundahl, M. (2010) 'Kvinnor, vithet och de andras litteratur' [Women, whiteness and the other's literature], *Tidskrift för genusvetenskap*, vol 1–2, pp 113–37.

Lundqvist, Å. (2011) *Family policy paradoxes: Gender equality and labour market regulation in Sweden, 1930–2010*, Bristol: Policy Press.

MacLeavy, J. and Peoples, C. (2009) 'Workfare–warfare: neoliberalism, "active" welfare and the new American way of war', *Antipode*, vol 41, no 5, pp 890–915.

Mankell, H. (2011 [1991]) *Faceless killers*, London: Vintage Books.

Mankell, H. (2013 [2001]) *The shadow girls*, London: Vintage Books.

Martinsson, L. (2001) 'Marmorhallen' [The marble hall], in B. Lundgren and L. Martinsson (eds) *Bestämma, benämna, betvivla* [*Decide, denominate, doubt*], Lund: Studentlitteratur, pp 17–45.

Martinsson, L. (2006) *Jakten på konsensus: Intersektionalitet och marknadsekonomisk vardag* [*Struggle for consensus: Intersectionality and neoliberal everyday life*] Malmö: Liber.

Martinsson, L. (2014) 'Intersektionell normkritik' [Intersectional critique of norms], in P. De los Reyes (ed), *Inte bara jämställdhet* [*Not merely gender equality*], Stockholm: Fritzes förlag, pp 247–72.

Mattsson, K. (2010) 'Genus och vithet i den intersektionella vändningen' [Gender and whiteness in the intersectional turn], *Tidskrift för genusvetenskap*, vol 1–2, pp 7–22.

McCall, L. (2005) 'The complexity of intersectionality', *Signs*, vol 30, no 3, pp 1771–800.

Melby, K., Ravn, A.-B. and Wetterberg, C.K. (2009) *Gender equality and welfare politics in Scandinavia*, Bristol: Policy Press.

Mohanty, C.T. (2003) *Feminism without borders: Decolonizing theory, practicing solidarity*, Durham, NC: Duke University Press.

Mouffe, C. (2005) *On the political*, London: Routledge.

Mulinari, D. and Neergaard, A. (2014) 'We are Sweden Democrats because we care for others: exploring racisms in the Swedish extreme right', *European Journal of Women's Studies*, vol 21, no 1, pp 43–56.

Mulinari, P. and Selberg, R. (2013) 'Intersectional directions in working life research: a proposal', *Nordic Journal of Working Life Studies*, vol 3, pp 81–98.

Nordberg, M. (2005) *Jämställdhetens spjutspets* [*The spearhead of gender equality*], Göteborg: Arkipelag.

Norocel, O.C. (2013) '"Give us back Sweden!" A feminist reading of the (re)interpretations of the folkhem conceptual metaphor in Swedish radical right populist discourse', *NORA: Nordic Journal of Feminist and Gender Studies*, vol 21, no 1, pp 4–20.

Pereira, M. do Mar (2012) '"Feminist theory is proper knowledge, but ...": the status of feminist scholarship in the academy', *Feminist Theory*, vol 13, no 3, pp 283–303.

Peters, J. (2012) 'Neoliberal convergence in North America and Western Europe: fiscal austerity, privatization, and public sector reform', *Review of International Political Economy*, vol 19, no 2, pp 208–35.

Pred, A. (2000) *Even in Sweden*, Berkeley: University of California Press.

Puar, J.K. (2007) *Terrorist assemblage*, Durham, NC: Duke University Press.

Razack, S.H. (2004) 'Imperilled Muslim women, dangerous Muslim men and civilised Europeans: legal and social responses to forced marriages', *Feminist Legal Studies*, vol 12, no 2, pp 129–74.

Reimers, E. (2014) 'Asexuell heteronormativitet' [Asexual heteronormativity], in L. Martinsson and E. Reimers (eds) *Skola i normer* [School in norms], Malmö: Gleerups, pp 81–110.

Rofel, L. (2007) *Desiring China. Experiments in neoliberalism, sexuality, and public culture*, Durham: Duke University press.

Rönnblom, M. (2011) 'Vad är problemet? Konstruktioner av jämställdhet i svensk politik', [What's the problem? Constructions of gender equality in Swedish politics], *Tidskrift för genusvetenskap*, vol 2–3, pp 33–55.

Schierup, C.-U. and Ålund, A. (2010) *Beyond liberal politics*, Linköping: Remeso.

Schierup, C.-U. and Ålund, A. (2011) 'The end of Swedish exceptionalism? Citizenship, neoliberalism and the politics of exclusion', *Race and Class*, vol 53, no 1, pp 45–64.

Sjögren Lindquist, G. and Wadensjö, E. (2014) *Jämställd försäkring* [Equal insurance?], Stockholm: Fritzes förlag.

Sjöstedt Landén, A. and Olofsdotter, G. (2013) 'The tiring practices of gender mainstreaming: As Sisuphus' sisters push new stones, how do we get to mess with the hill', in *Mobilizing gender research: Challenges and strategies*, Sundsvall: Mid Sweden University, pp 159–65.

Statistics Sweden (2014) *Women and men in Sweden: Facts and figures*, at: http://www.scb.se/Statistik/_Publikationer/LE0201_2013B14_BR_X10BR1401ENG.pdf, accessed 29 November 2015.

Ström, P. (2007) *Mansförtryck och kvinnevälde* [Men's oppression and women's power], Stockholm: Den nya välfärden.

Svensson, E.-M. et al (2011) *På vei: Kjønn og rett i Norden* [On the way: Gender and justice in the Nordic countries], Göteborg: Makadam.

Tollin, K. (2011) *Sida vid sida: En studie av jämställdhetens genealogi 1971–2006* [Side by side: A study of the genealogy of gender equality], Stockholm: Atlas.

Van der Vleuten, A. (2013) *The price of gender equality: Member states and governance in the European Union*, London: Ashgate.

Verloo, M. and van der Vlauten, J.M. (2009) 'The discursive logic of ranking and benchmarking: understanding gender equality measures in the European Union', in E. Lombardo, P. Meier and M. Verloo (eds) *The discursive politics of gender equality*, London: Routledge, pp 166–82.

Wasshede, C. (2010) *Passionerad politik* [Passionate politics], Malmö: Bokbox.

Wottle, M. and Blomberg, E. (2011) 'Feminism och jämställdhet i en nyliberal kontext 1990–2010' [Feminism and gender equality in a neoliberal context 1990–2010], *Tidskrift för Genusvetenskap*, vol 2–3, pp 97–115.

Yuval-Davis, N. (2006) 'Intersectionality and feminist politics', *European Journal of Women's Studies*, vol 13, no 3, pp 193–209.

ONE

When feminism became gender equality and anti-racism turned into diversity management

Paulina de los Reyes

Introduction

Swedish historiography on social movements has largely been concerned with the actions of particular groups and social antagonisms defined on the basis of conflicting interests derived from structural conditions. The history of the women's movement in Sweden is no exception. Its historical accounts have generally focused on gender inequality as a fundamental social contradiction, and women as a group are commonly depicted as a homogenous political subject. Studies dealing with mobilisations against racism and racist organisations show a different and somehow less clear trajectory. For a long time Sweden was considered a country where racism is a marginal problem or something that could be relegated to the past (Pred, 2000; Catomeris, 2004). When racism has been touched upon it has principally been in connection with far-right nationalist organisations, but seldom in relation to everyday practices embedded in institutions and organisations. In this way the impact of racism on social structures, ideologies and cultural perceptions has historically been ignored, denied or played down. At present, and despite important social mobilisations against racism and abundant research evidence (Molina, 1997; Pred, 2000; Azar, 2004; Mulinari and Neergaard, 2004; Mulinari, 2007; Kamali, 2008; Jämte, 2013), the consequences of institutional racism for social inequality are still a matter of discussion and profound political controversies. The different patterns of feminist and anti-racist organisations are significant not only for a historical account of the politics of gender and race but also to analyse how social inequality is conceptualised and politicised in the context of neoliberal reforms. A historical analysis of the political arenas where measures against racism and gender-equality policies have been negotiated and (re)formulated can therefore illustrate how perceptions of racism and gender are articulated within a framework of neoliberal citizenship.

The neoliberal reforms implemented during the 1990s are often described as a paradigmatic change in Swedish public discourses and policies, not least because of these reforms' negative impact on social and economic equality (Domej and Flodén, 2009; Hartman, 2011; Lapidus, 2015). Paradoxically, as is discussed in this chapter, it was also during this period that many policies aimed at achieving gender equality and the integration of immigrants were produced and put into practice. While many researchers have focused on the remaking of gender-equality issues within a neoliberal framework (Tollin, 2011; Rönnblom, 2011; Manga and Vinthagen, 2015), there are few studies dealing with the transformation of anti-racist demands into diversity management (de los Reyes, 2001).

Researchers in Sweden have traditionally studied gender and the ethnic/race divides separately. However, the intersectional turn has opened up the possibility of new insights and perspectives in relation to the importance of the articulations of gender and race for understanding the particular conditions favouring the implementation of neoliberal policies in Sweden. A point of departure in this chapter is that the intertwining of different relations of oppression and the discursive construction of difference are central to understanding how the idea of singular identities is co-articulated with structural inequalities. This is particularly relevant in a context where the formation of unequal subjectivities has been conceptualised as diversity.

The focus on diversity as a political and management strategy tends to hide the impact of power relations and structural inequalities at the social level. It also creates a 'paradigm of difference' (de los Reyes, 2001; de los Reyes and Martinsson, 2005), that is, an analytical and political framework where the existence of different subject positions in terms of gender, ethnicity, race, sexuality and class become an axiom that does not need to be verified. The impact of this paradigm of difference is central to understanding the conditions that create different political subjects and also to elucidating how political struggles for justice and recognition can be incorporated into state practices that operate within a neoliberal logic.

This chapter examines the various ways in which social mobilisations regarding feminist politics and anti-racism have become state policy in a general context of neoliberal reforms. The first section examines feminist collective organisations with a special emphasis on different forms of women's mobilisation and networking during the late 1900s. The second section analyses anti-racist mobilisation and the conditions leading to the transformation of stances against racism into diversity policies. The third and last section concentrates on the political and theoretical impact of intersectional approaches to inequality in a context of neoliberal hegemony. A central issue is the extent to which intersectional perspectives represent a way out of the limitations of earlier theorisations about race and gender. The radical potential of intersectional political strategies is examined in the light of a polarised political debate in which subordination on the bases of racism, homophobia and sexism is considered as separate from the logic of capitalist exploitation and reduced to identity struggles instrumental for the implementation of neoliberal politics.

From the women's movement to the women's lobby

Feminist mobilisation in Sweden has historically tended to emphasise the common interest of women, thus reinforcing the idea of a homogeneous political subject that, as a collective of historically contingent agents of social change, is capable of formulating emancipatory goals. In this context, demands directed at the welfare state have also been formulated on the assumption of a shared interest and common goals among women. Historical research reveals how divergent voices have been systematically marginalised from the movement's narrative (Manns, 2000; Rönnberg, 2000), yet our knowledge of the concrete strategies, practices and priorities contributing to the formation of a hegemonic feminism is still limited. A spirit of consensus that characterises feminism's accounts of its own history has undoubtedly influenced theoretical developments within feminism, and also the legitimacy of gender policies formulated in the name of all women. However, the implementation of neoliberal reforms during the 1990s was accompanied by high unemployment rates, the dismantling of the welfare state and the growing precariousness of working conditions (Engstrand and Thörnquist, 2011; Gavanas and Calleman, 2013). This development makes inequalities in women's living conditions across lines of class, ethnicity and sexuality a burning issue for feminist theoretical work and political mobilisation.

When one examines historical narratives of the Swedish women's movement critically it becomes evident that hegemony is constructed not only on the basis of privileged positions but also on a particular conceptualisation of gender inequality as the principal antagonism in society. Inequalities among women are thus marginalised not only from the dominant narratives but also from the formulation of a feminist political agenda. When addressed, these inequalities have often been conceptualised as 'variations' among women or as an expression of diversity (Florin et al, 1999; Abrahamsson and Gonäs, 2014), but rarely as the consequence of power relations between women. As a consequence, different living conditions among women, as well as the existence of diverse and hierarchical forms of exploitation and subordination, have been accompanied by the particularisation of subjectivities formed by experiences related to class position, racist hierarchies or sexual identity.

Gender equality is often referred to as a success story in which women's mobilisation and women's strategies are given a central role. Even though different ideological positions are identified, the Swedish movement's capacity to create unity around specific question is emphasised (Florin et al, 1999; Isaksson, 2007). Women's struggles for the right to vote in late 18th century are commonly seen as the starting point of a long tradition of political organisation involving, in the first place, an educated middle-class elite, but also women from other backgrounds and ideological affiliations. According to historian Josefin Rönnbäck (2000), the achievements of the suffragist movement are closely related to a strategy that actively reinforced a collective gender identity at the same time that class conflicts and ideological differences were played down. The struggle for equal civil rights, rather than for specific rights for women, thus became an important ideological position in order not only to increase the political representation of women but also to preserve a united movement.

The idea of a collective identity is central to understanding the particular circumstances characterising the emergence of the Swedish welfare state in the post-war period, and especially to what has been called a 'gender-friendly welfare model' (Sainsbury, 1999). In contrast to other countries, where access to welfare benefits has been reserved for specific groups, Swedish welfare policies were formulated on the idea of universal rights based on a common citizenship (Bergqvist et al, 2007). According to this model the social rights of women were not conditioned by marital status or economic deprivation but recognised within a framework where national belonging, paid work and social engineering played a central role. For instance, the introduction of general maternal leave and other allowances during this period was discussed in a context where definitions of deserving and undeserving (female) beneficiaries were permeated by bio-political perceptions of (un)desirable citizens. Official recommendations pointed out that women categorised as 'zigenare' (Romanies) 'tattare' (Travellers),[1] 'sinneslöa' (the mentally disabled) or 'asocial' would be not allowed to receive maternity benefits unless they agreed to be sterilised (de los Reyes, 2014).

Gender research on the Nordic countries underlines the links between gender equality-friendly policies and women's political organisation (Mahon and Michels, 2002; Bergqvist et al, 2007). In the case of Sweden, most of these political measures aimed to increase women's labour-force participation. The expansion of the public sector during the 1960s became possible due to a rapid incorporation of women into the labour market. Universal childcare provision, taxation policies, parental insurance and access to part-time jobs in the public sector have been considered important factors in enabling women to combine paid work and family work (Stanfors, 2007). Thus the idea of gender equality became closely linked to women's participation in the labour market and equal rights in working life. Although gender-friendly policies provided many important incitements to women's labour-market participation, they also created important pitfalls; part-time jobs in the welfare sector not only reinforced gender segregation in the labour market and the responsibility of women for care work, but also resulted in low incomes, few possibilities for advancement and low retirement pensions for many women. From a longer-term perspective it is also necessary to interrogate the political consequences of a gender-equality model based on the subordination of women to salaried work in a framework of (welfare) capitalism.

Since the 1970s, and concurrently with a growing presence of women in paid work, working life has been the arena where theoretical discussions, empirical studies and political statements have created, reproduced and conveyed perceptions of gender. To be sure, women's political mobilisation and representation in the Swedish Parliament and government also increased, thus opening up new conditions for the formation of political subjects able to formulate gender demands. Although ideological questions dealing with women's oppression, subordination and liberation articulated many of the demands discussed within the women's movements during the 1970s (Isaksson, 2007), Swedish reforms concerning gender-equality issues were mainly focused on the labour market. In this context the enactment of the Gender Equality Law in 1979, addressing equal treatment in working life, can be read not only as an important political achievement for women but also as a juridical reinforcement of the discursive co-articulation of equal rights and wage work.

As equal opportunities for women and men became institutionalised, gender equality was also established as a constitutive component of Swedish national identity and, as such, as a demarcation line vis-à-vis immigrants (de los Reyes, 1998; Towns, 2002; Mulinari et al, 2009). If the Swedish model was internationally already perceived as a successful combination of economic growth and social equality, gender policies became a further example of Swedish exceptionalism. On a discursive level, gender equality was transformed from an ongoing political project to a distinctive national characteristic. In this way, gender equality became a national (essential) attribute closely connected to the idea of Swedish supremacy. Postcolonial feminist research in Sweden identifies this idea as central to understanding the construction of immigrants, and particularly immigrant women, as essentially deviant from Swedish norms and, consequently, a target group for gender disciplining (de los Reyes, 1998; de los Reyes and Martinsson, 2005; Mulinari et al, 2009).

During the post-Second World War period Sweden received a growing and highly heterogeneous group of migrant women and men. The economic expansion during the 1950s and 1960s demanded not only increased labour inputs but also mobile workers who could be employed in low-paid service work or in other less-attractive occupations. Until 1955 the majority of these newcomers were women who made a living as industrial workers, care workers or low-paid workers in the agricultural sector (de los Reyes, 1998). A small group of refugees who survived the exterminations camps of the Nazis had arrived in Sweden already during 1945. Due to shortages of labour in agriculture, many of these women started to work in the fields soon after their arrival (Olsson, 1997). According to historian Lars Olsson (1997), gender and ethnicity became important principles in the organisation of work during this period, not only in agriculture but also in other sectors.

Historical and economic-historical research highlights the importance of migrant women for an analysis of differentiation processes in the labour market and stresses the need for an intersectional analysis in order to understand how social hierarchies were constructed during the post-Second World War period (de los Reyes, 1998, 2001; Strollo, 2012; Thörnquist, 2013). The division of labour along the lines of gender and ethnicity, as well as the significance of work for the construction of social identities, illustrates the complex imbrications of class, gender and ethnicity in the Swedish context. Until the late 1970s the labour-force participation among migrant women exceeded that of Swedish women (de los Reyes, 1998). However, not only have female migrants been invisible in gender analyses of the Swedish labour market, but also they are often depicted as a problem and as a group who need to learn about 'Swedish gender equality' (Knocke, 1991; de los Reyes, 1998; Mulinari et al 2009). Thus, at the same time that a new ideal of femininity based on active labour market participation was established during the 1970s, the experiences of immigrant women and their contribution to the Swedish industry and welfare sectors during the 1950s and 1960s were silenced and marginalised in discourses about gender equality.

The Swedish gender-equality model is inscribed within a paradigm in which a high rate of female labour-market participation is considered an important achievement not only for women as group but also for the whole nation (de los Reyes, 1998; Towns, 2002; Mulinari et al 2009). Women's wage work has been conceptualised both as a step in an emancipation process and as a sign of efficiency, modernity and progress, at the same time that demands for equal rights became indissolubly tied to labour rights. However, the particular conditions of women's work – in most cases care work within the public sector – have also contributed to making the (welfare) state the main counterpart in political negotiations about the gender order. In contrast to conflicts between capital and labour that traditionally have been managed by agreements between the labour market parties, the achievement of gender-equality goals has been considered as an issue to be negotiated with the state.

This particular characteristic became evident during mobilisations for equal representation during the 1990s. In a period of deep neoliberal restructuring of the Swedish model, characterised by privatisation, deregulation and the implementation of New Public Management in the welfare sector, a new wave of feminist organisations emerged in the Swedish political arena. An important background to this mobilisation was the paradox represented by women's increased participation in wage work and their low representation in politics. In 1987 an official inquiry (SOU 1987:19) suggesting the enforcement of gender quotas in order to increase women's representation was rejected by almost all political parties, with the exception of the Left Party. The Swedish Trade Union Confederation (LO), the Swedish Confederation of Professional Employees and the Confederation of Swedish Enterprise (SN) were all against the proposal, arguing that gender quotas were inconsistent with democratic traditions (Eduards, 2002).

According to political scientist Maud Eduards (2002), a central argument against the proposal was that gender equality would gradually be achieved when political parties and organisations realised the potential of women's competence. However, when the results of the 1991 elections showed that the proportion of women in Parliament had gone down from 34% to 31%, the demands for equal representation became ever more urgent and loud. A network formed by prominent women with a strong voice in the public arena was organised, with the purpose of increasing female representation in Parliament. This network, whose name, the Supporting Stockings, ingeniously indicated both affinity with and distance from the radical feminist Red Stockings of the 1970s (see Dahlerup, 2002), emerged as a powerful challenge to traditional political parties and as a voice putting feminist issues on the political agenda.

With the return of the Social Democrats to government after the elections in 1994, gender issues gained both legitimacy and political relevance. A commission of inquiry into power was initiated, with a special focus on the relationship between women and men (SOU 1998:6). The main task of the commission was to describe how power, influence and economic resources are distributed between women and men. The inquiry was also expected to suggest measures in order to address gender inequality and to improve the economic situation of women (SOU 1998:6). As inequality between women and men was central to the enquiry, its methodology was basically comparative, and both problems and solutions were mainly focused on gender differences. Even though certain categories of women were specifically targeted (different professions, organisational levels, occupations, marital status, migrant position and so on), a binary gender division was central to the framing of gender (in)equality and influenced the measures proposed by the inquiry.

A binary perception of gender was thus reinforced at the same time that gender differences and power relations between women were overlooked or played down. An illustration of this is access to tax-deductible household services, which was presented as a gender-equality measure since it provides a solution to gender imbalances within the family and enables women to face new challenges in working life (SOU 1997:137). As in earlier periods, working life was the arena where gender equality was expected to be realised. But to the extent that the implications of class, sexuality and ethnicity for this measure (implemented 2007) were ignored, it is also possible to read these claims as an expression of the privilege of the interpretation of feminist politics as formulated from a white, heterosexual, Swedish and middle-class position.

The implementation of gender-equality policies with a focus on gender mainstreaming involved not only the establishment of a new field of knowledge but also the proliferation of professionals, experts and advisors with special competence in gender issues. Many of the efforts of this new political field were directed at educating on gender matters and teaching politicians, managers and stakeholders about the imperatives of gender equality. This strategy not only contributed to constructing gender equality as a method to be learned (see Chapter Seven in this volume); it also shifted the focus from political mobilisation to gender expertise, thus depriving gender politics of a power dimension. Additionally, the emphasis on equal representation was closely linked to administrative practices and to an audit culture that 'measures' advances and backlashes in different sectors: the labour market, welfare, education, social security and so on all contributed to the launching of gender equality policies.

The method of 'counting bodies' as an instrument for implementing gender equality and for measuring its achievements has not been uncritically accepted. Auditing, it has been argued, is not neutral but productive, and implies a particular understanding of what kind of gender equality it is possible to achieve (Rönnblom, 2011; Tollin, 2011; Manga and Vinthagen, 2015). Still, the establishment of hegemonic articulations not only makes these practices possible but also legitimates them. To elucidate this, a closer examination of the relationship between feminist mobilisation and state policies is necessary.

Feminist researchers provide different explanations for the transformation of feminist political mobilisations, represented by the Supporting Stockings, into a self-evident national goal implemented by the government. According to Ulmanen (1998), who gives an account of this process from an inside activist position, the feminist movement was 'kidnapped' by a reformist faction that managed to translate feminist demands for equal representation into a neoliberal logic. Further, the movement lost autonomy and strength when many of its most prominent representatives were co-opted by the Social Democrat government after the election 1994 (Ulmanen 1998). In this narrative the ambivalent position of the Supporting Stockings is underlined, as well as the weakness of political pressure groups that never consolidated into political parties. In this context, the government's initiative to create the Women's Lobby 1997, an umbrella organisation representing an important number of member organisations and financed by the state (SOU 2004, p 59), can be seen as the emergence of new spaces of negotiation between the state and organised women, and also as the expression of new forms of political agency that shifted the focus from political mobilisation to lobbyism.

Analysing gender politics in Sweden, political scientist Maud Eduards (2002) points out that the fate of the Supporting Stockings and, particularly, the traditional political parties' strategies towards the network can be read as a reaction of the political establishment against the potential threat represented by the politicisation of gender antagonisms. Against this background, the incorporation of gender-equality goals, meaning in most cases equal representation of women and men, into the agenda of the traditional parties can be seen as a strategy to address (one of) the effects rather than the causes of gender inequality.

From a longer-term perspective it is also necessary to interrogate why equal representation became one of the most important demands of women's mobilisation during this period. The centrality of equal representation of women and men can be seen as a paradox in a political context of neoliberal reforms entailing not only labour market deregulation and a gradual dismantling of the welfare state but also growing unemployment rates and increased social inequality. Rather than focusing on women's mobilisations or public policies, sociologist Maria Törnqvist (2007) underlines the discursive embedding of visions and strategies, making gender equality a legitimate target for political action and change. A central issue in this is how the consensual values of Swedish politics (class agreements and negotiations between labour and capital) discursively articulated ideas of gender equality as a general goal for women and men.

In line with this analysis, political scientist Katharina Tollin (2011) argues that the formulation of gender-equality proposals has been conditioned by the imperatives of economic policy. The separation of feminism and gender-equality politics from general labour politics is, according to Tollin, an important precondition for this development. In this analysis, the emergence of women as political subjects is directly connected to the (im)possibilities that class alliances may create in the labour market. Paradoxically, it is not the character of the antagonisms between labour and capital that permeates this analysis, nor the lack of political strategies to counter new models of capitalist exploitation. The labour movement's historical incapacity to deal with gender and ethnic divisions in working life remains unproblematised. Instead, the focus is on the common lines between the neoliberal state and demands for gender equality, articulated from a rather hegemonic feminist position.

Considering the growing fragmentation in working conditions that characterises current neoliberal models of capital accumulation, and labour market instability emerging along lines of class, age and ethnicity, the formation of a feminist political subject cannot be other than unstable and contingent. However, the trajectory of the Women's Lobby illustrates continuities and changes that characterise the close relationship between the state and promoters of gender equality. In the work towards a gender-equal society, issues of (equal) representation have been a central task. When gender equality is prioritised (and other inequalities are silenced) the perception of women as a unitary political subject is reinforced and the idea of the state as a counterpart in negotiations to solve gender conflicts is confirmed. Furthermore, to the extent that the Women's Lobby privileges activities aimed at influencing politicians and decision making on behalf of the common interest of women, it also represents a significant shift from traditional political mobilisations among women, and in fact reduces the political spaces available for the formulation of feminist demands outside established channels.[2]

Growing inequalities in the living conditions of women make gender politics an arena where the emergence of hegemonic femininities is closely related to exclusionary practices and a systematic silencing of the differentiation processes that reproduce power relations among women. Despite a widespread and well-established conceptualisation of gender relations as a power issue, gender equality is still formulated as a national goal that benefits the whole of society. This understanding is consistent with a hegemonic feminism that ignores power relations between women and negotiates consensual solutions. In this context, demands to the state have replaced other political antagonisms such as, for instance, between labour and capital. The importance of state interventions for dealing with gender demands and implementing gender reform is not only expressed in the orientation of feminist mobilisation and its gradual transformation into a lobby organisation. National boundaries have also been constructed as a natural arena for the negotiation of the gender order – boundaries that are still manifested in a strong tradition of theoretical and methodological nationalism within Swedish gender research.

From anti-racism to diversity management

The dynamics of anti-racism are a largely unexplored issue in Sweden. Even though extensive research efforts have been directed to understanding different expressions of racism, and to revealing how racism permeates social hierarchies and how it is challenged in everyday practices (Molina, 1997; Tesfahuney, 1998; Osman, 1999; Pred, 2000; de los Reyes, 2001; Mulinari, 2007; Kamali, 2008), until now few studies have concentrated on political mobilisations against racism. To be sure, anti-racism is a phenomenon that goes beyond traditional political organisation and must therefore be understood in a context of power where racial oppression is largely unrecognised and resistance is commonly denied political legitimacy. However, these forms of resistance are to a great extent beyond the reach of this chapter, which is principally devoted to an account of political mobilisations against racism and to an analysis of the diversity strategies implemented by the government.

The question whether there is or has been an anti-racist movement in Sweden is not easy to answer. Political mobilisations against racism have occurred within different historical contexts and on the bases of diverse ideological principles. Political scientist Jan Jämte (2013) identifies four different waves of anti-racist organisation. The first one goes back to the 1930s and the political struggles against fascism and Nazism. The trace of these struggles is remarkably absent from the traditional Swedish historical understanding of the period, which commonly appears as a relatively stable epoch where racism and racist organisations were a marginal issue. A second period is related to the anti-apartheid movement and the formation of a solidarity movement with oppressed people in South Africa. Anti-racism's third wave is chronologically placed in the 1980s and characterised by struggles against racist extremists, a mobilisation that has continued in a fourth wave in the last few decades and involves mobilisations against right-wing populism and other manifestations of structural racism. A common ground for these different organisations has been their central focus on struggling against racism.

These different waves involve not only different expressions of racism but also a variety of political strategies for coping with racism. The political framing of anti-racism has influenced the capacity for mobilisation during these different periods. However, it is important to make a distinction between mobilisations that place racism in other geopolitical spaces such as South Africa, and mobilisations that address contingent issues affecting people in Sweden. According to Jämte (2013), the internal diversity of the anti-racist movement has been a factor contributing to the diffusion of anti-racist ideals. The existence of an anti-racist movement is thus attributed an ideological function that transcends concrete goals and contributes to preserving ethical values threatened by racist ideologies. However, diversity has also been a source of fractional strife and disagreements that have immobilised the movement and obstructed collective action. To the extent that anti-racism is articulated on the basis of different ideological positions, it also mirrors a variety of perceptions of racism, a fact that influences historical accounts of anti-racist struggles. In contrast to the history of women's mobilisation, anti-racist historiography is fragmented and discontinuous, a feature that has hindered the formation of a unified anti-racist political subject.

The obstacles identified by Jämte shed light on the limitations of a movement that lacks a distinct political subject. A central problem has been the incapacity of the movement to articulate mobilisations against other forms of racism than those represented by right-wing extremism. The existence of exclusionary practices, patronising attitudes towards women and migrants and sectarian divisions within the anti-racist movement have also been pointed to by separatist groups such as the *svartskallebrigaden*[3] (Black Skull Brigades), an organisation that unites anti-racist activists with personal experiences of racism. Thus, the pervasiveness of racism and its wider implications in everyday practices, even within anti-racist contexts, have often remained obscured. Additionally, the political dimension of everyday racism, attacks on refugee camps and the persecution of anti-racist activists have seldom been recognised. Nor have the racist motivations of crimes committed against migrants.[4]

When far-right nationalism and openly organised racists are identified as the principal exponents of racism, mobilisations against these organisations become defined as the main, if not the only, focus for anti-racist struggles and policy measures. Institutional racism and diverse manifestations of everyday racism are made not only invisible but also incontestable. In this context the absence of political actors with direct experience of racism is remarkably unproblematised in historical accounts, and also consistent with an understanding of anti-racism as more of an ethical stance than a political problem. In a broader perspective, this can be related to the reluctance among politicians, experts and researchers to understand structural racism as a power issue and to deal with its political implications.

The absence of a recognised anti-racist political subject with the capacity to articulate different ideological positions towards a common definition of an anti-racist policy became particularly evident when politicians and experts decided to deal with racism by integrating migrants. The conception of migrants or racialised groups of people as 'different' and in need of being integrated was the underlying assumption of integration policies during the 1990s (Pred, 2000; de los Reyes, 2001; Kamali, 2008). However, that essentialist understanding of difference also gave rise to exclusion and discrimination (Pred, 2000; de los Reyes 2001; Bredström, 2008). When a migrant background provides the basis for policies, there is a serious risk that people's individual needs, capacities, desires, experiences and so on will be overshadowed by the anonymising of references to their ethnic affiliation. According to Balibar and Wallerstein (1991), the idea of an ethnically and culturally homogenous nation is fundamental to maintaining the order of power that entitles the majority of the population to make demands on those who should be integrated. But this requires a two-fold process, one of separation and differentiation and another of homogenisation and creating consensus and community; in other words, a process where an active and constant recreation of community and separation takes place and confirms the nation's double function.

The idea of a different (ethnic) other became a point of departure for the diversity policies of the 1990s; initiatives celebrating the benefits of ethnic diversity also reinforced national(istic) boundaries. Diversity strategies mirrored not only what was defined as a primary task for labour market policies and organisational management but also the model for dealing with an ethnically differentiated and racialised labour force in a context of high unemployment, market reforms, the privatisation of the welfare sector and demands for a flexible labour force (de los Reyes, 2001; Lapidus, 2015). To the extent that growing inequalities in the labour market and in society were conceptualised in terms of diversity, new patterns of exploitation in the wake of new liberal models of capital accumulation remained invisible. Racism became a problem to be addressed by information, training and good advice. In a foreword to the final report of the National Coordinating Committee for the European Year Against Racism 1997,[5] the minister in charge, Mona Sahlin, declared:

> The work against racism, hostility towards foreigners, and anti-Semitism touches upon questions that are central for all of us but at the same time fairly uncomplicated and obvious. To accept! Accept that we as people are different. Different in terms of gender, physical appearance, skin color, background, opinion. We are different – but of equal value. (Swedish Government Official Report SOU 1998:99)

The use of diversity strategies to face racism and discrimination had several implications. In a context of anti-racist mobilisation, blatant and hidden discrimination and growing ethnic differentiation, the stance of the Social Democratic government was to affirm differences and ignore inequalities. Structural social inequality and relations of power were discursively reduced to differences that must be accepted in the same way that 'we' are expected to accept 'opinions'. In this way, the authorities redefined racism and discrimination within a framework of tolerance and called for a politics of acceptance where there was an 'us' that was invited to accept 'them'.

The impact of diversity strategies must be also understood within an economic rationality that suggests that celebrating a diverse labour force also favours imaginaries formed by 'flexible' workers and by a fragmented working collective. The assertion 'diversity pays', which became a catch-phrase among Swedish politicians and labour market parties, points to the economic gains promised by diversity strategies in a context where the existence of racism and discrimination was denied or simply justified as rational and necessary:

> An absolutely overwhelming portion of all discrimination is without doubt not an expression of truly racist or foreigner hostile convictions on the part of producers and employers, but instead based on more or less rational, often economically conditioned considerations. (Swedish Government Official Report SOU 1998:100)

Diversity discourses are closely connected to an understanding that celebrates difference at the same time as inequality is silenced and racism is played down. Diversity strategies have been pushed for by authorities, experts and actors in the labour market but without the participation of social movements and in the absence of autonomous anti-racist political subjects. In contrast to gender equality, there is no connection between the anti-racist movements and the promoters of diversity. This imbalance constitutes not only a bias influencing the formulation of the problem and the political forces behind possible solutions. It also affects the legitimacy of the strategies that were proposed. The subsequent transformation of anti-racist policies in Sweden actualised the urgency to formulate a different understanding of the centrality of racism in order to identify the limits of the Swedish model and also the political challenges that Swedish society faced at the end of the millennium. In spite of the absence of anti-racist political subjects in politics, issues of racism found their way into academic research, specifically into postcolonial feminist scholarship that introduced intersectional perspectives and explored the latter's relevance to the Swedish context.

The intersectional challenge

When discussing the uses and abuses of intersectionality and the multiple and varying interpretations of the concept since it was introduced into Swedish feminist debates at the threshold of the new millennium, a few central issues tend to disappear or to be neglected. One of these issues concerns the centrality of racism in understanding complex and intertwining forms of subordination, oppression and exploitation in Sweden. Drawing on the theoretical work of Black Feminism (Hull et al, 1982; hooks, 1984; Crenshaw, 1989; Hill Collins, 1990) and postcolonial feminists (Anzaldúa, 1987; Brah, 1996; McClintock, 1995; Trinh, 1989; Tomlinson, 2013), the silence about racism has been identified not only as a problem related to mainstream feminist demands for gender equality and diversity strategies promoting the integration of the immigrants. Racism has also been considered as a main component in discourses legitimating structural discrimination and in practices that penalised individuals who failed (or refused) to accomplish the demands of the neoliberal order (Osman, 1999; de los Reyes, 2001; Mulinari and Neergaard, 2004). However, it is also necessary to recall that racism is not an invention of neoliberalism. The historical continuity of different forms of racism and their impact on the systems of privileges that articulate ideologies, institutions and practices in Swedish society has been a major argument for the introduction of intersectional analyses (Molina, 1997; de los Reyes, 1998; de los Reyes and Martinsson, 2005).

When the imbrications of class, gender, race and sexuality are focused on in intersectional analysis, this implies a redefinition of the limits of gender research and a critical revision of practices of power within feminist organisations. Paradoxically, the operations of power in feminist contexts are to a great extent an unattended political and theoretical issue. The idea of a unique (and superior) *feminist ethos* permeated by values of solidarity, inclusion and loyalty reflects not only an essentialist perception of womanhood but also an incapacity to deal with issues of power within feminism. While the theoretical openness to intersectional analysis has generated a considerable quantity of studies under the umbrella of intersectionality, most of the interest has been directed at the interplay of different norms and also at theoretical models dealing with the complexity of systems of multiple oppressions (see Lykke, 2007; Mählck, 2013; Carbin and Edenheim, 2014; Farahani, 2015). However, the logic behind these norms and the ways that different structures of power operate in a neoliberal context demand further discussion and analysis. This is particularly manifest in discussions dealing with racism and heteronormativity, the status of which in intersectional analysis is often considered optional or unimportant.

The marginalisation of racism in Swedish intersectional analyses and the lack of effective political strategies against racism have being accompanied by renewed demands for equal ethnic and racial representation and for the accountability of antidiscrimination measures and equal-treatment policies (Hübinette et al, 2014). These demands are articulated not only in academia but also by ethnically organised groups. For instance, the Afrosvenskarnas Riskförbund (Swedish–African organisation) stresses the need for so-called 'equality data', that is, for statistical records based on voluntary racial identification, in order to make race inequality visible (Sabuni, 2014).

Even though issues of equality, power and subordination are present in intersectional debates dealing with representation, methodologies and ontologies, there is a noticeable lack of critical analysis linking the formation of different subjectivities to current modalities of capitalist exploitation. To the extent that intersectional analyses fail to disclose how different forms of subordination are related to the diverse forms of exploitation historically characterising capitalist accumulation, there is a risk that intersectionality becomes nothing more than a reinvention of diversity approaches. It is against this background that leftist voices in public debates associate the influence of intersectionality in research and politics with the reinvention of an identity politics that is based on the assumption of essentially defined political demands and political subjectivities consistent with neoliberalism.

We must talk about class! This is a recurrent claim among leftist voices that see intersectional perspectives in politics and in academia as a threat to traditional political mobilisation and a devaluation of working-class perspectives (Skeggs, 2008; Linderborg, 2014). From this stance, both anti-racism and queer mobilisations are defined as identity politics, incapable of transforming the conditions of capitalism. This fear of identity, which in some situations provokes reactions comparable to a moral panic, can to some extent be related to a western intellectual tradition that considers identity as essential and fixed (Hobsbawm, 1990). However, decentring knowledge in a postcolonial spirit invites us to think in a different manner than that based on European historical experience. According to philosopher Achille Mbembe (2013), western understandings of identity as an ontological category can be confronted with ideas of multiplicity, circulation and composition that describe what is meant by becoming a person:

> a process of becoming as a relation; a relation in which the 'I', meaning the subject, is understood as being made and remade through the ethical interaction with what or who is not him. In fact, the idea that other is another me, the other is the other only to the extent that he or she is another me. (Mbembe 2013)

Rather than following a traditional logic that establishes a dichotomy between identity politics and political mobilisation based on ideological stances or structural conditions, Mbembe proposes an understanding where historical, material and symbolic conditions shaping multiple subjectivities (becoming a person) are central. The recognition of the other as 'another me' enables at the same time a conceptualisation of the other as non-hierarchical and not subordinated.

In the present postcolonial world, the formation of multiple and varying subaltern subjectivities implies the need for a critical analysis of capitalism not only in its neoliberal form but also in its colonial constitution. Thus an intersectional perspective of the imbrications of class, race, sexuality and gender can be a point of departure for understanding the different ways that current capitalist accumulation models are recreating bio-political assumptions of the human through processes of commoditisation and the emergence of new modalities of governance. In recalling the logic of capital accumulation I do not reify the economy as a fundamental and determining force (in the last instance). Instead I argue for the need to rethink the potential of intersectionality in the light of the historical transformations of capitalism.

In order to realise this potential, intersectional analysis must develop a theoretical framework that articulates the shaping of differentiated identities with the subjectivities emerging from the logic of capitalist exploitation. To be sure, processes of identity formation cannot be reduced to the logic of capitalism and the expansion of profit. The challenging point for intersectional analysis is, however, to uncover how and in what circumstances identity formation is instrumental for capitalist accumulation. In this context it is necessary to analyse how genderised and racialised subjectivities premise the commoditisation of different forms of life and the expansion of working conditions that exploit human capabilities beyond the limits needed (and paid) for the reproduction of the labour force (Virno, 2004). Furthermore, the expansion of capitalist exploitation is not limited to the organisation of work and the expropriation of the means of survival of subaltern people in the global South (Harvey, 2006; de Sousa Santos, 2011). It also implies the devastation of natural resources, the exploitation of human and non-human life and the naturalisation of bio-political practices that reify ideas about desirable and undesirable people, deserving and undeserving citizens and grievable and ungrievable bodies (Butler, 2009).

In analysing historical processes of subject formation, intersectionality can interrogate the circumstances that shape perceptions of the human and uncover the paradoxes emerging from an idea of universal human rights and the acceptance of structural and persistent inequality. Postcolonial feminist Margaret Denike (2008) has pointed to the fact that the idea of human rights also involves what it is possible to do in the name of humanity. In the light of the militarisation of borders around fortress Europe, in Gaza and in Rio Grande and in front of the impossible task of stopping displaced people, asylum seekers and refugees, the issue of the rights of the other is once again on the political agenda. In this context, intersectionality can develop alternatives to disembodied political strategies that ignore experiences of diaspora, exile and colonial exploitation and instead explore the potentials of a stance where the other is nothing more and nothing less than 'another me'.

Final remarks

In this chapter social mobilisation around feminist politics and anti-racism deployed in the general context of neoliberal reforms has been examined. Starting with feminist collective organisation with an emphasis on different forms of women's mobilisation and networking during late 1900s, I then followed this with an analysis of anti-racist mobilisation and a discussion of the conditions leading to the transformation of stances against racism into diversity policies. In the last section, the political and theoretical impact of intersectional approaches in a context of neoliberal hegemony was discussed. A central argument in this chapter is that intersectional perspectives represent a way out of the limitations of earlier theorisations about race and gender. However, this is not seen as an evolutionary development but, rather, as an ideological conflict between different perceptions of the possibilities of achieving gender equality and anti-racist goals within capitalism. The radical potential of intersectional political strategies must therefore be realised through a critical analysis that anchors issues of identity formation and subjectivity into a logic of capitalist exploitation. To this end it is necessary to think of capitalism as something that transcends its neoliberal form and instead also takes into account its historical foundation in a (post)colonial world.

Notes

[1] It is important to point out that these categories are not fully translatable into contemporary, non-discriminatory concepts. In official documents the Swedish public authorities used the word 'tattare' as a derogatory term to designate Travellers and,

to some extent, the Roma. The word 'gypsies' was reserved for Roma people. See Ministry of Culture (2015).

[2] The tensions between lobbyism and feminist organisation were clearly exposed during the so-called Nordic Forum 2014 and in debates following this event. See Martinsson's chapter in this book. See also Manga and Vinthagen (2015).

[3] Nabila Abdul Fattah writes about her experience in the Brigadas in the newspaper *ETC* (4 March 2014). See also a public declaration of the Brigadas (Brigadas, 2004).

[4] This is the case of Peter Mangs and John Ausonios. Ausonios, also called 'the laser man', operated during 18 months without being apprehended. He shot eleven immigrants in Stockholm and Uppsala during 1991–92 before the police realised a common pattern in these crimes (Tamas, 2002).

[5] The committee was appointed after a resolution of the Council of Ministers of the European Union that declared 'the European year against racism' in July 1997.

References

Abrahamsson, L. and Gonäs, L. (eds) (2014) *Jämställt arbete? Organisatoriska ramar och villkor i arbetslivet* [*Equal work? Organisational frames and working conditions*], Stockholm: Fritzes.

Anzaldúa, G. (1987) *Borderlands/la frontera: The new mestiza*, San Francisco: Aunt lutte.

Azar, M. (2004) 'Den koloniala bumerangen och kulturdiskursen' [The colonial boomerang and the discourse of culture], in O. Pripp (ed) *Mångfald i kulturlivet* [*Diversity in life of culture*], Tumba: Mångkulturellt centrum, pp 13–23.

Balibar, E. and Wallerstein, I. (1991) *Race, nation, class: Ambiguous identities*, London: Verso.

Bergqvist, C., Olsson Blandy, T. and Sainsbury, D. (2007) 'Swedish state feminism: continuity and change', in J. Kantola and J. Outshoor (eds) *Changing state feminism*, London: Palgrave Macmillan, pp 224–45.

Brah, A. (1996) *Cartographies of diaspora. Contesting identities*, London and New York: Routledge.

Bredström, A. (2008) *Safe sex, unsafe identities: Intersections of 'race', gender, and sexuality in Swedish HIV/AIDS policy*, Linköping: Linköping University.

Brigadas (2004) 'Segregerad antiracism, segregerad kamp' [Segregated anti-racism, segregated struggles], *Brand*, vol 1.

Butler, J. (2009) *Frames of war: When is life grievable?* London: Verso.

Carbin, M. and Edenheim, S. (2014) 'The intersectional turn in feminist theory: a dream of a common language?', *European Journal of Women Studies*, vol 20, no 3, pp 233–48.

Catomeris, C. (2004) *Det ohyggliga arvet* [*The terrible heritage*], Stockholm: Ordfront.

Crenshaw, K. (1989) 'Demarginalizing the intersection of race and sex: a black feminist critique of antidiscrimination doctrine, feminist theory, and antiracist politics', *The University of Chicago Legal Forum*, vol 40, pp 139–67.

Dahlerup, D. (2002) 'Three waves of feminism in Denmark', in G. Griffin and R. Braidotti (eds) *Thinking differently: A reader in European women's studies*, London: Zed Books, pp 341–50.

de los Reyes, P. (1998) 'I skärningspunkten mellan genus och etnicitet' [The crossroads between gender and ethnicity], *Arbetsmarknad & arbetsliv*, vol 4, no 1, pp 13–31.

de los Reyes, P. (2001) *Diversity and differentiation*, Stockholm: SALTSA, Arbetslivsinstitutet.

de los Reyes, P. (2014) *Inte bara jämställdhet* [*Not gender equality only*], Stockholm: Fritzes förlag

de los Reyes, P. and Martinsson, L. (2005) *Olikhetens paradigm* [*Paradigms of difference*], Lund: Studentlitteratur.

Denike, M. (2008) 'The human rights of others: sovereignty, legitimacy and "just causes" for the "war on terror"', *Hypatia*, vol 23, no 2, pp 95–121.

de Sousa Santos, B. (2011) 'Between Prospero and Caliban: colonialism, postcolonialism, and inter-identity', *Luso-Brazilian Review*, vol 39, pp 10–43.

Domej, D. and Flodén, M. (2009) 'Inequality trends in Sweden 1978–2004', *Review of Economic Dynamics*, (13): 179–208.

Eduards, M. (2002) *Förbjuden handling: Om kvinnors organisering och feministisk teori* [*Forbidden act: on women's organising and feminist theory*], Stockholm: Liber.

Engstrand, A.K. and Thörnquist, A. (eds) (2011) *Precarious employment in perspective: Old and new challenges to working conditions in Sweden*, Brussels: Peter Lang.

Farahani, F. (2015) 'Home and homelessness and everything in between: a route from one uncomfortable zone to another', *European Journal of Women's Studies*, vol 22, no 2, pp 241–47.

Florin, C., Sommestad, L. and Wikander, U. (eds) (1999) *Kvinnor mot kvinnor* [*Women against women*], Stockholm: Nordstedts.

Gavanas, A. and Calleman, C. (eds) (2013) *Rena hem på smutsiga villkor? Hushållstjänster, migration och globalisering* [*Clean homes on dirty conditions: Household services, migration and globalisation*], Stockholm: Makadam.

Hartman, L. (2011) *Konkurrensens konsekvenser* [*The consequences of competition*], Stockholm: SNS-förlag.

Harvey, D. (2006) *Spaces of global capitalism: A theory of uneven geographical development*, New York: Verso.

Hill Collins, P. (1990) *Black feminist thought: Knowledge, consciousness and the politics of empowerment*, Boston: Hyman.

Hobsbawm, E.J. (1990) *Nations and nationalism since 1780: Programme, myth, reality*, Cambridge: Cambridge University Press.

hooks, bell (1984) 'Black woman shaping feminist thought', in *Feminist theory: From margin to center*, Boston: South End Press, pp 1–16.

Hübinette, T., Beshir, S. and Kawesa, V. (2014) *Afrofobi: en kunskapsöversikt* [*Report on Afrophobia*], Tumba: Mångkulturellt centrum.

Hull, P., Bell Scott, P. and Smith, B. (eds) (1982) *All the women are white, all the blacks are men but some of us are brave*, New York: The Feminist Press.

Isaksson, E. (2007) *Kvinnokamp. Synen på underordning och motstånd i den nya kvinnorörelsen* [*Women's struggle: Subordination and resistance in the new women's movement]*, Stockholm: Atlas.

Jämte, J. (2013) *Antiracismens många ansikten* [*The* many faces *of* anti-racism], Umeå: Umeå universitet, Statsvetenskapliga institutionen.

Kamali, M. (2008) *Racial discrimination: Institutional patterns and politics*, London: Routledge.

Knocke, W. (1991) 'Invandrade kvinnor: Vad är problemet?' [Migrant women: what is the problem?], *Kvinnovetenskaplig tidskrift*, vol 3, pp 4–15

Lapidus, J. (2015) *Social democracy and the Swedish welfare model: Ideational analyses of attitudes towards competition, individualization, privatization*, Gothenburg: Gothenburg Studies in Economic History 13.

Linderborg, Å. (2014) Solidaritet slår identitet' [Solidarity more important than identity], *Aftonbladet*, 2 December, http://www.aftonbladet.se/kultur/article19954737.ab.

Lykke, N. (2007) 'Intersektionalitet på svenska' [Intersectionality in Swedish], in B. Axelsson and J. Fornäs (eds) *Kulturstudier i Sverige*. Malmö: Studentlitteratur, pp 129–47.

McClintock, A. (1995) *Imperial leather: Race, gender and sexuality in the colonial context*, New York: Routledge.

Mählck, P. (2013) 'Academic women in the global knowledge economy: bodies, hierarchies and resistance', *Women's Studies International Forum*, vol 36, pp 65–74.

Mahon, R. and Michels, S. (eds) (2002) *Child care policy at the crossroads: Gender and entitlements at the crossroads*, New York: Routledge.

Manga, E. and Vinthagen, R. (eds) (2015) *Utvägar* [*Ways out*], Stockholm: Ordfront.

Manns, U. (2000), 'Så skriver vi historia: den svenska kvinnorörelsen ur ett historiografiskt perspektiv' [The Swedish women's movement: a historiographic perspective], *Kvinnovetenskaplig tidskrift*, vol 4, pp 5–28.

Mbembe, A. (2013) 'Africa and the future: An interview with Achille Mbembe', http://africasacountry.com/africa-and-the-future-an-interview-with-achille-mbembe/.

Ministry of Culture (2015) *The dark unknown history: white paper on abuses and rights violations against the Roma in the 20th century*, Stockholm: Fritzes.

Molina, I. (1997) *Stadens rasifiering* [*Racialisation of the city*], Uppsala: Geografiska regionsstudier.

Mulinari, D. and Neergaard, A. (2004) *Den nya svenska arbetarklassen* [*The new Swedish working-class*], Umeå: Borea.

Mulinari, D., Keskinen, S., Irni, S. and Tuori, S. (eds) (2009) *Complying with colonialism: Gender, race and ethnicity in the Nordic Region*, Farnham: Ashgate.

Mulinari, P. (2007) *Maktens fantasier och servicearbetets praktik.* [*The imagination of power and service work*], Linköping Studies in Arts and Science. Linköping; Linköpings universitet.

Olsson, L. (1997) *On the threshold of the people's home in Sweden: A labour perspective on Baltic refugees and freed Polish concentration camp prisoners in Sweden at the end of World War II*, New York: Center for Migration Studies.

Osman, A. (1999) *The 'strangers' among us: The social construction of identity in adult education*, Linköping: Linköping Studies in Education and Psychology No 61.

Pred, A. (2000) *Even in Sweden. Racisms, racialized spaces, and the popular geographical imagination*, Berkeley: University of California Press.

Rönnbäck, J. (2000) 'Rösträttsrörelsens kvinnor i konflikt och samförstånd' [The suffrage movement's women in conflict and consensus], *Kvinnovetenskaplig tidskrift*, vol 4, pp 51–63.

Rönnblom, M. (2011) 'Vad är problemet?' [What is the problem?], *Tidskrift för genusvetenskap*, vol 2–3, pp 33–5.

Sabuni, K. (2014) 'Gör afrofobi till en valfråga!' [Make Afrophobia into an election question], *Dagens arena*, 7 February.

Sainsbury, D. (1999) 'Gender and social democratic welfare states', in D. Sainsbury (ed.), *Gender and welfare state regimes*, Oxford: Oxford University Press.

Skeggs, B. (2008) 'Om moralismens ekonomi och arbetarklassens värdighet' [On moralist economy and working class dignity], *Fronesis*, vol 25–26.

Stanfors, M.(2007) *Mellan arbete och familj. Ett dilemma for kvinnor i 1900-talets Sverige* [Between work and family], Stockholm: SNS förlag.

Strollo, E. (2012) *Det städade folkhemmet* [German domestic workers in the people's homes of Sweden], Stockholm: Makadam.

Tamas, G. (2002) *Lasermanen: En berättelse om Sverige,* [The laser man: A story of Sweden], Stockholm: Ordfront.

Tesfahuney, M. (1998) *Imag(in)ing the other(s)*, Uppsala: Uppsala University.

Thörnquist, A. (2013) *Mångfaldens marknad och arbetets villkor. Om följder av kundval (LOV) i hemtjänsten* [Marketisation and working condition: consequences of the customer choice system (LOV) in Swedish home-based elderly care], Arbetsliv i Omvandling No. 2, 2013, Lund: Lund University.

Tollin, K. (2011) *Sida vid sida* [Side by side], Stockholm: Atlas.

Tomlinson, B. (2013) 'To tell the truth and not get rapped: desire, distance and intersectionality at the scene of argument', *Signs*, vol 38, no 14, pp 993–1017.

Törnqvist, M. (2007) 'Varannan damernas väg till parlamentet'[Every other women's way to the parliament] *TGV* vol 4, pp 25–46

Towns, A. (2002) 'Paradoxes of (in)equality: something is rotten in the gender equal state of Sweden', *Cooperation and Conflict: Journal of the Nordic International Studies Association*, vol 37, no 2, pp 157–79.

Trinh, T.M. (1989) *Woman, native, other*, Bloomington: Indiana University Press.

Ulmanen, P. (1998) *(S)veket mot kvinnorna och hur högern stal feminismen,* [*The perfidy to women and how the Right stole feminism*], Stockholm: Atlas.

Virno, P. (2004) *A grammar of the multitude: For an analysis of contemporary forms of life*, London: The MIT Press.

Statens offentliga utredningar (SOU) (Swedish Government Official Reports)

SOU 1987:19 *Varannan damernas.* [*Every other woman*] Slutbetänkande från utredningen om kvinnorepresentation, Stockholm: Allmänna förlag.

SOU 1997:137 *Glasstak och glasväggar? Den könssegregerade arbetsmarknaden* [*Glass ceilings and glass walls. The gender segregated labour market*], Rapport till utredningen om fördelning av ekonomisk makt mellan kvinnor och män. Stockholm: Fritzes.

SOU 1998:6 *Ty makten är din* ...[*The power is yours* ...], Slutbetänkande från utredningen om fördelning av ekonomisk makt mellan kvinnor och män. Stockholm: Fritzes.

SOU 1998:99 *Acceptera!* Betänkande från den nationella samordningskommittén för Europaåret mot rasism. Stockholm. Inrikesdepartementet. Stockholm: Inrikesdepartementet.

SOU 1998:100 *Har rasismen tagit slut nu?* [*Is racism over now?*] Bilaga till betänkande från den nationella samordningskommittén för Europaåret mot rasism, Stockholm: Inrikesdepartementet.

SOU 2004:59 *Kvinnors organisering* [*Women's organisations*] Utredningen om kvinnorepresentation, Stockholm: Fritzes.

TWO

Normalisation meets governmentality: gender equality reassembled

Katarina Giritli Nygren, Siv Fahlgren, Anders Johansson

Introduction

This chapter explores the ways in which discourses of gender equality have become intertwined with neoliberal discourses and policies in Sweden today and thus (re)assembled and (re)interpreted in different ways, and what this does to feminist theory. The Nordic countries in general have an enviable reputation for gender equality politics and practices, and an important aspect of the national self-image of Swedes is being gender equal and tolerant (de los Reyes, Molina and Mulinari, 2002; Edenheim and Rönnblom, 2012). At the same time, even though Sweden has maintained a stronger commitment to the welfare state than many other capitalist economies, neoliberal policy and governmentality have today penetrated the Nordic welfare state to the extent that they have made Sweden a highly marketised country. In spite, of this many researchers, in Sweden and elsewhere, are unaccustomed to discussing neoliberalism in relation to the Swedish case, still regarding it as a good example of the so-called third way (Edenheim and Rönnblom, 2012). And, according to Dahl (2012, p 284), this also has important implications for feminism: 'Despite the amount of research on neoliberalism, surprisingly little has been written from a feminist perspective, although the changes brought about by neoliberalism have had an immense impact on welfare issues that have traditionally been of substantial importance for feminist research and activism.' Even though the assigning of equality rights to women and other marginalised groups continues, the gradual retreat of the Swedish welfare state from the public sphere has impacted on the ways in which gender equality is being reinterpreted (Wottle and Blomberg, 2011). Against the background of the national self-image of Sweden as gender equal and tolerant, concepts such as equal rights and gender equality have also been made important aspects of neoliberal discourses in ways that, we will argue, act as a serious challenge to feminist theory and practices.

In neoliberalism, new types of techniques of governing have emerged. We use the concept of neoliberalism following Foucault (2008), that is, as a certain development of liberal governmentality during the second half of the twentieth century. It is thus neither reduced to mere political ideology nor raised to the status of a new epoch. Rather, it is thought in the plural but still marked by certain traits, such as marketisation and competitiveness, 'a way of doing things', as Foucault put it, that today can be seen in technologies of governing such as New Public Management and the audit culture (Dean, 2010, p 73).

Foucault's (1990) analysis of the way in which normality (in terms of the normal distribution curve) has functioned in the power regimes of modern society during the last two centuries illuminates how normalisation processes, concerning the control of reproduction, birth, mortality, health and domestic hygiene, are administered through various power techniques in a number of different institutions such as the family, school, healthcare, the police and the social services. Foucault refers to this administration as the bio-politics of the population and regards a normalising society as the historical result of a power regime centred upon life itself.

In neoliberal governance we see new types of governing technique. Wendy Brown (2003) has defined neoliberalism as a political discourse that tends to extend the rationality of the market to all institutions and all social actions. In that discourse, even welfare and social politics are used to serve the economy and the neoliberal subject is produced as one who is calculating rather than rule abiding. In accordance with this, political interventions are limited to that which ensures that the market works. They become nothing but administration or 'active policy without state control' (Foucault, 2008, p 133). The state is not less active but its involvement is restricted to creating the framework and the conditions for the market to function freely, and the simple distinction between normal and pathological that was central to earlier bio-political analysis shifts. The distribution of normality has become a matter of (in terms of economic arguments) regulating individual choices, re-signified as individuals exercising their freedom. Human beings, those to be governed, are now conceived as individuals active in their own government. But the normalisation of the neoliberal subject, as all normalisation processes, takes place within the ordering of power structures (Foucault, 1990). On the one hand, there is openness towards pluralism and freedom of choice; on the other, freedom of choice also means individual responsibility to choose, and to choose 'right'. Norms and normalisation are to some degree inscribed by discipline, but to a great degree produced through individuals exercising their freedom. Individualisation thus conceals processes of normalisation beneath the cloak of the strong neoliberal emphasis on freedom and individual choice. In so doing, it perhaps makes these processes even more powerful and almost impossible to criticise, since freedom and individual choice become supposedly a good in themselves. Individual choices become the node through which governing works. In this, way structural inequalities such as gender, class and race/ethnicity become mystified, invisible and de-politicised in ways that we will exemplify with our research.

This obscuring of structural relations means a serious challenge to the possibility of taking a position of (collective) solidarity and feminist agency. But it is not enough to let the social or the structural be explanations in themselves, just as taken-for-granted as the freely choosing individual in neoliberal discourses. As we will discuss, in those discourses the individual and structure are intertwined, presuppose each other, in ways that mean that a solely structurally based critique will not necessarily be able to question that which binds them together.

To discuss the issues raised above we will use examples from our previous research concerning gender equality in welfare institutional settings (Fahlgren, 2011), in school documents (Johansson, 2011) and within contemporary Swedish policy discourses (for example, Giritli Nygren et al, 2015). By comparing the articulation of gender equality in different welfare settings it becomes possible to analyse how gender equality has diverse meanings and ambivalences in different contexts in Sweden today. In re-reading our previous research we note that the notion of gender equality has become significant in the construction of what is considered normal, in the form of a 'trademark' of the neoliberal, assumingly rational and freely choosing subject. And in the following we show how the intertwining of different articulations or interpretations of gender equality with neoliberalism is 'done' in current welfare institutions and policy discourses, and what this 'does' to the (im)possibility of feminist theory and agency.

The normalisation of different articulations of gender equality

Although gender equality is often used as an unequivocal and supposedly well-understood concept, it carries multiple meanings and emerges out of different contexts. Skjeie (2011, p 43) describes how a 'travel metaphor' is embedded in the Nordic gender equality discourse – treating gender equality rights as consensual and free of controversy and, moreover, gradually achievable as a linear process of evolvement where we all take new steps towards the goal. However, in our analysis we show how the significations of gender equality continuously slide and change in relation to different contexts, rather than having such a linear structure.

In discussions of gender equality there is also often a confusion of practices that take place on different levels such as social policies, political promises, legal frameworks, academic work and so forth. According to de los Reyes (2010, p 3), it therefore becomes difficult to delimit all the social spaces where equality is being done. It is easier to identify the limitations of gender equality, as well as the exclusions it carries (often through the inclusions of some) and the invisibilisations that takes place in its name – that is, what it *does*. This is the case, for example, in the Swedish Minister for Gender Equality, Maria Arnholm's speech before the Union for the Mediterranean on 9 September 2013, where she strongly denounced violence against women:

> In all societies – including Sweden – we witness various forms of violence against women and girls that must cease immediately: domestic violence, marital rape, early and forced marriage, honour crimes, female genital mutilation, gender-based killings and trafficking. Women's and girls' access to sexual and reproductive health and rights are not always provided and ensured. This is unacceptable! (Arnholm, 2013)

The importance of fighting the crimes that Arnholm points to cannot be denied. That struggle is part of what everybody 'cannot not want', to use a phrase of Gayatri Spivak's (1994, p 278). However, the list is also deconstructable. No matter what Arnholm's intentions, the list depends on juxtaposing *tradition* with modern civil rights. What allow violence against women to prevail are the traditions of those not (yet) 'enlightened':

> Preventing this violence requires addressing its root causes. It is imperative to challenge the traditional gender stereotypes, social norms and attitudes that hinder the achievement of gender equality, and the elimination of all forms of violence against women and girls.

> Neither custom, tradition nor religion can ever be invoked to avoid the obligations we as states have in protecting our citizens' fundamental human rights. (Arnholm, 2013)

The narrative of enlightenment and progress here provides the skeleton of the minister's speech. Tradition, custom, stereotypes and religion are what hinder not only the fight for gender equality, but 'the *elimination of all forms* of violence against women and girls' [our emphasis]. They are the 'root causes'. Enlightenment and progress, coupled with 'fundamental human rights' and 'we as states' will prevent tradition from hindering women's being 'entitled to the same rights and to equal power to shape society and their own lives'. The underlying presupposition is, thus, that there is an opposition between tradition and the state. Here, a complex web of notions of historical progress, utopianism and acquired rights is woven round the notion of a 'we as state', comprising all of 'us' real agential individuals opposing the darkness of tradition. One could perhaps describe this as a performative slide from the promise of progress and coming equality to the substantial position of the enunciating 'I' as representative of states protecting *already* achieved rights, and the (Swedish) state is implicitly articulated as good, rational and modern.

Our intention is not to suggest that Arnholm is wrong in any simplifying way. Rather, we want to highlight some traits in the discursive logic that animates her speech, traits that we think have become important nodes in today's political discourse, with its strong neoliberal influences, concerning values and agency, nodes that have important consequences for feminist theory. First, an opposition is stated between tradition and the state that turns progressive promises of equality and rights into something associated with the Swedish state. Second, rights and values are fundamentalised into something given, needless to define, obviously true. And finally, the border established between traditions and critical, enlightening (anti-)tradition that belongs to the state is based on the assumption that 'we as state' form a collective that is rationally and critically transparent to itself, that has transcended the limitations of tradition. Here, quite an interesting contradiction occurs, a contradiction that might tell us something about the ways in which neoliberalism is articulated and translated within the Swedish welfare state. One of the most important traits of neoliberalism has been argued to be the weakening of the state (see, for example, Foucault, 2008; Harvey, 2008) that should be used only for securing appropriate market conditions. But what emerges here is a 'we as state' that, through the establishment of fundamental values and rights, can create the possibility that violence against women may 'cease immediately' by the implementation of rational preventions against the residuals of tradition. By this articulation, Swedish gender equality seems to be able to be used as a way to produce equality as positioned within the frame of a Swedish national community that, as we will show in the following, also becomes an instrument for maintaining a racialised and dichotomous view of gender (see also Towns, 2002; de los Reyes, 2010). This is done, first, by letting 'at risk' policies replace real political contestation. It is done, second, through reducing gender equality to questions of measuring and auditing, based on the old thinking of gender complementarity. And last, it is effected by appropriating gender equality as an element in the creation of an 'us', of a Swedish neoliberal rational identity in consensus.

Gender equality as something we have already accomplished and the disappearance of gender: reassembling the normal in terms of risk

Giritli Nygren et al (2015) analysed a governmental policy document: 'Sweden's national reform program 2011 – Europe 2020 – the EU's strategy for smart, sustainable and inclusive growth' (Reg. 2011). In the place of a Swedish welfare discourse, this document produces a neoliberal market discourse. According to the logic of this discourse, the challenge of politics has become the challenge of working with at-risk groups (Reg. 2011, p 19) – groups at risk of what in Sweden is called 'utanförskap' or 'outsiderhood'. Relational concepts such as gender, class, race/ethnicity and age become recoded as risk factors to be administered by policies in order to avoid outsiderhood. Combatting that risk means reducing exclusion from the labour market, 'increasing long-term employment, and making it more attractive to start and run a business' (Reg. 2011, p 27). 'Outsiderhood', at the same time as it reiterates the identity logic of us and them, also becomes a risk category that is understood in market terms as not profitable. The meanings of welfare normalisation have at the same time changed from being a question of including people in (the welfare) society, to a question of making individuals choose the 'right' engagement with the market (Giritli Nygren et al, 2015).

A construct such as 'outsiderhood' cannot by itself support the market discourse's legitimatisation. For such a pronounced market discourse to have any sort of legitimacy in a welfare society such as Sweden's, the meaning of the old, politically privileged welfare state's watchwords such as welfare reform, justice, equity, gender equality (*jämställdhet*) and justice must be framed by and written into the market discourse, acquiring new meanings in the process. Implicitly the reform programme was, for example, witnessing a discursive shift in the meaning of the term 'reform', for reform (unlike welfare reforms, meaning interventions with normalising and equalising ambitions on behalf of vulnerable groups) should in this context *promote growth* in the market, and thus 'be used in structurally targeted measures that strengthen employment and improve the functioning of the economy … among other things by a pro-growth tax and business policy' (Reg. 2011, p 16). Reforms of the type supported by the market discourse are thus entirely different in nature from those advocated within the welfare discourse (Giritli Nygren et al, 2015).

In another passage of the reform programme of 2011, Swedes were depicted as almost already being (gender) equal, a position that would be safeguarded by ensuring that a fair distribution of welfare was adjusted to the market so that it could offer better and more:

> A fair distribution of wealth is a central point. Sweden should defend its position as one of the most equal and gender-equal countries. The government has implemented a number of reforms for higher quality, more choice, and greater access to welfare. (Reg. 2011, p 17)

This quotation shows how neoliberalism and gender equality are co-articulated. (Gender) equality is not depicted as a question of power or political dispute, or indeed disagreement between the sexes or between different economic or ethnic groups (see Carbin and Rönnblom, 2012). Rather, it becomes rewritten as the policy of fair distribution and redefined here entirely in administrative terms as something that can be administered within the realms of the market. As Rose (1996, p 347) writes, the social logic of welfare bureaucracies is replaced by a new logic of market segmentation. The question of equality is rewritten in accordance with the market discourse and thus seems to become nothing but a question of distribution, individual choice and availability on the market.

Meanings are shifting, and are possibly renormalised by the market discourse, with a different, new closure, towards a neoliberal interpretation, far from the welfare-policy interpretations of the twentieth century. In this way, the 'normal' position is not depicted as a class or as a race or a gender defined position. This makes it appear as if the market does not create privileged locations from which some individuals actually never need to seek a job. To be administered and forced into the labour market so as not to be considered at risk is the implicit future prospect of those who cannot secure their livelihoods and their purchasing power in the market.

Thus, the notion of being 'at risk' seems to be central for the doing of normality in contemporary society (see Rose, 2001; Pickard, 2009). The change, revealed in the individualised concept of being 'at risk', is that the responsibility for 'performing normality' and living a risk-free life is placed at the feet of individuals, and thus renders any structural inequalities invisible. The mechanisms of the general normalisation of a unified population are turned into normalisation through individualised 'at risk' policies. It seems as if power hierarchies in terms of gender, race/ethnicity or class no longer exist and as if they do not still prop up the structures of power inequality, and injustice. Structural inequalities are made invisible by 'at risk' politics.

At the same time, in these normalisation processes, those who are *not* considered at risk of outsiderhood are reassembled as the same in terms of having made the right choice in relation to the market. Denying or mystifying differences and specificity in terms of power relations and other circumstances when this choice is made, and the individualisation and privatisation of the responsibility of the choices made, mean that we seem to be witnessing the discursive disappearance of relational categories such as gender, race/ethnicity and class.

Gender equality as a measurable quantitative complementarity: reproducing gender/power relations

An ordinary way of defining gender equality in Sweden has for a long time been – and still is – to do it quantitatively: if there are as many men as women, or perhaps 40–60%, gender equality supposedly prevails. And of course this is important: you have to be there to be able to make a difference! Such a view makes it possible to discuss how women as a group still have worse conditions than men as a group within a whole range of different areas; for example, when it comes to health, working life, levels of wage or pension, the taking of parental allowances and so forth. At the same time this way of defining gender equality focuses on already defined categories of men and women rather than questioning the very premises for the making of differences and the doing of gender – that is, those norms, values and practices that are responsible for certain individuals or groups being treated unequally, how it is done, legitimated and reproduced (de los Reyes, 2010). The old idea of gender complementarity (Parsons, 1951) is easily co-articulated with the neoliberal view of society as depending on competition producing unity, rather than as filled with contentions and antagonisms. When this articulation takes place the link between gender and power disappears, the issue of gender equality is not politicised and becomes one of many computing operations within neoliberal audit culture. In this way a complementarity discourse of gender equality is supported by the neoliberalist focus on figures and audits. This is exemplified by the following account of how the idea of gender complementarity may function in working life.

The ideology of gender equality and the provision of good public childcare in Sweden have resulted in a high level of participation by both women and men in the workforce. However, Sweden has an extremely gender-segregated labour market: women work in the public sector and men in the private sector. In striving for gender equality, there is a rationale for not decreasing this gender segregation in the Swedish labour market. A gender-equal organisation becomes a workplace where the same number of men and women work to complement each other in productive ways. This notion of gender – and thus also of gender equality – has proved to play a central role in the organisation of social work in Sweden today (Eriksson and Eriksson, 2002; Mattsson, 2005; Palm, 2006; Laanemets and Kristiansen, 2008). Similar constructions of gender have also been observed in other countries (Petrelius, 2003; McConkey et al, 2007). This rationale rests on an assertion of the value of gender differences and of complementarities between the genders, for example, in youth care (Fahlgren, 2013), in the care of substance abusers (for example, Mattsson, 2005; Johansson, 2006; Laanemets and Kristiansen, 2008), in family law (for example, Eriksson and Eriksson, 2002; Eriksson, 2003) and in healthcare (for example, Eriksson and Eriksson, 2002).

Fahlgren (2013) researched a Swedish home – working with families with severe social problems, and with problems in providing care for their children – as a workplace. Since its inception some 20 years previously, its workforce had been deliberately made up of five men and five women. Such absolute gender balancing is very uncommon in this kind of institution in Sweden, but in this case was considered important for working with troubled families. In their interviews the social workers all attached great importance to their gender-balanced workplace. To justify the importance and value of this, gender differences were normalised as *gender complementarity*: there are inherent differences between women and men, and thus also similarities within genders, so they complement each other, or, as one social worker said:

I think there are masculine and feminine ways of thinking within the social services and I reckon that in situations in which men and women work together, then its best to combine the two, it makes things more effective and the social services get closer to getting a nine out of ten score. Unfortunately, the social services tend to be dominated by women and that explains some of the problems with them; they're dominated by a female way of thinking. That may sound as though I think that women think wrongly, but it doesn't need to mean that, it can be about thinking more broadly. (Fahlgren, 2013, p 4)

The interesting thing is that this notion of complementarity may at once contain biologist, essentialist and constructivist dimensions. As the quotation shows, the idea of complementarity assumes gender differences, but can be very vague about what these differences consist of. Rather, a pragmatic view of this kind of essentialism prevails. This form of pragmatic essentialism, which may take on different meanings depending on the organisational context, is an important feature of the idea of gender mainstreaming that plays a significant role in Swedish gender policies (Fahlgren, 2013). Gender equality becomes a means for organisational effectiveness rather than struggle against inequality or injustice. Female 'dominance' and female ways of thinking are thus, in the quotation above, constructed as a *problem* creating *shortcomings* in the workplace that only a male contribution can overcome. Gender differences are here naturalised (it is the way things are) and normalised (it is the way things should be) through the very blend of rationalist and essentialist choices, biologism and constructivism that can be contained within the notion of complementarity (Fahlgren, 2013).

Although there are examples of the opposite (see, for example, Martinsson, 2006), in a predominantly female workplace male workers often become a coveted commodity who are in short supply. Men are framed as a scarce and valuable resource, by both women and men, while women's value is made invisible (compare Cross and Bagilhole, 2002; Eriksson and Eriksson, 2002; Mattsson, 2005, p 230). This makes it harder for the workers to understand and reflect upon the way in which gender ordering creates a power hierarchy in the valuing of their work. The question of gender power differences disappears and becomes depoliticised while the heteronormative dichotomy between men and women is reproduced and naturalised (Fahlgren, 2013). Being a man was said to be valuable both among the staff and in meetings with parents of both genders (Fahlgren, 2013). The presence of men may also signal neutrality and professionalism (Eriksson and Eriksson, 2002; McPhail, 2004), which gives male social workers greater value and therefore increased space of action, silently granting men privileges and reproducing a gendered hierarchy (Pease, 2010). When gender equality is rendered as a question of numerical balance (50–50 or 40–60) or pragmatic decisions, the effect is to conceal the hierarchical gender order and the way in which one of the sexes is privileged.

Gender equality as pragmatic complementarity does not deal with complicated and messy relations of power but with a heteronormative ideal expressed in numbers. To criticise this normalised meaning of gender equality is often interpreted as taking a stance *against* a dominant gender-equality discourse. Problematising this sex-based, dichotomised and complementary way of describing gender equality has even been interpreted as if the gender researchers who do this are taking a position *against* gender equality in Sweden (see Rothstein, 2012; Fahlgren and Sjöstedt Landén, 2014). As feminists, we are thus left with an ambivalent feeling that the meaning of gender equality as a quantitative question of equal numbers is both important and very problematic. It opens itself to essentialist interpretations and uses. Most of all, it enables a view of gender equality as something everyone can agree upon that is good, and that is possible to achieve through administrative decisions.

Gender equality as a narrative of and for 'us' – by producing the 'other'

The use of gender equality in the formation of an 'us' is a narrative of gender equality that can be seen in different policy discourses of Sweden today. It is a normalisation of gender equality as something for 'us' that at the same time is built on the production of 'the other'. Such normalising social processes were found in Johansson's (2011) re-reading of the Swedish national school curriculum that permits the establishing of certain 'normal' values as undeniable 'core values' that anyone sharing the same cultural heritage ought to identify with. Even when it comes to enhancing respect for the other, the idea of a community of individuals able to choose rationally controls the idea of any kind of meeting, through the inevitable perspective of 'us'. The 2011 Swedish curriculum for compulsory schooling shows how this logic appears in an official school document:

> The school should promote understanding of other people and the ability to empathise. Concern for the well-being and development of the individual should permeate all school

activity. No one should be subjected to discrimination on the grounds of gender, ethnic affiliation, religion or other belief system, transgender identity or its expression, sexual orientation, age or functional impairment or other degrading treatment. Such tendencies should be actively combated. Xenophobia and intolerance must be confronted with knowledge, open discussion and active measures.

The internationalisation of Swedish society and increasing cross-border mobility place high demands on the ability of people to live with and appreciate the values inherent in cultural diversity. Awareness of one's own cultural origins and sharing in a common cultural heritage provides a secure identity which it is important to develop, together with the ability to understand and empathise with the values and conditions of others. The school is a social and cultural meeting place with both the opportunity and the responsibility to strengthen this ability among all who work there. (Swedish National Agency for Education, 2014)

Here the 'awareness of one's cultural origins' in itself replaces and seems to explain what 'understanding and compassion for others' means. The same is a prerequisite for the other; one must first of all have 'a secure identity', in order to be able to meet the other. Of course, this is not wholly wrong, at least not since this is how modern society has conceptualised itself since the 18th century, but we need to point out that it is set within the conditions of a certain governmental rationality that fails to explore the tensions between two potentially incompatible positions, that is, insisting on one's own value and accepting others, making them a prerequisite for each other.

Here the concept of 'core values' comes into play. They point to the complementarities of, on the one hand, essentialism or fundamentalism and, on the other, relativist culturalism. Core values, as we find on the home page of the Swedish National Agency for Education: 'should not be taken as something given but be interpreted and conquered every day by all of us' (2014). It might seem contradictory that core values should be open to continuous interpretation. However, as Rose has pointed out, the notion of core values has from the beginning relativist and social constructivist roots in the so-called communitarian thinking of the 1980s (Rose, 1999, p 183). In contrast to traditional liberals, communitarians think beliefs and values come not from a contract between free individuals, but through 'community', 'history, traditions, culture' (Rose, 1999, p 183). It is thus neither any essential core substance of the values nor any specific interpretative conclusion that is most important in the definition offered by the National Agency for Education; it is 'all of us'. What makes values into core values is that they are *our* values. The emphasis on core values is as much about certain values as it is about the creation of consensus around what 'anyone normal' ought to agree upon. It is a consensus about the individual's critical reflection and choices that will produce values within the confines of a community of supposedly free and rational individuals. There is thus the creation of seemingly very open, changing and nominalistic (non-)definitions of ethical values pertaining to *one good tradition*, in contrast with traditions formed by those assumed to be unfree, uncritical and non-reflecting individuals who only follow given norms.

Such culturalist relativism does not, however, reduce the *importance* of norms, even if it sees them as in constant change and as effects of freedom of choice. Norms and normality are instead based on what is seen as rational. It is a certain kind of rationality that is the condition of possibility for neoliberal values and freedom. According to Foucault it is an individual rationality that is *calculable*. Calculability and predictability are what, from the beginning of modern liberal governmentality, unites the individual with the community, not least through the notion of the norm – equally important in inventing individual bodies as in inventing social communities (Foucault, 2003, pp 252f). Being normal comes to mean adhering to norms that individualise me as a foreseeable rational subject and, at the same time, create belonging to a predictable community, a population, a people, a nation. Explicitly constructivist, there is no problem for neoliberal governmentality to accept values produced by 'enlightened free choices', since there are no other ways through which values can be legitimated. Openness towards pluralism and freedom of choice therefore goes hand in hand with the individual responsibility to choose. Notably, however, the normalisation of freedom of choice makes the limits of what is accepted as normal narrower.

The point in terms of our argument is that the ethics of this kind of governmentality are purely formal. Governing does not need to take any interest in the *content* of the norms that are created within its field of governance, as long as that content does not threaten the very fabric of belonging that defines the community. And the limits for this are that they are calculable, predictable, recognisable and understandable – a logic of the same, as well as of contextual, cultural relativism. What this means, however, is that this discursive logic is easily appropriated by racism, in fact it is perhaps the very logic that makes racism possible

(Foucault, 2003). So, when gender equality becomes appropriated by neoliberalism as part of what constitutes rational, western normality, it also risks becoming part of racist discourses, which can be seen in the way the right-wing Sweden Democrats party uses gender equality in opposition to what is, for instance, described as Muslim misogyny. Feminist theory thus has to deal with the fact that neoliberal governmentality, at the same time as it opens up possibilities for gender equality, reinscribes it in a culturalist logic of the same kinds that it shares with racism. Here the deconstructivist predicament of continually criticising what we 'cannot not want' (Spivak, 1994, p 278) makes itself felt.

How is feminist critique possible when reflective critique has become part of normalisation processes, and freedom of choice the very ground for politics?

Newman and Tonkens (in Dahl, 2012) have shown that the transnational discourses of neoliberalism have travelled and have been translated into new and hybrid forms, stressing for example 'participation' and the 'responsibility' of 'the active citizen' (Dahl, 2012), and have even co-opted discourses from below. In a similar way gender equality becomes translated and articulated in relation to discourses of neoliberalism; for example, as a quantitative question of equal numbers of women and men, as a narrative of enlightenment of and for 'us' Swedes, and as something 'we' have already accomplished – making freedom of choice the very ground of politics. The question is whether, and in that case how, the Swedish gender regime is redefined and transformed by these new forms of freedom. Through our analysis we have shown how the ongoing struggle for gender equality in different policy documents and discourses tends to be described as a unified process almost already accomplished (see, for example, Giritli Nygren et al, 2015; Johansson, 2011), and how concepts such as equal rights and gender equality have been made important parts of neoliberal discourses, and therefore have also been subjected to the possibilities and the restrictions inherent in the kind of freedom these policy discourses produce. Thus, what neoliberal discourses also do, on the negative side, is to mystify and obscure the impact of feminist theory and political practice.

A first conclusion to be drawn from this is that the pragmatic relativism of neoliberal policies makes traditional critique – that either uncovers illusion or reveals structural or causal determinism by showing their contingency – seem like revealing nothing but what is already known. Critique has become an inseparable part of defining the rational individual as someone that is aware of her or his blindnesses, as opposed to those that are not aware of theirs.

The common critique of neoliberal forms of government – that they are concerned only with individuals and not with structures or social contexts – must accordingly also be qualified. When it comes to the role of the market and freedom of choice it is certainly the case that individuals and their choices have become nodes through which governing works. But this does not mean that the social has any less importance. Civil society is still, no matter how marketised it has become, that environment in which politics can intervene in order to control possibilities and limit individual choice. The astonishing interest in school and education that neoliberal governments show, the interventionist politics that go with it and the will to use education as a tool for the implementation of core values prove that institutions or contexts are important within neoliberal governmentality. A culture produces its values. Once formed, however, these values are reducible to prerequisites for individual choice, reducible to behaviourist simplicity or, in other words, thought of as controllable mechanisms for producing the rational individual. And with this comes the belief that knowledge of fundamental values such as gender equality can be implemented in school; that knowledge in itself should lead to the removal of traditions that hinder equality.

A critique of neoliberal thought that only says 'structure' rather 'individual' risks missing the point. Individual and structure are both parts of the neoliberal world-view. It is the form of rationality that binds together individual and structure that is key to understanding neoliberal governmentality and how it functions. For gender theory this means that one has to avoid making either the individual or social structure into final *explanations* of gender and gender inequality. Relativist and constructivist, pragmatic and in constant change, neoliberal governmentality is also nomadic, differential, emergent, becoming as well as indeterminate. A sense of impossibility permeates much of present-day feminist thinking. Even if the research that is being done seldom lives up to the hopes of political fast fixes, there is nevertheless, in the search for excellence and grants, a danger of complicity with neoliberal governmentality that has problematic dimensions.

What we have tried to show above is that this poses some challenges for feminist theory. Empowerment and refusal of victimisation are strategies for resistance that are intimately bound to the political landscape that has been shaped by neoliberalism into management of possibilities rather than conflict. All this we know already. But to know this does not mean that one can control or manage it. We do not want feminist theory today to get into an impasse, or feminist researchers to be caught in a 'political depression', trapped in neoliberal measures of success, that is, the activities that count, to borrow a phrase from Ann Cvetkovich (2012). As feminists, we 'cannot not want' to build alliances, in order to get political recognition. Gayatri Spivak once called this 'strategic essentialism' (1996, pp 204f). This is still what it is all about; not about choosing between relativism or fundamentalism because they are both parts of what constitutes the field that continues to produce the other as not us, but about to some degree having to talk their language in order to oppose them. However, our chapter is about the ambivalences and aporias that feminist theory is living through at the present. We must not forget these, remembering that we are essentialists only strategically, because the landscape in which we have to develop strategies is filled with ambivalences and aporias.

References

Arnholm, M. (2013) 'Anförande vid Union for the Mediterranean, våld mot kvinnor och flickor' [Speech at the Union for the Mediterranean; Violence against women and girls], Regeringskansliet (Government Offices of Sweden). http://www.government.se/sb/d/17107/a/224337, accessed 15 June 2014.

Brown, W. (2003) 'Neoliberalism and the end of liberal democracy', *Theory and Event*, vol 7, no 1, pp 1–19.

Carbin, M. and Rönnblom, M. (2012) 'Jämställdhet i akademin: en avpolitiserad politik?' [Gender equality in academia: a depoliticised politics?], *Tidskrift för Genusvetenskap*, vol 1–2, pp 75–94.

Cross, S. and Bagilhole, B. (2002) 'Girls' jobs for the boys? Men, masculinity and non-traditional occupations', *Gender, Work and Organisation*, vol 9, no 2, pp 204–26.

Cvetkovich, A. (2012) *Depression: A public feeling*, Durham, NC: Duke University Press.

Dahl, H.M. (2012) 'Neoliberalism meets the Nordic welfare state: gaps and silences', *Nora*, vol 20, no 4, pp 283–88.

de los Reyes, P. (2010) *Vad händer med jämställdheten? Nedslag i jämställdhetens synfält. [What happens with gender equality?]*, Uppsala: Uppsala University.

de los Reyes, P., Molina, I. and Mulinari, D. (2002) *Maktens (o)lika förklädnader: kön, klass och etnicitet i det postkoloniala Sverige. [The different disguises of power: Gender, class and ethnicity in postcolonial Sweden]*, Stockholm: Bokförlaget Atlas.

Dean, M. (2010) *Governmentality: power and rule in modern society*, 2nd edn, Thousand Oaks, CA: Sage.

Edenheim, S. and Rönnblom, M. (2012) 'Tracking down politics and power in neoliberal society', *Nora*, vol 20, no 4, pp 227–9.

Eriksson, K. and Eriksson, M. (2002) 'Kön har ingen betydelse men könsblandning är bra: "könsgörande" i två professionella sammanhang', [Gender does not matter but gender mixing is good: the doing of gender in two professional settings], *Kvinnovetenskaplig tidskrift*, vol 1, pp 53–72.

Eriksson, M. (2003) *I skuggan av pappa: Familjerätten och hantering av fäders våld.* [*In the shadow of daddy: Family law and the handling of fathers' violence*], Stehag: Förlags AB Gondolin.

Fahlgren, S. (2011) 'About getting a daily life going: social work, time and normalization', in S. Fahlgren, A. Johansson, and D. Mulinari (eds) *Normalization and 'outsiderhood': Feminist readings of a neoliberal welfare state*, UAE: Bentham eBooks, pp 28–38.

Fahlgren, S. (2013) 'The paradox of a gender-balanced work-force: the discursive construction of gender among Swedish social workers', *Affilia*, vol 28, no 1, pp 19–31.

Fahlgren, S. and Sjöstedt Landén, A. (2014) 'När genusforskningen blir ett hot mot jämställdheten: en diskursanalys av en debattartikel' [When gender research becomes a threat against gender equality: a discourse analyses of an article], *Tidskrift för Genusvetenskap*, vol 1, pp 7–26.

Foucault, M. (1990) *The history of sexuality. Vol. 1. The will to knowledge*, Harmondsworth: Penguin.

Foucault, M. (2003) *'Society must be defended': Lectures at the Collège de France, 1975–76*, ed M. Bertani and A. Fontana, New York: Picador.

Foucault, M. (2008) *The birth of biopolitics: Lectures at the Collège de France, 1978–1979*, Basingstoke: Palgrave Macmillan.

Giritli Nygren, K., Fahlgren, S. and Johansson, A. (2015) '(Re)assembling the "normal" in neoliberal policy discourses: tracing gender regimes in the age of risk', *Nordic Journal of Social Research*, vol 6, pp 24–43.

Harvey, D. (2008) *A brief history of neoliberalism*, New York: Oxford University Press.

Johansson, A. (2011) 'Democratic values as normal values: on normalization as a social process', in S. Fahlgren, A. Johansson and D. Mulinari (eds) *Normalization and 'outsiderhood': Feminist readings of a neoliberal welfare state*, UAE: Bentham ebooks, pp 80–90.

Johansson, H. (2006) 'Brist på manliga förebilder' [A lack of male role models], unpublished dissertation, Göteborg: Göteborg University.

Laanemets, L. and Kristiansen, A. (2008) *Kön och behandling inom tvångsvård: En studie av hur vården organiseras med avseende på genus* [*Gender and treatment in compulsory care: A study of how healthcare is organised in terms of gender*], Research Report 1: 2008, Statens institutionsstyrelse SIS.

McConkey, R., McAuley, P., Simpson, L. and Collins, S. (2007) 'The male workforce in intellectual disability services', *Journal of Policy and Practice in Intellectual Disabilities*, vol 4, no 3, pp 186–93.

McPhail, B.A. (2004) 'Setting the record straight: social work is not a female-dominated profession', *Social Work*, vol 49, no 2, pp 323–6.

Martinsson, L. (2006) *Jakten på konsensus: Intersektionalitet och marknadsekonomisk vardag,* [*Struggle for consensus: Intersectionality and neoliberal everyday life*], Malmö: Liber.

Mattsson, T. (2005) *I viljan att göra det normala: En kritisk studie av genusperspektivet i missbrukarvård* [*In an effort to do normality: A critical study of gender perspectives in the care of substance abusers*], Malmö: Égalité.

Palm, J. (2006) *Moral concerns: Treatment staff and user perspectives on alcohol and drug problems*, Stockholm: Stockholm University.

Parsons, T. (1951) *The social system*, New York: Free Press.

Pease, B. (2010) *Undoing privilege: Unearned advantage in a divided world*, London: Zed Books.

Petrelius, P. (2003) 'Gender and orientation towards social work', *Nordiskt Socialt Arbeid*, vol 3, pp 144–53.

Pickard, S. (2009) 'Governing old age', *Sociology*, vol 43, no 1, pp 67–84.

Reg. 2011 'Sweden's national reform program 2011 – Europe 2020 – the EU's strategy for smart, sustainable and inclusive growth', Stockholm: Government Offices of Sweden.

Rose, N. (1996) '"The death of the social?" Refiguring the territory of government', *Economy and Society*, vol 25, no 3, pp 327–56.

Rose, N. (1999) *Powers of freedom: Reframing political thought*, Cambridge: Cambridge University Press.

Rose, N. (2001) 'The politics of life itself', *Theory, Culture and Society,* vol 18, no 6, pp 1–30.

Rothstein, B. (2012) 'Fel av staten att stötta genusforskningen' [State-supported gender research is wrong], *Göteborgsposte*, 4 April.

Skjeie, H. (2011) 'Gender equality: on travel metaphors and duties to yield', in D. Sainsbury, and M. Soininen (eds) *Kön makt nation*, Stockholm: Stockholm University.

Spivak, G. (1994) 'Bonding in difference', in A. Arteaga (ed) *An other tongue: Nation and ethnicity in the linguistic borderlands*, Durham, NC: Duke University Press, pp 273–85.

Spivak, G. (1996) 'Subaltern studies: deconstructing historiography', in D. Landry and G. MacLean (eds) *The Spivak reader: Selected works of Gayatri Chakravorty Spivak*, New York: Routledge, pp 203–35.

Swedish National Agency for Education (2014) Värdegrundsarbetet [Working with Core Values], http://www.skolverket.se/skolutveckling/vardegrund/vardegrundsarbetet, accessed 14 June 2013.

Towns, A. (2002) 'Paradoxes of (in)equality: something is rotten in the gender equal state of Sweden', *Cooperation and Conflict*, vol 37, no 2, pp 157–79.

Wottle, M. and Blomberg, E. (2011) 'Feminism och jämställdhet i en nyliberal kontext 1990–2010' [Feminism and gender equality in a neoliberal context 1990–2010], *Tidskrift för Genusvetenskap*, vol 2–3, pp 97–115.

THREE

Emotionally charged: parental leave and gender equality, at the surface of the skin

Kajsa Widegren

Introduction

In the mid-1970s a young member of the Swedish Parliament articulated the political aim of Swedish gender equality politics as 'getting mom a job and making dad pregnant' (Klinth, 2008, p 20).[1] This statement should be read in the context of the notion of Swedish gender equality politics as 'the double emancipation', based on the idea that both men and women should cast off their old traditional 'sex-roles' (Palme, 1972; Klinth, 2002; Mellström, 2005). This chapter analyses images from brochures published and distributed by the Swedish Social Insurance Agency with the aim of informing parents and soon-to-be parents about their right to parental leave. The political aim of achieving gender equality through parental leave has been a recurring theme ever since the parental leave insurance was gender-neutralised in 1974. From being an insurance programme directed at mothers, it was renamed and directed at both the mothers and fathers of new-born infants (Klinth, 2002; Lind Palicki, 2010). The images used to promote parental leave are thus analysed as part of the gender equality politics that intended to 'make dad pregnant'.

Sweden has the most generous state-funded parental leave insurance in the world. Insurance as a bureaucratic and political tool for governance has been extensively researched in Sweden (Widerberg, 1993; Klinth, 2002; Johansson and Klinth, 2010), as have the normative claims concerning who should use parental leave and under what circumstances (Lind Palicki, 2010). However, as a political tool for gender equality, if 'gender equality' is defined as more fathers using their parental leave, the insurance has not been particularly successful. Mothers still use approximately 80% of the insurance (Statistics Sweden, 2008; Johansson and Klinth, 2010). Since the 1970s the Swedish

Social Insurance Agency has launched repeated campaigns and has continuously produced information brochures about parental leave insurance directed at fathers, as a part of its political assignment from various governments (Klinth, 2002). Although the campaigns have been directed at fathers, the information material such as brochures, posters and televised information films have been directed at all parents. However, it is clear from just a brief look at the material produced from 1974 and onwards that it addresses fatherhood. Out of ten different brochures, seven have front illustrations of men and children. Two have illustrations of infants alone and one shows a heterosexual nuclear family. In the 1980s – according to Lind Palicki's (2010) study – several images showed nuclear families and some depicted women.[2] Since my study is not quantitative but, rather, builds on a close reading of case studies, this first glance at the material only confirms that the images are mainly part of what Roger Klinth (2002) calls 'daddy politics'. So a starting point for this chapter is the state-endorsed construction of parents as men, and of men as parents. How are the images related to a wider contextual production of visual meaning, connected to parenthood and the emotionally and embodied relation between infant and adult? How is fatherhood constructed visually and emotionally? In research on these campaigns and information brochures it is the *normalising* textual address that is in focus (Lind Palicki, 2010). Images are included in some research (see Klinth, 2008; Johansson and Klinth, 2010), but as visual effects of dominant political discourses on gender equality. However, this chapter will analyse this particular political scene from another perspective: images can never fully represent a political project such as the efforts to make fathers use their parental leave more equally. They will always participate in producing new meanings and emotions and thus change the political efforts, since images are not mimetic in relation to political discourse.

Image is a concept that relates to the sensory function of eye and visuality, but since images can be constructed in many ways, with many different technologies and thus with different effects, the analysis of images calls for specification. I use the concept of genres, in which I include technique, material, publication context and address (Rose, 2012). Intimisation of communication between authorities and citizens often takes the form of image practices that are close to the notion of the everyday use and production of pictures. The photographic snapshot is one such image practice, as is the comic drawing. But the professionalisation of the production of information material has also led to an increased use of images that are produced by advertising agencies. Commercial images are often well executed in terms of lighting, composition, colouring and portraiture of humans, and they are also effective in managing the viewers' emotional response (Rose, 2012). Images are performative as well as affirmative: they both create and reproduce ideals and emotions (Rose, 2012). This non-dualistic character of images can make them ambiguous, and sometimes contradictory, overflowing with meaning. On the other hand, the rhetoric of the image, and historically developed and reiterated genres, limit the meaning and emotional response to images. Photography uses light composition, closeness/distance, definition of depth and colour saturation as well as printing techniques to create an emotionally charged image. These techniques are often naturalised, due to the photographic images' indexical relation to 'reality'. This constitutes the performative force of photographs, their potential to seem 'real' (Tyler, 2001; Rose, 2012).

Of the at least 50 different images produced over 40 years of gender-neutral parental leave insurance, six images – and the campaigns they were part of – will be discussed in this chapter. They are all examples of images that create tensions and conflicts regarding how fatherhood is imagined in Sweden. I have excluded most of the images that show only infants, as well as images that depict heterosexual nuclear families, since these are not directly linked to what Klinth calls 'daddy politics'. From an analysis of the technologies used to create embodied relations between adult and child, or between child and the (adult) preferred viewer of the image, this chapter will argue that fathers who are depicted as 'mothering' and 'modern' are visually idealised.

The analyses locate the construction of the parent–infant relation at the surface of the skin. Skin colour and texture, the transcorporeal interactions between parents and infants, and cultural positions expressed by the attire of the photographic subjects all contribute to the constructions of fatherhood. I will try to avoid language that presupposes biological sex 'beyond' the image surface, with the exception of persons in images who are already known in the public sphere. This has to do with theoretical points that I want to make about corporeality as part of human existence (Alaimo, 2010).

Pregnant subjectivity

Imaginations of other possible understandings of gender relations and new ways of perceiving masculinity and reproduction have been produced in art as well as in mainstream culture. In 1991 the American artist Barbara Kruger (1999) used the *New York Times* as an exhibition area with ads that highlighted differences in men's and women's life situations. One of these ads presented an image of a white, smiling, white-collar man in his thirties, a typical yuppie of the 1980s. The text of the poster reads: 'Help! I've worked hard. Business is booming and I've decided to enter politics. The campaign is going very well but I just found out that I'm pregnant. What should I do?' The man in the image has a far-off gaze, and reflections from a large window are projected over his body. His dreamy smile and the reflections give the impression that he is secluded from the busy world around him. Should we read the text and image ironically? Or is this an image that tries to capture aspects of pregnancy that are expelled from a dichotomous structure where public and private are mutually exclusive, where being pregnant is always an obstacle in the world of political and economic success? Another look at the image shows that the man's smile seems to be directed inwards, to his inner stream of consciousness. Maybe he holds a secret, something that goes beyond his business suit and the powerful environment that we might imagine he is in. An ironic reading of this work would point at the constrained situation of a woman, who cannot easily combine professional life, political ambitions and parenthood. As it is a Kruger work, it could also be seen as an intervention in the growing political conflict regarding women's rights to abortion in an increasingly conservative US context. However, some aspects of the image – the man's dreamy look, his content, inward-looking smile, the surreal ambiance of being behind/in front of the glass – all point at the possibility that this is a person experiencing the secret and transformative miracle of pregnancy. Is Kruger's image an ironic reference to the ironic interpretation? Or is it just that the photograph she is using for her artwork contains an interpretable overabundance, a surplus of meaning, that is actually enhanced by the words on the poster, rather than the two – image and text – contradicting and undermining each other?

In an analysis of *Junior*, a Hollywood production featuring Arnold Schwarzenegger, Nina Lykke (2003) uses the notion of 'the body as a trickster' (Haraway, 1987) to approach the film's theme. Schwarzenegger plays a man who, as the result of a medical experiment, becomes pregnant and gives birth to a child. The cyborgic notion of the body's unpredictable agency challenges both dualistic models of gendered differences and the conceptual link between woman and body. In *Junior* the male pregnancy departs from the monster narrative of, for example, Frankensteinian violations of the laws of nature. Instead, the pregnant body acts on its own, with its own agency that transforms masculinity into an embodiment of nurturing and care. The pregnant body thus challenges both traditional forms of masculinity and the notion of the subject as unitary and autonomous. Imogen Tyler (2001, p 74) describes this as 'Neither one nor two, it is the fleshy in-betweenness and irreducible simultaneity of pregnant subjectivity'.

Reading against the ironic grain of Barbara Kruger's *Help* poster might lead to the same conclusion: the pregnant body is largely left out of our cultural imaginary, since it undermines the notion of the body as the property of the sole and autonomous individual. It challenges borders and, as such, it can serve as a figure of material permeability (Tyler, 2001, p 71; Alaimo, 2010). This concept underlines the material connectedness and potentiality of intra-active transformations, with the starting point in the materiality of both our bodies and the world we inhabit. Transcorporeal permeability can thus help us to understand the political goals of gender equality as relational, emotional and embodied transformations of gender relations.

Equality politics – a politics of reversal?

The formulation 'getting mom a job and making dad pregnant' could be dismissed as populist, simplified or absurd. As a statement, it has a ring to it that makes it sound serious, as if this reversal of men's and women's activities could be achievable, even easy. However, the slogan is politically and theoretically problematic on many levels: it threatens to conceal and flatten important structural differences between the labour market and the private sphere in terms of resources and influence in society. Previous research has highlighted the heteronormative assumptions implicit in the Swedish gender equality discourse, when it is centred on, and thus structured by, the heterosexual couple (Dahl, 2005; Martinsson, 2006; Martinsson and Reimers, 2010). Ideas of the reversibility of 'men's' and 'women's' positions and activities can be criticised in much the same way: it is a politic that reinforces the group 'men' as homogenous, universal, eternally differentiated from the group 'women'. I would like to make a different point, though, in terms of the levelling out of differences in power between the locations that men and women would be switching with each other: the politics of reversibility conceals that men who have positions in the labour market actually lose power when they give up these positions. This is part of what Malin Rönnblom (2008) calls the 'de-politicisation' of gender-equality politics, the idea that gender equality is merely a question of administration and 'attitudes', and not about struggles over political and economic power.

The structure of an assumed 'reversibility' between men's and women's positions thus disguises the power struggle that permeates the gender system. Nonetheless, this dichotomous idea of reversibility has in many ways guided and structured both state politics and research in the field of gender equality. From a feminist materialist perspective, reversibility as equality reinscribes dichotomies based on gender, and risks reproducing signification chains culturally associated with 'woman' and 'man'. However, just as important is the feminist materialist critique of the reproduction of dichotomies between mind and body. This dichotomy is often gendered so that masculinity is constructed as an ideal of de-corporalisation, a fantasy of the free-floating, transcendent subject, distanced from the messy realities of the material world (Alaimo, 2011). This ideal of course goes very well with constructions of the autonomous and self-serving neoliberal subject, and works as depoliticisation that constructs masculinity as naturally detached from parenting, embodiment and activities that take place in the unpaid 'private' sphere.

Or of corporeal permeability?

What would it mean if, instead of criticising and dismissing the slogan 'getting mom a job and making dad pregnant' and its dichotomous structure, we were to take it seriously? From the point of view of new material feminist theory, which includes on its agenda the deconstruction of gender dichotomies, and also of dichotomies such as that between mind and body, one could think about the concept of 'pregnancy' in an extended way (Lykke, 2003; Alaimo, 2011). With the material body in focus, and its affective and emotional capacity to develop new embodied relations with the material world around it, 'pregnancy' can no longer be seen as a function only of the female uterus, or as relying on a discrete, autonomous and self-contained being (Young, 1984; Tyler, 2001). Instead, pregnancy in this chapter will be understood as a corporeal process that involves all human beings that take care of the fundamentally incapable creature that is the new-born infant. To take seriously the idea that fathers could be pregnant, if by 'pregnant' we mean something other than just the possibility of harbouring a foetus inside one's body, would be to acknowledge the corporeality of contact that affects and changes humans regardless of their gender. Pregnancy in this extended account would mean constant involvement in another human being's corporeality, an embodied reciprocity between adult and infant. Stacey Alaimo (2010) calls this reciprocity of the body and its surface a starting point for a transcorporeal ethics, a sense that humans are inevitably entangled in a transcorporeal material sphere. Alaimo, who has worked extensively in the field of 'environmental humanities', writes specifically on the permeability of human and non-human corporealities. In 'The naked word' the visual material she analyses is of naked humans forming political statements in different landscapes, underlining the shared vulnerability of humans and nature. Wiping, cleaning, carrying, leaning, wrestling, catching. The intricate action of dressing a tiny, squirming, surprisingly strong but still fragile infant in small and unnecessarily complicated clothes is not something one learns without changing one's material and embodied being in the world (Rossi, 1977; Lykke, 2003). To theorise the pregnant father is to focus on the corporeal permeability between adult and infant and their involvement in a reciprocal, embodied moulding of the surface of the caretaker. In relation to an analysis of images of parenting as an embodied activity, it is crucial to take into account the fetishising of bodies in contemporary visual culture. In *Thinking through the skin* Sarah Ahmed and Jackie Stacey (2001) argue that there is a tension between the body as a privileged object of study in feminist theory and the risk of fetishising this body within the same theoretical framework. Theorising the skin is an intervention into the risk of totalising 'the body' as well as fetishising it. Ahmed and Stacey argue that zooming in on the skin can be a way to elaborate the body in its locatedness as well as its constructedness in contact with other bodies. However, the skin is also an object of racialised normativity and gendered and normative ideas of beauty. Besides touch and the earlier-mentioned permeability of bodies through the skin, the focus on the skin always entails a risk of reinscribing the objectifying gaze, and the difference between the one who sees and the one who is visually exposed (Phelan, 1993). Analysing the visual dimensions of the process of 'making dad pregnant' as part of a state-endorsed gender equality project, the risks of visual idealisation call for critical theoretical perspectives. One such perspective is offered by Ulrika Dahl (2011), who uses the concept 'surface tension' – in a context outside of natural science – to point to the social and cultural conflicts connected to the surface of the human body and at the same time challenge the dichotomy between depth and surface, which has gendered and racialised implications.

> If by the surface and the contours of the body we also mean the skin, it is in no way a superficial issue. That is apparent by the fact that the colour, shape and decoration of the surface are what at first *glance* determine who is a stranger and who belongs, white or not, 'real' women or not. The surface is thus a pertinent part of racialisation and other deep line drawing of categorization. As an arena for

making meaning it is just like feminist politics, seldom as smooth as the ideals dictate. [...] Closer contact, visual or tactile, with this seemingly distinct surface reminds us that it is through the skin, our largest sensing organ, that emotions and affects are expressed: it sweats and leaks, it blushes and gets stained, shivers and creeps. The skin is our contact surface with the world, that which touches and gets touched. (Dahl, 2011, p 21)

Along with other feminist scholars Dahl highlights the skin as a reciprocal surface that, when made visual or haptic, contains a potential for shared vulnerability, corporeal permeability and non-deterministic perceptions of the body. If Alaimo underscores the particular meanings of the naked body, Dahl theorises the skin in both its bare and exposed as well as adorned and technologically fashioned state, but also as always already racialised. For the purpose of this chapter, which is to analyse images that are included in the Swedish Social Insurance Agency's information brochures and campaigns, all these aspects are equally important. The visual construction of fatherhood uses both corporeality and clothes to create surface tensions: to challenge or reinstate traditional hegemonic masculinity in relation to parental leave and Swedish gender equality politics.

Approaching images

In her ground-breaking article 'Situated knowledges' (1988) Donna Haraway challenges the notion of a scientific gaze that could 'see[ing] everything from nowhere'. Her argument is epistemological, and her answer is 'partial perspectives', but I have always understood this in the most concrete way. The seeing eye is always attached to – or rather, is a part of – the sensuous network of functions that we usually call the body. The body is always located in a specific place that determines the perspective of the one who is looking, scientifically or not. Images in this particular account are actualised in an embodied situation; the act of seeing is always embodied, and emotional. So, how have the images on the brochures constructed a permeability for fathers and children that can account for this expanded notion of pregnancy? Two different layers of permeability characterise the relation between image and viewer. First, there is the construction of the corporeal relation that is being depicted in the image – taking into consideration the technology involved in producing the image as well as references to different image genres that carry certain meanings and emotions – in this case, meanings and emotions traditionally connected to parenting. Second, the construction of the image allows for a permeability of the relation between image and viewer. Does the image make intertextual connections to visual traditions that naturalise the motif? Or does the image create a surface tension, a visual resistance?

The visual material that I analyse in this chapter is part of the 'intimisation' that the Swedish authorities mobilise in their communications with citizens. This process of intimisation started during the late 1960s and early 1970s and was part of reforms that aimed at bridging the gap between authorities and citizens (Mårtensson, 1988). During the 1980s and 1990s Swedish authorities also professionalised their work with information material, increasing their use of professional public relations and advertising bureaus to refine their communication (Lind Palicki, 2010). This was in part an effect of the need to communicate a growing number of public insurance programmes (along with their complex regulations).

Soft touch

In 1976 the most famous image representing Swedish gender-neutral parental leave was produced as part of a campaign aimed at encouraging fathers to use it (Figure 3.1). The image is a half-length photographic portrait of a bearded man holding a small child. The man is a well-known Swedish wrestler, Lennart 'Hoa-Hoa' Dahlgren, and the image has been iconised to the extent that it is now almost equated with the Swedish gender equality politics of the 1970s. The infant in the image is approximately three months old, seemingly naked, bold and gender-undifferentiated, which also contributes to the notion of Swedish gender equality norms that emphasised gender-neutrality for children (Ambjörnsson, 2011). The infant is held in the arms of the large man, and the man smiles at the infant, while the infant looks content, but also a bit surprised, as if having been caught in the middle of an involuntary movement. This gives the photo the directness and closeness of everyday embodied intimacy. The child is not depicted in sentimental or idealised 'perfection', and the look on the man's face seems heartfelt and affectionate.

The image is shot in a warm light, which underlines the colours of the man's reddish curly hair and beard. The infant's skin is very fair. Richard Dyer (1997) discusses light aesthetics in film and photography and the construction of whiteness in terms of affinity: light technologies and the effects of making the white skin's glow work together with the discourse of whiteness as holiness. In the case of the infant, the light is used to enhance an appropriate 'childlike' fragility, and at the same time it produces the warm and fuzzy ambience in which this corporeal fragility can be kept safe. The differentiated way of constructing adult and child underlines the fleshy in-betweenness of them; the man is

Figure 3.1: 'Hoa-Hoa' Dahlgren on the front of 1976 version of Swedish Social Insurance Agency information brochure

Source: Photo by Reio Rüster. Reproduced by permission of the Swedish Social Insurance Agency.

simultaneously depicted as part of this neither-one-nor-twoness and as the responsible and caretaking part of the corporeal assemblage.

This image has accompanied me throughout my life (born 1974) and could potentially be hard for me to analyse; its iconic status in Swedish public life is an effect of its constant reproduction and paraphrasing.[3] Considering both the construction of corporeality in the picture and the genre of the image as expressed in its content, one might argue that the image is iconic not only because of its status, *it is* an icon, more precisely produced in the genre of the iconicity of Madonna and baby Jesus pictures. The glowing light of the image and the embracing touch around the infant's body place the image in the frame of mothering, and at the very same time it promotes 'the new father' (Johansson and Klinth, 2010). 'Hoa-Hoa' Dahlgren's effortless ability to take the Virgin Mary's place in the image shows a readiness to abandon imaginaries of masculinity as distanced from and transcending the matter of parenting (Alaimo, 2011). Does this image 'make dad pregnant' and contribute to a more gender-equal parental leave insurance? The analysis show that it does: it challenges traditional notions of masculinity and contributes to new imaginations of fatherhood.

The technology of garments

The skin is not the only part of the visual construction of identity positions and embodied relations, such as the parent–infant relationship. Clothing contributes just as much to the construction of embodied positions, and can be seen as a technology (de Lauretis, 1989) of gender. The technology of clothing is perhaps most important when the image is not a photograph but a drawing. The drawing often simplifies and accentuates, where the photograph overflows with interpretable detail. The drawing in question is from the very first parental leave brochure that was produced by the Swedish National Insurance Agency, in 1974. It shows a male adult leaning over an infant lying on a nursing table. The adult smiles at the baby. The drawing technique creates a sense of 'togetherness' of the two persons in the image as they are formed in fundamentally the same way, within the same discourse, with the same type of pencilled contours. However, there is no bodily closeness between the two, and the adult wears typical white-collar business attire – white shirt, pullover and tie. The office attire and the distance between the adult and the child give the impression that the situation is pleasant but temporary. The adult is on a short visit to the baby's world. Both in the execution of this particular drawing and as a general difference between photograph and pencil drawing, corporeal permeability, as in embodied closeness and reciprocity between the two persons in the image, is not constructed in this image. In the clothing, in the depicted relation and in the technology of image making, the image reinstates a traditional view of fatherhood as distant and uninvolved, although with a sympathetic attitude towards the child.

There are various differences (as well as similarities) between this first brochure and the ones that were produced later in the 1970s. One difference is that in the later brochures, photography was used instead of drawings. A similarity is that the images continued to focus on the adults. A new brochure produced in 1977 features a photograph of three adults. No children are shown at all.[4] The three men are casually dressed, in jeans and T-shirts; they have (fashionably) long hair and two have beards. Two are public figures: one is the actor Janne 'Loffe' Karlsson and the other the wrestler 'Hoa-Hoa' Dahlgren. Each man is turned towards a baby's pram. The three prams face away from the camera so that the viewer sees them from behind. All three men are looking down into the prams and smiling. These are men of their time, laid back and relaxed, transcending the traditional masculine breadwinner role and career-focused path. Collectively, the three adults in this image reflect a social change – the men affirm each other in their new parenting responsibilities. At the same time, the image does not imply at all what these responsibilities are, other than admiring the babies as they lie in their prams. Life as a full-time parent seems easy and relaxed, just as this type of 'alternative' masculinity implies. The social and cultural changes around masculinity seem to be connected to working life, represented by persons who do not have traditional office occupations and who are not subjected to set office hours and organisational hierarchies. In these two images, the drawing from 1974 and the photograph from 1977, the ambivalent relations between masculinity and the public sphere of productive labour are played out in different ways. I call it ambivalent, since the drawing brings the 'office' into the nursery, while the photograph presents parenting as a leisure activity, without any acknowledgement that taking care of a child could be considered labour as well. The men's garments create their own 'surface tensions' when considered as part of the emotionally charged landscape of parent imaginaries. At the surface of the image the garments produce this shift from professional masculinity to stay-at-home dad. However, the bodily distance between parent and infant is consistent.

The peculiar absence of the children from the image is echoed in a later campaign, from 1997. This campaign included four different brochures and three leaflets, the leaflets explicitly directed at fathers, and the brochures directed at all parents. The graphic form is common to all the products. Each page of the brochures has a Polaroid snapshot with a handwritten comment beneath it. The snapshots are organised so as to present a narrative of pregnancy, preparations for the labour and the parental leave. The three leaflets also include Polaroid images, but no handwritten captions. They introduce three different conflicts that a man could find himself in when he plans to use his parental leave: with his boss, with his workmates and with women – apparently wife and mother – hovering over him when he holds the child. The headlines of these leaflets are ironic: 'Your boss will be so happy!' and the image shows a young male adult standing behind and forcing the older man's mouth into a false smile. Similar scenes are depicted with the assumed workmates and with one younger and one older woman watching over the man's shoulder, advising and admonishing. It would appear that any man who wants to use his parental leave is under attack from three different fronts: the management at his workplace, the apparently all-male workplace and the women surrounding him and questioning his abilities in matters of childcare. The solidaristic collectivist grouping of the 1977 image is completely gone, and the nuclear family seems like a place of suspicion and conflict rather than one of joint parental responsibility.

Through the lens of the camera

The four brochures that accompany the leaflets from 1997 also employ Polaroid photos with everyday-life motifs.[5] What is peculiar about these brochures is that, although there are images on almost every page, nowhere is the child in question depicted. There are images of the child's 'first shoes', 'first bike' and self-portraits of the father loading the car and going for a 'routine check-up at the doctor's'. As these images are supposed to represent Polaroid snapshots taken by first-time parents as a record of this important time in their lives, the exclusion of the child from the images is not only odd, it carries an 'unheimlich' sense of denial and disavowal. The images of fathering activities are connected to documenting everyday life as a stay-at-home dad, but the central figure of this life is invisible. In focus is not the activities connected to caring for a helpless infant but the gadgets – the car seat, the nursing bottle, the clothing and toys – and the man with the camera. The camera and its connotations of control, distance and surveillance have been the objects of considerable theoretical debate in relation to gendered structures of meaning (Mulvey, 1975; Irigaray, 1980; Phelan, 1993). The photographic image's ontological claim, its 'being-there-ness' has also theoretically connected photography to death and loss (Barthes, 1993). Empirically, new camera technologies have often been marketed to the heterosexual male consumer with advertising strategies that put forward the possibilities of capturing a desired woman's image as a possession for the male amateur photographer (Vettel-Becker, 2005). Do these images contribute to a politics that 'make dad pregnant'? No; rather, they contribute to traditional notions of masculinity as non-involved when it comes to the possibility of corporeal permeability through parenting, and they do so by reinstating a traditional 'male gaze' (Mulvey, 1975).

In the images of the non-existent child, the parenting father is the manager of the camera, a distanced figure, hidden behind the lens. The photographs create a tension between the viewer and the cultural imaginaries of parental corporeality, closeness and care. Connections between masculinity and technology, distanced surveillance and autonomy are strengthened and the embodied relationship between parent and child is replaced with an interest in the practicalities and managing aspects of parenting. Emphasising these aspects of parenting can be interpreted as a way to establish a certain 'male' approach to parenting activities, rather than corporeal permeability guiding the relation between adult and infant.

The white gaze

As Dahl points out, skin colour and thus notions of race and/or ethnicity create surface tensions and should be included in an analysis that takes its departure at the surface of the skin (and the image). Dyer notes that camera technologies reproduce notions of white skin as naturalised and charged with positive connotations. The white gaze can be used to put forward both the idealisation of white skin in image production and the naturalisation and reproduction of racist imaginaries and stereotypes. In a brochure from 1996 titled 'Why is it so important that dad be at home with his child?' the Swedish Social Insurance Agency takes a new stand to encourage fathers to use their parental leave insurance. This was part of the renewed focus on fatherhood in Swedish gender-equality politics during the 1990s (Klinth, 2002). This brochure is different from the usual information material in that it does not describe the technicalities of the use of parental leave insurance. Instead, it presents historical, anthropological and psychological accounts of fatherhood and everyday life with a child. It is written in simple language and illustrated with drawings. The drawings are humorous and cartoon-like (including caricatures and stereotypes),[6] reflecting the kind of accessible, undemanding type of communication that characterises so much of 'intimised' information by the state. The content of this brochure concerns subjects that are complex and hotly debated. Maybe that is why the text references an 'expert', an associate professor of pedagogy. The image genre chosen for the brochure is in contrast to the serious textual content, but it also underlines the simplification and popularisation of the arguments of the texts. Under the headline 'Can we change the course of nature?' the text explains changes in human societies in regard to the division of labour between men and women with examples from anthropological research from tribal cultures. This section of the brochure is accompanied by a drawing of a group of four people standing under a palm tree (Figure 3.2). They appear to be a family, according to the nuclear-family model, with two children, one woman and one man. The man seems to be dancing, holding a spear in his hand. He throws his head backwards, his oversized mouth is open and he spreads out his arms and legs. The three other figures stand in the background, not participating in the dance. All four of the figures have dark hair and brown skin, which is a first in the history of the Swedish Social Insurance Agency's production of information about parental leave.

Figure 3.2: Illustration from the 1996 brochure 'Why is it so important that dad be home with his child?'

Source: Illustration by Hans Lange. Reproduced by permission of the Swedish Social Insurance Agency.

We can understand that the previous absence of images of brown skin in previous campaigns may be accounted for by the very slow withering of a self-perception of Swedes as blond and blue eyed, and the notion of the Swedish population as homogenous. This caricature of the 'uncivilised' browned-skinned people in the context of an anthropological discourse constructs a naturalisation of the white gaze, 'scientifically' endorsed by the expert professor. It also brings with it more than just another racist stereotype. In this context it also inscribes modernity as something in contrast to 'traditional' societies, combined with the headline's reference to 'nature'. Since the explicit aim of the brochure is to encourage fathers to stay at home with their children, the combining of this practice with the notion of Swedish exceptionalism and national modernisation is dependent on the possibility of pointing out the 'Other' as less modern, less civilised and less fit for modern parenting (Sawyer and Habel, 2014).

Symbolic marks of 'Swedishness' have been used in the visual material since 1976, with the image of 'Hoa-Hoa' Dahlgren wearing his T-shirt with yellow crowns on a blue background. These crowns and colours are widespread in Swedish visual culture. 'Tre Kronor' (Three Crowns) has been the name of the national ice-hockey team since the World Championship in Prague in 1938 and the crowns are featured on the team's logo. The Swedish currency is called the crown (krona), and blue and yellow are the colours of the national flag. The 'three crowns' are the national symbol of Sweden as a state under the first 'Swedish' king, Gustav Vasa, and are part of Sweden's coat of arms. The crowns stand for national sovereignty and were also the name of the former royal castle that was destroyed in a fire during the 17th century. The pattern on 'Hoa-Hoa's T-shirt conjoins a wide range of connotations: royal independence, ruling and control, economy, masculinity, nationality, strength and sports such as ice hockey, which also points back to 'Hoa-Hoa' himself, as a public persona known for his wrestling career, with strength and masculinity as his main characteristics. The 1976 image was followed by a new campaign in 1979, with 'Hoa-Hoa' Dahlgren cast as a stay-at-home dad.[7] This time he was depicted more in line with the typical playful dad, rather than the caring mother. He sits at the top of a playground slide, with a child approximately three years old on his lap, ready to go down the slide. In an accompanying information film, Dahlgren is cast in the role of a dad who picks up his child from pre-school. He enters the pre-school with a lion-like roar, staging a chasing game that includes all of the children in the room. After some chasing he takes one of the children – presumably the one he has come to pick up – under his gigantic arm and leaves the room, without any words, and accompanied by excited and delighted screams and laughter from the children.[8]

'Hoa-Hoa' Dahlgren is thus cast as the new dad, loving and intimately close and present when the baby is new-born, fun and playful when it enters the pre-school age. His wordless game is set in a context of intelligibility – as a game – while the brown-skinned man of the 1996 brochure is neither cast as corporeally close to his children nor set in any other context that makes his body language intelligible. 'Hoa-Hoa's blue and yellow T-shirt bluntly states that this particular masculinity, strong but emotionally and bodily engaged with a small infant, is a Swedish phenomenon. The whiteness of his skin and his clothing differentiate and make a hierarchy on the basis of skin colour. The new father is modern (as the adjective 'new' indicates) and white skinned (Klinth, 2002).

Even though none of the other images discussed here includes symbols that so explicitly refer to Swedish nationality, they are very similar in constructing 'Swedishness' at the surface of the skin. Children and adults alike are white skinned, fair haired and blue eyed from 1974 onwards. In the 1996 brochure, however, fatherhood is presented in a historical perspective. That perspective articulates social continuities as well as social change. The drawing of the brown-skinned family may be seen as an answer to this construction of Swedish modernity – the imperative of engaged fathers is a modern phenomenon that makes its affirmative claim to fathers who can distance themselves from the uncivilised ways of the 'tribal man'.

The effortlessness with which the white-skinned man enters corporeal permeable parenthood can be theorised with Dahl's concept of 'surface tension'. A naturalised connection between white skin and valuable features like the 'soft touch' of 'Hoa-Hoa's interaction with the infant reproduces a white gaze, seemingly tensionless. Sara Ahmed's notion of the non-white body as halted, stopped and obstructed when moving through a 'white space' (Ahmed, 2007, p 161) has its parallel in the imaginaries that cast the brown-coloured skin as stuck in the past. The 'Hoa-Hoa' pictures contribute to an understanding of masculinity as nurturing and mothering, and at the same time construct whiteness as a naturalised part of this masculinity.

... and the sentimental gaze

What is the policy behind the publication of an image of a little brown-skinned girl in the brochure from 2010? Swedish public policy has used images of people of various cultures and skin colours as a diversity strategy at least since the turn of the millennium (see further Chapter One in this volume) and its contrast to all the fair-skinned toddlers and babies in the brochures from the entire campaign history is hard to miss. Current Swedish visual popular culture also increasingly depicts brown-skinned bodies, although these are idealised and to a great extent fetishised. In photographs of black celebrities such as entertainers and sports stars, the visualisation technique emphasises the shimmering qualities of the brown-skinned surface (hooks, 1992; Wallace-Sanders, 2003). In the 2010 image (Figure 3.3) the child is at the centre, rather than the parent–child relationship, but since the brochure targets adults, the relation is rather that between the depicted child and preferred viewer.

The image shows a toddler in a red-and-white checked skirt. The summertime surroundings and the child's activity – blowing the fluffy seeds off a dandelion – combine the two most important elements of Swedish pictorial sentimentality: nature and child (Werner and Björk, 2014). The child's clothing reflects idyllic notions of rural childhood

Figure 3.3: Photo from the 2010 Swedish Social Insurance Agency information brochure

Source: Reproduced by permission of the Swedish Social Insurance Agency.

as depicted in, for example, Astrid Lindgren's stories about life in pre-industrial times. The image captures the child just as the seeds from the dandelion are caught by a breeze that blows them right back into her face. The game and the seeming spontaneity of the image emphasise the natural sweetness of the young child. In the image of this particular child the emphasis is not on the colour but on the softness of her baby skin. The photographic technique, the printing technique and the quality of the paper, which is lustreless, enhance the softness of the child's skin and her chubby body. The fluffy parts of the flower that blow into her face show the childlike lack of control and create a visual effect of viscerality and tactility; one can almost feel the seeds that cling to her moist lips and face. Jasbir Puar (2007) suggests that viscerality – rather than visuality – is a useful concept when theorising 'race', since it points to deeply embodied cognitions that construct emotional responses to the racialised body. I would argue that the same can be said about the child-body. Corporeal permeability in the relation between image and viewer makes it possible to virtually feel the child's body on a visceral level, underlined by the repeated use of a sentimentalised image language. The image thus constructs a sweet innocence and unawareness of any (adult) gaze; the child as caught in the moment, in play and sensuousness. It also gives the adult viewer unrestricted access to the child, as it does not make any claims on the viewer (Higonnet, 1998). The surface of the skin and of the image collapse into each other; no tension is created, as the child is made completely available for the adult's gaze. This image was most likely produced in the professionalised setting of an advertising agency, taken by a professional photographer (not mentioned in the printed brochure). It has the intimate style of a parent's candid snapshot of a child. It reproduces the preferred relationship between adult and infant where the adult is the viewer, the one in control of the camera, and visualisation technology that provides visual access to idealised childhood. There is no tension at the surface, only the naturalisation of children's to-be-looked-at-ness, which in relation to age and generation and in combination with other signs of 'Swedishness' does not exclude the sentimentalised and adorable brown-skinned child.

Conclusions

'Making dad pregnant' is a tricky business – as analyses of Swedish parental politics have previously shown (Klinth, 2002; 2008; Johansson and Klinth, 2010; Lind Palicki, 2010) – but it seems even harder to challenge and resist the imaginaries of the progressive, modern parent as white skinned, while the visual fetishisation of children allows a diversity of skin colour, as long as they are cute and inscribed in a 'Swedish' imaginary of idealised childhood and closeness to nature.

Images can be seen as part of dominant political discourses, but they also produce meaning beyond policy production. The images analysed in this chapter are very different from each other, they use different techniques to create their visual effects. Instead of looking at how the images confirm or reproduce gender equality politics, their manifold ways of participating in the policies of 'making dad pregnant' have been analysed.

The case studies included in this chapter show an increased professionalisation of image use in the Swedish state authorities' communications with its citizens. The 2010 image is strikingly similar to advertising images, with a well-modulated use of photographic technique to enhance the appeal of the depicted child. This professionalisation also seems to lead to images that do not produce the overabundance of meaning that makes earlier images polysemic and more contradictory. Many of the images analysed here show no closeness at all between fathers and children, either emotional or corporeal. One could say that they do not contribute to a daddy politics that aims at 'making dad pregnant'. These dads are nevertheless depicted as legitimate caretakers, although within the realm of a traditional hegemonic masculinity: distanced, efficient and autonomous. Comparing the collectivity of the fathers depicted in the 1970s and the autonomy of the 1990s dad underlines this conclusion. However, the main characteristic of an idealised father in the image material is the way he is depicted as modern. *Skin contact* between parent and infant – the potentiality for a corporeal permeability and 'making dad pregnant' – is not the focus, but rather *skin colour*. With the concept 'surface tension' embodied, technologically developed, visually available surfaces are made important in the process of constructing parent–infant relationships. Surface tension potentially both enables and obstructs the process of 'making dad pregnant' in the context of Swedish equality politics and the parental leave information material. The very same materiality of the sensing skin that makes embodied relations possible can also harbour surface tensions that distance child from caretaker, sometimes to the extent that the child is not even visible. When the adult, and not the parent–child relation, is at the centre, the images are emptied of parenting as an activity with a particular content and aim, as well as of its transcorporeality. The images that depict fathers alone construct them as autonomous in their choice of active parenting; these construct a new identity, with political implications, rather than a specific form of relationship. This construction is framed as modern, white skinned and 'Swedish'. When the embodied relation between parent and child is emphasised the images rely on well-established genres and modalities, where 'mothering' is used as a way to shape the meaning of the parent–child relationship, regardless of gender position.

Transcorporeal permeability emphasises the fundamental togetherness of human materiality and co-dependence. It challenges the notion of an autonomous, mind-centred and disembodied subject and its political context as well as its political effects. The parent–child relationship already 'knows' this, whether it is thought of as a relationship that starts with the foetus enclosed by the uterus, or with the infant in the arms of the adults who are assigned to be its caretakers. Images participate in this corporeal permeability by managing and producing emotions and meanings. In Swedish state-endorsed parental politics, images manage tensions around who should – and can – be involved in the transcorporeal permeability of reproduction.

Notes

[1] This is the translation Roger Klinth (2008) uses in 'The best of both worlds?', but the statement could also be translated as 'getting mom a job and letting dad have the baby ', to avoid the medicalised terminology that is implicit in the word 'pregnancy'.

[2] Lind Palicki used the archives of the Social Insurance Agency. After reading of the specific problems that she faced, I decided to collect and analyse the material at the Swedish National Library in Stockholm, which is the copyright library for Sweden.

[3] See, for example, the hilarious paraphrase by Ulrika Stahre on the cover of the Swedish feminist magazine *bang*, 2004, issue 3.

[4] This image can be found in the Swedish National Insurance Agency's brochure from 1977.

[5] These images can be found in the Swedish National Insurance Agency's brochure from 1997.

[6] Cartoons and illustrations in children's books have been fiercely criticised for reproducing racist stereotypes in Swedish (and Euro-American) visual cultures (see Martinsson, 2014). In Sweden, particularly the children's book illustrations by Stina Wirsén, the racist stereotypes in *Pippi Longstocking* and in the comic books about Tintin have been criticised. The connections between children's book illustrations, cartoons and the 1920s construction of stereotypes of African-Americans is based on a specific notion of 'humorous' representations, which seems to have spread easily

to children's books when they transformed from sense-moralistic and sentimental to entertaining and 'crazy'.

[7] This image can be found in the Swedish National Insurance Agency's brochure from 1979.

[8] This film can be found on Filmarkivet [The Swedish Film archive] http://www. filmarkivet.se/sv/Film/?movieid=594, accessed 8 June 2015.

References

Ahmed, S. (2007) 'A phenomenology of whiteness', *Feminist Theory*, vol 8, no 2, pp 149–68.

Ahmed, S. and Stacey, J. (2001) *Thinking through the skin*, London: Routledge.

Alaimo, S. (2010) 'The naked word: the trans-corporeal ethics of the protesting body', *Women & Performance: A Journal of Feminist Theory*, vol 20, no 1, pp 15–36.

Alaimo, S. (2011) 'New materialisms, old humanisms, or, following the submersible', *NORA: Nordic Journal of Feminist and Gender Research*, vol 19, no 4, pp 280–4.

Ambjörnsson, F. (2011) *Rosa: den farliga färgen* [*Pink: The dangerous colour*], Stockholm: Ordfront.

Barthes, R. (1977) *Music, image, text*, New York: Hill and Wang.

Barthes, R. (1993) *Camera lucida: Reflections on photography*, London: Vintage.

Dahl, U. (2005) 'Scener ur ett äktenskap: jämställdhet och heteronormativitet' [Scenes from a marriage: gender equality and heteronormativity], in D. Kulick, (ed) *Queersverige* [QueerSweden], Stockholm: Natur och Kultur, pp 48–71.

Dahl, U. (2011) 'Ytspänningar: Feminister, feminismer, femmefigurationer' [Surface-tensions: feminists, feminisms, femme figurations], *Tidskrift för genusvetenskap*, vol 1, pp 5–27.

de Lauretis, T. (1989) *Technologies of gender: Essays on theory, film, and fiction*, Basingstoke: Macmillan.

Dyer, R. (1997) *White: Essays on race and culture*, London: Routledge.

Haraway, D. (1987) 'A manifesto for cyborgs: science, technology, and socialist feminism in the 1980s', *Australian Feminist Studies*, vol 4, pp 1–42.

Haraway, D. (1988) 'Situated knowledges: the science question in feminism and the privilege of partial perspective', *Feminist Studies*, vol 14, no 3, pp 575–99.

Higonnet, A. (1998) *Pictures of innocence: The history and crisis of ideal childhood*, London: Thames & Hudson.

hooks, b. (1992) *Black looks: Race and representation*, Boston: South End Press,.

Irigaray, L. (1980) 'When our lips speak together', *Signs*, vol 6, no 1, pp 69–79.

Johansson, T. and Klinth, R. (2010) *Nya svenska fäder* [*New Swedish fathers*], Umeå: Boréa.

Klinth, R. (2002) *Göra pappa med barn: den svenska pappapolitiken 1960–95* [*Making dad pregnant: the Swedish daddy politics 1960–95*], Umeå: Boréa.

Klinth, R. (2008) 'The best of both worlds? Fatherhood and gender equality in Swedish paternity leave campaigns, 1976–2006', *Fathering: A Journal of Theory, Research, and Practice about Men as Fathers*, vol 6, no 1, pp 20–38.

Kruger, B. (1999) *Thinking of you*, Cambridge, MA: MIT Press.

Lind Palicki, L. (2010) *Normaliserade föräldrar: en undersökning av Försäkringskassans broschyrer 1974–2007* [*Normalised parents: An investigation of the Swedish National Insurance Agency's brochures 1974–2007*], Örebro: Örebro universitet.

Lykke, N. (2003) 'Corps-cyborg et bioéthique féministe: le cas de "Junior"' [Cyborg bodies and feminist bio-ethics: the case of Junior], in A.G. Pinsart (ed) *Genre et Bioéthique*, Paris: Vrin, pp 15–26.

Mårtensson, E. (1988) 'Den familjära myndigheten: Intimiseringen av det offentliga språket' [The familiar authority: intimisation of the official language], in O. Löfgren (ed) *Hej, det är från Försäkringskassan! Informaliseringen av Sverige* [*Hi, it is from the social insurance agency*], Stockholm: Natur och Kultur, pp 105–27.

Martinsson, L. (2006) *Jakten på konsensus* [*Hunting for consensus*], Malmö: Liber.

Martinsson, L. and E. Reimers (2010) *Norm-struggles*, Newcastle: Cambridge Scholars.

Martinsson, L. and E. Reimers (2014) *Skola i normer* [*School in norms*], Malmö: Gleerup.

Mellström, U. (2005) 'Doing critical men's studies in a state feminist country: reflections on gender research in Sweden', *Schriften des Essener Kollegs für Geschlechterforschung*, vol 5, no 1, pp 5–27.

Mulvey, L. (1975) 'Visual pleasure and narrative cinema', *Screen*, vol 16, no 3, pp 6–18.

Palme, O. (1972) 'Emancipation of man', *Journal of Social Issues*, vol 28, no 2, pp 237–46.

Phelan, P. (1993). *Unmarked: The politics of performance*, London: Routledge.

Puar, J.K. (2007). *Terrorist assemblages: Homonationalism in queer times*, Durham, NC: Duke University Press.

Rose, G. (2012) *Visual methodologies: An introduction to researching with visual materials*, London: Sage.

Rossi, A. (1977) 'A biosocial perspective on parenting', *Daedalus*, vol 106, pp 1–31.

Rönnblom, M. (2008) 'De-politicising gender? Constructions of gender equality in Swedish regional policy', in E. Magnusson, M. Rönnblom and H. Silius (eds) *Critical studies of gender equalities: Nordic dislocations, dilemmas and contradictions*, Göteborg: Makadam, pp 112–34.

Sawyer, L. and Habel, Y. (2014) 'Refracting African and Black diaspora through the Nordic region', *African and Black Diaspora: An International Journal*, vol 7, no 1, pp 1–6.

Statistics Sweden (2008) *Women and men in Sweden: Facts and figures*, Stockholm: Gender statistics unit, Statistics Sweden.

Tyler, I. (2001) 'Skin-tight: celebrity, pregnancy and subjectivity', in S. Ahmed and J. Stacey (eds) *Thinking through the skin*, London: Routledge, pp 69–83.

Vettel-Becker, P. (2005) *Shooting from the hip: Photography, masculinity, and postwar America*, Minneapolis: University of Minnesota Press.

Wallace-Sanders, K. (2003). *Skin deep, spirit strong: The Black female body in American culture*, Ann Arbor: University of Michigan Press.

Werner, J. and Björk, T. (2014) *Blond och blåögd: Vithet, svenskhet och visuell kultur* [*Blond and blue-eyed: Whiteness, Swedishness, and visual culture*], Göteborg: Göteborgs konstmuseum.

Widerberg, K. (1993) 'Kvinnoperspektiv på rätten: den svenska föräldraledighetslagstiftningen som ett belysande exempel' [Women's perspective on the law: The Swedish parental leave legislation as an enlightening example], in L. Jakobsen and J. C. Karlsson (eds) *Jämställdhetsforskning* [*Research on gender equality*], Karlstad: Högskolan, pp 31–47.

Young, I.M. (1984) 'Pregnant embodiment: Subjectivity and alienation', *The Journal of Medicine and Philosophy*, vol 9, no 1, pp 45–62.

FOUR

Rethinking gender equality and the Swedish welfare state: a view from outside

Gabriele Griffin

It is difficult to keep local instances local in their significance. (Appadurai, 2006, p 40)

Introduction

A quick search on search engines such as JSTOR and Google Scholar reveals that researchers continue to have more to say about 'Sweden and equality' than about 'Sweden and inequality'. This indicates the persisting hold that the equation of Sweden with equality has in certain public imaginaries. However, investigating the gendered constructions of racism in Swedish internationalised popular culture – in particular, in this instance, in the works of Henning Mankell (2011; 2013), whose writings serve as a cultural barometer of changing Swedish attitudes to the socioeconomic realities of immigration – challenges this image. That investigation reveals how the construction of Sweden as the most gender-equal nation in Europe – if not in the world – has for some considerable time been called into question, not least by the effects of globalisation and their impacts on Sweden. This chapter will draw on the theoretical elaborations of Arjun Appadurai's work on the *Fear of small numbers* (2006; 2009) to suggest that the fears Appadurai diagnoses as central to neoliberal regimes are operant in Sweden, where their articulation throws light on the inequalities that govern that country. I will argue in this chapter that changes to the Swedish welfare system and the weakening of the Swedish nation-state as an effect of certain globalising forces, in particular the movements of people, capital and information, have led – inter alia in popular culture – to the construction of Sweden as embattled territory with strongly delineated gendered contours.

Migration, welfare changes and racialised violence

Mankell's *Faceless killers*, the first volume in his Wallander series, came out in 1991, at a time when Sweden was experiencing a significant increase in immigration numbers (Table 4.1). Indeed, 'by the mid-1990s, over 10 per cent of all Swedish inhabitants [9.1 million] were foreign-born, and 13 per cent were either foreign-born or Swedish-born with two foreign-born parents' (Eger 2010, p 205). This means, as Eger suggests, that Sweden turned into a multi-cultural society in a very brief period of time.

Table 4.1: Residence permits granted, Sweden, 1990–96

Residence permits granted	1990	1991	1992	1993	1994	1995	1996
Refugees	12,839	18,663	12,791	36,482	44,875	5,642	4,832
Family reunification	22,221	21,230	19,662	19,769	25,975	19,707	18,816

Source: Adapted from the Swedish Migration Board, http://www.migrationsverket.se/English/About-the-Migration-Board/Statistics/Overview-and-time-series.html (accessed 14 May 2014).

The surge in immigrant numbers that Sweden experienced went together with significant shifts in Swedish immigration policies. At the same time the welfare state was increasingly in retrenchment and being supplanted by a workfare ideology, and neoliberalism in the form of marketisation, privatisation and the rhetoric of individual choice came to the fore. It is in this context that Kurt Wallander, middle-aged male police inspector and one of the heroes of the post-2000 expansion of so-called Scandinavian crime fiction (Saarinen, 2003; Nestingen and Arvas, 2011; Forshaw, 2012; Nestingen, 2012), makes his first appearance as he asks, à propos of the unprovoked murder of a Somali refugee:

> What's behind this whole thing? Neo–Nazis? Racists with connections all over Europe? Why would someone commit a crime like this anyway? Jump out into the road and shoot a complete stranger? Just because he happened to be black? (Mankell, 2011 [1991], p 232)

In response to these questions his colleague answers: "'No way of knowing," said Rydberg. "But it's something *we're going to have to learn to live with*." (Mankell, 2011 [1991], p 232) Rydberg's 'having to learn to live with' suggests an inevitability of being compelled to accommodate, to accept such violence. By 2014 racialised violence – in the 1991 novel still mainly an expectation – had, one might argue, become the 'new normal'. Racism in Scandinavia – in its many forms, and always with the threat of shadow networks of neo-Nazis and fascists reaching across Europe in the background – has become 'everyday' (Essed, 1991). Anders Breivik's killings in 2011 are but the last, highly publicised instance of this. At the end of *Faceless killers*, Wallander muses: 'Again he thought about the violence. The new era, which demanded a different kind of policeman. We're living in the age of the noose, he thought. Fear will be on the rise' (p 298).

'Fear on the rise': cultures of violence, whiteness and facelessness

When I first came to Sweden for an extended period of time, in the winter of 2008, I knew nothing of the Wallander series[1] and I had no sense at all of 'fear being on the rise' of any culture of violence or racism. I remember that I was quite taken aback to discover, in the free local newspaper, a column entitled 'Polisreporten' that detailed all the crimes that had occurred in the previous week in the very well-to-do quarter of Stockholm, Ostermalm, where I was housed by the university. I had always imagined Sweden as a very safe culture, and, actually, I still think of it as such. What really struck me about Stockholm at that time in 2008 was how white it was[2] – rather like the covers of the Mankell novels as published in the UK by Vintage, which frequently feature a snowy-white landscape in the foreground and a city or isolated house in the background, set back at a distance, with few or no people around. For me coming from the UK, this whiteness was particularly noticeable, since, especially in the cities in which I had lived – London, Leeds, Leicester – multiculturalism visibly prevailed.[3] The street scene in Stockholm was very different – certainly in the quarters I frequented the most, which appeared to be largely mono-ethnic, something that is not quite the case just six years later, in 2014.

What also struck me in 2008 were the multiple exhibitions around Stockholm testifying to the horrors of mass killings and deaths elsewhere, outside of Sweden: Lars Lerin's installation at Walldemarsudde, commemorating the 26 December 2004 tsunami in Thailand, featured a row of abandoned shoes washed up on the shore, and was reminiscent of another memorial articulated through shoes, that of Hungarian Jews in Budapest;[4] at Magasin 3 in Stockholm there were works such as Être et avoir by Christian Boltanski, memorialising the Holocaust. In all these exhibits it was not the faceless killers conjured up by Mankell's first Wallander novel that one confronted, but the faceless victims. Whiteness, and the cultural construction of the faceless victim – these seemed dominant. But they were also, importantly, accounts of what had happened *elsewhere*, rather than on Swedish soil. Mankell's work, however, returns these issues to Sweden, diagnosing, as Allan Pred already put it in 2000, that 'even in Sweden' 'racisms are currently flourishing' (p 6).

In examining the manifestation of inequality in Sweden, I want to explore these racisms and their gendered dimensions to reveal their intersectional imbrication that manifests itself in contemporary Swedish culture, and in particular as articulated in two works by Henning Mankell, *Faceless killers* and *The shadow girls*. I have chosen these texts for three reasons: (a) Scandinavian crime fiction, of which Henning Mankell and the Wallander series are outstanding and internationally renowned examples,[5] represents one window through which the wider world, including myself, looks in on Sweden; (b) simultaneously, these texts provide a cultural barometer of perceptions about inequality in Sweden from *within* Sweden; and (c) the two texts were first published in Sweden ten years apart (1991 and 2001) and hence cover a period in which significant changes occurred in Swedish immigration policy and actuality. It should be said straight away that *The shadow girls* is not a crime fiction, but its dissemination, I would argue, depends significantly on Mankell's reputation as the author of internationally acclaimed crime fiction.[6] Also, as I shall indicate, the text has certain thematic continuities with the Wallander series – in particular, *Faceless killers* – in its central male figures and its preoccupation with immigrants.

Facelessness was much debated in post-2000 academe, partly in response to Judith Butler's (2004, 2009) discussions of the rendering faceless of certain groups of people in the context of what she described as 'grievable lives', and partly in response to the media rhetoric of plurification, of 'floods' and 'masses', that had come to dominate some European, and certainly British, public discourse about immigration.[7] Here facelessness and sheer numbers, expressed through metaphors of quasi-natural disasters, were mobilised as a measure to dehumanise immigrants and to reinforce arguments about the limits of welfare state resources. In his 2001 novel *The shadow girls*, Henning Mankell attempts to address this facelessness. In the novel, a Swedish reporter arrives at a Spanish refugee camp to write 'a series on people without faces, refugees who are desperately trying to enter Europe. We want to tell your story. [he says] We want to give you back your face' (p 17) 'Tea-Bag', the female refugee to whom he proposes to give her face back, and who is one of the main female protagonists, is outraged by his suggestion, and claims her agency by demanding an apology, stating: 'I already have a face. What is he taking pictures of if I have no face?' (p 17). *She* is not faceless. 'I am here, Tea-Bag thought. I am in the centre of things here, in the centre of my life' (p 10). Facelessness is thus constructed as a matter of perspective – asserted of the other, but denied by the self.

Tea-Bag's encounter with the journalist early on in the text on one level sets the *gender* tone for the rest of the novel, where persecuted young females (damsels in distress in conventional romance parlance) are variously aided by older men – a gender dynamic of the most conventional heteronormative kind. On another level, Tea-Bag and the journalist's encounter translates into an uneasy confrontation between two people – a well-meaning white, paternalistic, middle-aged male and a young black female on the run – in different states of uncertainty, not least about the meaning of the other.

Taking the place of the subject: the fear of (small) numbers

Sarah Ahmed, among others, has written about such uncertainties, especially in a piece on 'The organization of hate' (2009). There, she discusses how hate is mobilised to generate 'a subject that is endangered by imagined others whose proximity threatens not only to take something away from the subject (jobs, security, wealth) but also to *take the place of the subject*' (p 252; my emphasis). This taking of the place of the subject, which is one way in which social groups might relate to each other, is what I want to discuss here. This issue underlies Appadurai's work on the 'fear of small numbers' where he seeks to account for the increasing numbers of large-scale ethno-nationalistically driven genocides that have occurred globally since the 1970s – in India, in Rwanda, in the former Yugoslavia and so on. He argues that we live in an age of social uncertainty, as the forces of globalisation – specifically the transnational flows of capital, people, information – have begun to marginalise nation-states' abilities to control their borders, and threaten their boundaries at every level. This results in an 'anxiety of incompleteness', as he puts it, and manifests itself in questions around identity that relate to the nation-state. He suggests:

> One kind of uncertainty is a direct reflection of census concerns: how many persons of this or that sort really exist in a given territory? Or, in the context of rapid migration or refugee movement, how many of 'them' are there among us? ... A further uncertainty is about whether a particular person really is what he or she claims or appears to be or has historically been. (Appadurai, 2006, p 5–6)

Appadurai's list of uncertainties is infinitely expandable and, as he suggests, 'these various forms of uncertainty create intolerable anxiety' (p 6) that may ultimately translate into violence that then becomes a technique for producing an order of 'them' and 'us'.

The question of numbers in conjunction with a sense of social uncertainty looms large in the context of migration, due to the expansion of the immigrant population in Sweden as in other European countries from the 1960s onwards. This expansion has led to increasingly restrictive legislation across Europe, including in Sweden. Goran Rosenberg (1995) suggests that from 1972, conceptually speaking, *labour* immigration to Sweden ceased as 'More or less overnight the Swedish political elite redefined the role of Sweden vis-à-vis its immigrants, from one of economic necessity to a moral duty' (p 211), with 'the word refugee [becoming] synonymous with immigration' and a shift in emphasis occurring from 'the needs of Sweden', that is its economic needs, to 'the needs of the refugees' (p 211). Indeed, Maureen Eger (2010) has argued that 'it is easier for foreigners who come to Sweden with asylum permits to apply for citizenship than it is for those who come with work or study visas' (p 205). However, as Tham et al (2011) have shown, two contradictory rhetorics have emerged in political and policy discourse. On the one hand there has been a rise in the construction of those whom the state should aid, as a function of the prevailing (though waning) welfare state ideology. In Tham et al's analysis this applies particularly to victims of crime. On the other, there has been a growing replacement of the welfare state approach by neoliberal values, including the stress on minimal government (p 595).[8] Tham et al further argue that as (in the context of globalization) 'the room available to politicians in economic questions decreases, efforts tend to increase in areas with a moral focus' (p 595). These areas with a moral focus include, one might suggest, not just crime victims but also refugees. However, although 'the suffering subject' may well, as Tham et al indicate, 'be presented as an object for social and moral engineering' (p 595) as expressed through legislative measures, such efforts are simultaneously hindered by the declining resources of the retrenching welfare state, where the need for support might be diagnosed and asserted, but the resources to grant such support are in ever-shortening supply.[9]

According to Rosenberg, the Swedish political rhetoric in the late 20th century around immigrants was that 'Refugees did not immigrate for the sake of helping Sweden; Sweden existed to help the refugees' (1995, p 211). This rhetoric, replicating the notion of the suffering subject alluded to above, led to the homogenisation[10] of immigrants and their redefinition *as refugees* and, in consequence, as an economic burden. Rosenberg blames the accompanying increasingly bureaucratised centralisation of immigration services and what he describes as the political elite's refusal to reconcile 'political and moral commitments with economic realities' (p 214) for the development of randomness in the processing of immigrants – a signal of the inability of the relevant services to cope. This manifested itself in 'increased insensitivity regarding individual refugees, i.e. … throwing people out after two or three years of investigation, forcing thousands of refugees into hiding' (p 214). This is precisely the issue that is thematised in *The shadow girls*.

Both *Faceless killers* and *The shadow girls* articulate concern about the Swedish state as an ailing structure, incapable of using its institutions – the police, the immigration service – effectively to control the influx and settlement of migrants. Confronted with the brutal murder of an elderly couple that is initially attributed to refugees, Wallander thinks, 'I really hope that the killers are at that refugee camp. Then maybe it'll put an end to this arbitrary, lax policy that allows anyone at all, for any reason at all, to cross the border into Sweden' (p 46). The failure to maintain borders adequately is linked to the inability of the state bureaucracy to do its work effectively. This is reiterated throughout the text, for instance through the assertion that 'There are files on everything' (p 59) in relation to the question of knowledge about foreigners who have committed crimes in Sweden. Indeed, there are files on everything, but they do not help Wallander to solve the crime. Towards the end of the novel Wallander tells the prosecutor, repeating his earlier thoughts: 'Right now we are living in a country where anyone for any reason can come across the border in any manner. Control has been eliminated. The customs service is paralysed. There are plenty of unsupervised airfields where the dope and the illegal immigrants are unloaded every night' (p 227). The result of this failure is that 'The insecurity in this country is enormous. People are afraid' (p 227). It is a fear that calls for change: 'Maybe the times require another kind of policeman, [Wallander] thought … Policemen who aren't distressed ... Policemen who don't suffer from my uncertainty and anguish' (p 19).

Masculinity in crisis

On one level – and this articulates the gender politics of this novel – Wallander's 'uncertainty and anguish' is the anxiety of a certain, conventionally dominant masculinity, especially in its middle-aged version, in crisis. In this Wallander is no different from the writer Jesper Humlin, the central male character of *The shadow girls.* Both men are adrift, feel embattled and hollowed out. They feel ambivalent and anxious about their work, are alienated from their partners, in an uneasy relation to their surviving parent, but with an unreflected heterosexually oriented sexual predatoriness that articulates their sense of entitlement, in this context to dominate women.[11] They represent the state (Wallander) and the cultural elite (Humlin), but they also stand for a failing male cultural majority. The women elude their control and, in fact, turn out to be *in control.* Jesper Humlin, for instance, experiences himself as the object of the comings and goings of the refugee girls whom he befriends but whose movements he cannot control, and as at the mercy of his mother. In *Faceless killers* Wallander finds that the men he expects to be in charge have vacated their function, and for a variety of reasons. The prosecutor is absent and his replacement is a young woman: 'Wallander stared at her. "Seen enough yet?" she said' (p 94). When Wallander rings the Head of Immigration Services he 'was surprised to be speaking to a woman. He assumed that all senior government officials were still elderly gentlemen full of arrogant self-esteem' (p 117). Ironically, Wallander fails to see himself in this image but in his bewildered response he does articulate his sense of the place of the subject, men like himself, being taken by another: women. The prosecutor, Anette, is instantly aware of his sexual objectification of her. Later in the novel that objectification turns into an actual sexual assault (p 228) by Wallander on her, thwarted only by Wallander's being too drunk to control the situation sufficiently.

The unreflexive sexual objectification of women is one main way in which Mankell signals masculinity in crisis in these texts, since this is constructed as the main way in which the heteronormative men he installs at the centre of his novels relate to women. Wallander has repeated erotic dreams about a black woman who functions as his object of desire. Humlin always and instantly focuses on women's appearance and their implicit attractiveness for him. Thus, for example, he is described as immediately 'falling in love' with his friend Pelle

Törnblom's wife, about whom he knows nothing other than: 'She had a beautiful face, with deep-set eyes. During his reading he directed his inner attentions towards her, reading his poems for her and no one else' (p 58). Neither Wallander nor Humlin really considers whether such attentions are in any way desired or reciprocated by the women in question; part of their sense of entitlement in relation to dominating women relies on their unquestioning projection of their own desires. The men's sexual subject position is thus consistently asserted in their unreflexive orientations towards women, and women's object status in these men's imaginaries is kept in place through that process. This mitigates the fear of the subject's (= men's) place being taken by the other (= women).

The absence of any equality in this domain is made plain when Wallander and Humlin are forced to confront the sexual in relation to the women either to whom they are related or with whom they are in a relationship – their mothers, their daughters, their wives or partners. Within a conservative gender politics, family members inhabit a space outside the sexual at best; at worst, their sexual desires and activities are meant to be contained. It therefore always comes as a shock to these men when their female family members appear to have independent sexual lives: Wallander's daughter dates a black man, and when Wallander discovers this, he gets very agitated and starts to spy on her, thus imbricating the racist in the sexist. Humlin's 90-year-old mother earns money on the side through phone sex, a source of agitation for Humlin. Neither man is able to intervene effectively in this situation because they recognise, morally, that it is not their place to do so. But the paroxysms into which these discoveries throw them are indicative of the difficulties they have in acknowledging women's agency in their own lives.

Importantly, throughout both texts a parallel is drawn between the state's being unable to control immigration and Wallander's and Humlin's being unable to dominate the women in their lives. Humlin feels himself to be the victim of his mother, whose bidding he reluctantly does, and of his girlfriend Andrea, whose desire for a child and for commitment he constantly evades rather than engages with. Depicted as a bumbling, self-obsessed egoist, in many ways still a child, Humlin feels constantly threatened in his subject position, telling Andrea, for example: 'Every time we have a serious talk it's as if I've been thrown into a play where I haven't even picked my own lines' (p 218–19). Characters in plays, of course, do not generally pick their own lines, but this irony escapes Humlin. His sense of not being in control is reiterated throughout the novel in his repeated assertion of having 'lost his footing' (for example, pp 133, 155, 172). Encouraged by his publisher to write a crime novel, a form of cultural populism in which he thinks he has no interest, he is nonetheless appalled to discover that both his girlfriend and his mother (as well as his male literary rival and his stockbroker) are writing such novels: 'Humlin felt an impending catastrophe speeding towards him. The final defeat would be when his own mother was hailed as a more accomplished writer then himself' (p 132).

In his analysis of 'how cultures of fear, humiliation and hope are reshaping the world' Dominique Moïsi (2009) discusses Europe as being dominated by a culture of fears of different kinds which altogether amount to 'the fear of loss of control over one's own destiny' (p 104). This, in a sense, is precisely the kind of fear both Humlin and Wallander articulate, the fear of their subject position being taken by another. It stems from a structural understanding of self that insists on the uniqueness of one's position which can be maintained only by the exclusion of others and in which only self can exist. Coexistence is not possible here. And, interestingly, in Mankell's texts the impossibility of coexistence is reiterated in relation to both women and refugees. In *Faceless killers* Wallander lives alone, separated from his wife, and the refugees are meant to live in segregated camps. In *The shadow girls* Humlin spends most of his time separately from his girlfriend, his mother lives on her own and the refugee girls exist either in camps or in temporary accommodation, or in other spaces where they are segregated from indigenous people.

As for other men, whether from the same or from another culture, they appear as menaces or threats, or as abjected and to be patronised. Male relations are mostly either confrontational or paternalistic. 'True' friendships between men where they coexist as equals in the same space are extremely rare. Men's interactions are structured through their relations to, or attempts at domination of, women. In that sense Mankell's novels replicate the homosocial triangle — where women function as objects of (quasi-)patriarchal patronage, contestation and exchange between men — so effectively diagnosed by Eve Kosofsky Sedgwick in 1985. Thus Humlin's friend Törnblom, another middle-aged male, mediates between Humlin and the girls, and between the girls and other males (their father, other male refugees and so on) in the boxing club where he arranges the meetings for Humlin and the refugee women. Humlin is meant to mediate between the women and the wider world by telling their story. And, indeed, in telling their story by interpolating it as a first-person narration, Humlin as narrator and Mankell as author both 'allow' or 'enable' — and these are the operant words here, given the embeddedness of the refugee girls' narratives – the women to take their, meaning the men's, place as subjects. The men thus produce their own narrative displacement, but through an act of incorporation that limits the notion of the women's agency. But the threat to the men's position is nonetheless there. In *Faceless killers* the Swedish Far Right makes its appearance in the shape of a male former policeman and his friend who kill refugees. Here we have another version of what I would describe as 'beleaguered masculinity', where indigenous men feel threatened in their subject position by immigrants whom they decide to kill for this very reason.

Predatory identities and the fear of numbers, large and small

It is in this triangle of masculinity in crisis, ailing nation-states and social uncertainty that Appadurai's (2009) 'Fear of small numbers' – which in important ways is concerned with fears of the other, rather than specifically or just small numbers – becomes relevant. In it he raises the question about what he calls the formation of so-called predatory identities (p 236). He argues that the anxiety of incompleteness about their sovereignty can turn majoritarian identities into predatory ones where discourses of how the majority could itself become the minority 'unless another minority disappears' function as incentives to become predatory and forestall the possibility of such reversals of fortune. In asking in particular when *liberal* majoritarianisms become illiberal, Appadurai links the idea of the number to the liberal imaginary. He suggests that liberals have a certain ambivalence about the legitimacy of collectives as political actors, since the critical number for liberal social theory is the number 1, 'the numerical sign for the individual'. The other important number is the zero, as it converts the one into tens, hundreds and thousands: 'in other words, zero is the numerical key to the idea of the masses' (p 239). However, according to Appadurai, the masses in liberal thought are associated with 'large numbers that have lost the rationalities embedded in the individual, in the number one' (p 240). They are viewed as the basis for both totalitarianism and fascism, and 'it is because of this . . . that much liberal thought has been rightly characterised by a fear of large numbers' (p 240). One might argue that the presentation of immigrants, refugees and asylum seekers in terms of faceless masses, not least in the media that Appadurai also indicts, fuels that fear within the neoliberal regime in which we live.

Appadurai contrasts this liberal fear of large numbers with the fear of small numbers, which is associated with 'oligarchies, elites and tyrannies', on the one hand, and 'the spector of conspiracy', in the form of 'the cell, the spy, the traitor, the dissident, the revolutionary', on the other (p 240). Part of Wallander's problematic in trying to understand the killings he has to deal with in *Faceless killers* is whether these are carried out by people who represent a movement, hence certain masses, or whether this is the work of a cell, a small group of people. Small numbers or minorities, according to Appadurai, carry with them 'special interest' claims, hence, especially as substantive minorities that are permanent, become problematic because of their rights claims. Appadurai argues that this has generated unease in western democracies where the struggle over cultural rights as they belong to national citizenship has led to the emergence and reinforcement of predatory identities.

Appadurai suggests that the fear of small numbers is linked to the majority's fear of 'becoming *minor* (culturally or numerically)' (p 249). But whereas in *Faceless killers*, his earlier novel, Mankell – like Appadurai in his work – focuses mainly on the fear of the majority, in *The shadow girls* he attempts to set against this the fear of the refugees, the minoritised. They, as illegals and, additionally and specifically, as women who are the objects of the predatory and proprietorial identities of men, suffer from fears that come in a series of guises: as the fear of poverty and violence that prompts fleeing; as the fear of the invisible illegal immigrant living in the shadows of becoming visible, hence vulnerable, not least to the authorities; as women's fear of men – their fathers, brothers, lovers, strangers. Visibility, the expression of a certain kind of freedom, prompts accountability, and hence, as the novel would have it, 'freedom – if it actually exists – is always threatened' (p 286).

Accounting for majoritarian fears

Mankell's attempts to account for majoritarian fears in his novels, which one might specify as the fear of the (cultural) majority (characterised as middle-aged indigenous men) that the other (women, immigrants) might take the place of the subject, come somewhat undone in the dénouement of his texts. These, as I shall indicate, reveal an undigested ambivalence, described by Anna Westerståhl Stenport as 'thematic contradictions about ideologies of immigration and nation' (2007, p 3), about the changes for which his texts act as a cultural barometer.

In *Faceless killers*, for instance, the majoritarian fear of the other is ultimately vindicated, since the brutal killers of the elderly indigenous couple turn out to be two Czech criminals, on the run from the police in their own country and from the Immigration Services in Sweden.

Thus, while the crime is solved it also serves to reinforce the notion of the criminal, particularly the vicious criminal, as foreigner,[12] a notion that is further reinforced by the actual, disproportionately high number of foreigners in Swedish prisons.[13] Through this resolution of the crime, the text by implication also (re)asserts a notion of Swedish purity – after all, and thankfully, the nasty murderers were not Swedish. Here we see some of the possibly unintended ambivalence in Mankell's work as it both queries and reasserts ideas of 'we-ness' and 'them'. At the same time the indigenous male population is also indicted, since it is discovered that the old man who was murdered had profiteered during the Second World War from doing business with the Nazis – a fact that had remained hidden from his family and neighbours – and the set of racist murderers turns out to be indigenous Swedish men.

In *The shadow girls* things are more complicated. This is partly because, while in *Faceless killers* the migrants still appear to exist in a segregated camp world, by *The shadow girls* they are constructed as part of the everyday fabric of Swedish society but living in precarity. Mankell attempts to counter the fear of the masses and the social uncertainty Appadurai diagnoses as arising from the effects of globalisation and migration, by giving 'faces', that is identities, histories and stories, to the migrant girls. But the intra-diegetic author, Jesper Humlin, also says at one point: 'I don't believe much of what people tell me, particularly not if they are young female refugees' (p 191). As he wonders increasingly 'which story really belonged to whom' (p 195) – since the girls' stories are full of contradictions and of fragments that seem to come from other stories – their unique tales turn into 'everywoman' or, rather, 'every-migrant-woman' tales that return the girls to the masses rather than keeping them in the state of radical individuation that supposedly unique narratives demand. And, unsurprisingly, Humlin finds that 'Suddenly, as if in a vision, he imagined thousands of small boats across the world filled with refugees on their way to Sweden. Maybe this is the way it is, he thought. We are living in the time of the rowing boat' (p 206). This 'new normal' is a faceless one where those who are rowing are metonymically supplanted by the boat, projecting the threat that the country will soon be swamped by immigrants who find it easy to enter illegally, who are then forced to lead criminal lives through burgling and so on to sustain themselves, and who end up in a Dantesque hell,[14] living in a parallel universe to the indigenous population.

Charting ambivalence: the conundrum of the individual versus the masses

The shadow girls, one might argue, seeks to chart an ambivalent course between the number one, the individual whose story is unique and who should be attended to, and the masses whose stories merge and become indistinguishable, hence a threat. The difficulties of balancing recognition of the individual with fear of the masses, as articulated in Mankell's/Humlin's juxtaposition of the notion of the unique story versus the merged account, is illustrated in Rosenberg's (1995) summary of events in Gimo, Sweden, where 500 refugees were placed in a village of 3,000 inhabitants with no supporting infrastructure, and in Sjöbo subsequently, where villagers refused to accept any refugees and put that issue to a local referendum (Max, 1988). As Rosenberg argues: 'the real issue was never discussed, namely the gap between official ideology and popular sentiment … Legitimate popular fears of social and economic disruption were transformed into flagrant racism' (p 216). This, one might suggest, is the crux of the matter, and one that in *Faceless killers* remains unanswered but in *The shadow girls* finds at least a tentative, if in Appadurai's framework somewhat utopian, resolution.

It could be argued that in *The shadow girls* Mankell attempts to show new ways of engaging with migrants, diverging significantly in this respect from Appadurai, by portraying the regime of fear that governs the minoritised – the fear of persecution, the fear of eviction, the fear of invisibility. Mankell produces this counter-narrative through three different devices, which I shall discuss in turn: first, the assertion of what I shall term the 'indifference of difference'; second, the repeated assertion and description of the fear and terror of the refugees, the minoritised; and third, the production of the refugee girls' stories.

A key device in Mankell's texts through which he challenges stereotypical notions of the 'them' and 'us' is through what I would describe as the construction of the 'indifference of difference'. By this I mean the implicit suggestion in Mankell's texts that perceived differences are not 'real' and need to be understood as the effects of affect and lack of knowledge. This is achieved through creating parallels between indigenous and migrant people. The most concrete example of this is perhaps the fictionalising of self, which not only the refugee girls but also Humlin himself engage in. Importantly, this is linked to questions of authenticity and truth as well as to the question of what difference difference makes. Humlin finds himself constantly confused by the shadow girls, not least because he is unclear about who they are and what their actual story is. It turns out, though, early on, that he himself has different versions of 'his journey to authorship' (p 43), which he produces for different audiences. These stories are of decreasing levels of truthfulness. The point, here, is that Humlin's life story, through the use of the metaphor of the journey, is very overtly compared to that of the migrant girls, who are also on a journey and trying to (re)construct their lives. Humlin, like the girls, fabricates stories to suit the occasion. In terms of their mode of operating, there is in this sense no difference between Humlin and the girls. The difference, which if anything makes *his* behaviour reprehensible, is that his lies are a function not of the necessities of survival but of his vanity. Simultaneously, as previously indicated, the telling of the girls' story threatens his subject position, not only through being displaced as narrator but also through the ways in which their stories, a genre quite different from his (autobiography versus obscure poetry), threaten his cultural position.

Mankell's second device to produce a counter-narrative to the fear of the masses is the repeated assertion of the fear and terror of the refugees, the minoritised. As the text asks: 'Why do people leave? Why do they pull up their roots and go? I suppose some people are chased away and forced to flee. Maybe it's war or hunger or fear – it's always fear' (p 307). Mankell, in other words, attempts to shift the perspective from the majoritarian to the minoritarian perspective. In a terrifying encounter on board a ship to Spain, for example, Tea-Bag meets a man whom she had known in a previous refugee camp and who has gone mad: 'I had seen madness in his eyes. Fear had eaten him up inside, as if it were an invisible parasite that had bored a hole through his skin' (p 148). Talk of fear pervades *The shadow girls*. When Humlin is taken to a flat the girls have broken into to seek temporary shelter there, he is afraid of being discovered and finds that one of them, Tanya, 'sees my fear, Humlin thought. If there's anything she knows all about it's insecurity since she lives with it constantly' (p 180). There are numerous invocations of this experience of fear, the point of which presumably is to generate empathy. Jennifer Harding (2009) discusses how what she terms 'emotion talk' participates in 'the production of specific subjectivities, social realities and power relations' (p 267). She suggests that 'Talk about fear, anxiety and anger features in [discourse on asylum in Britain] as part of the definition and management of different subject groups' (p 268) and shows how, in refugees' oral history narratives, fear is a constituting force of be(com)ing a refugee at the same time that it is 'a negative response among host communities' (p 272). As the latter version, Harding describes fear as 'a "hijacked" emotion word ascribed to members of the host community, which defines and locates them as likely victims of harassment or crime, economic deprivation and cultural and social change as a result of immigration and asylum in relation to threatening "migrant" others' (p 271). Simultaneously, 'fear is also deployed to describe and constitute the social realities and subjectivities of asylum seekers living with the daily threat of harassment and attack' (p 271). Harding points out that emotion talk serves to define boundaries, and to create distinctions between 'those who fear and those who threaten' (p 271), but also that 'Critics …have employed emotion language to make intelligible a politics of fear and inequality' (p 270). This, precisely, is what Mankell attempts to do in utilising emotion talk, specifically the repeated depiction of fear, to reduce difference between Humlin and the shadow girls, and to show that their fears are not of a different 'nature' but share common ground.

Mankell's third device is the actual production of the girls' stories. At one point Humlin is told: 'In this country immigrants are still treated like victims. Because of their circumstances, their poor language skills, for almost any other reason' (p 86). This reproduces Rosenberg's line about the shift of perspectives on migrants in Sweden from regarding them as contributors to the economy to seeing them as in need of assistance. However, Mankell suggests: 'most of them simply want to be treated like normal people' (p 86). The question, however, that is not asked is what kind of normal is envisaged here – who are these 'normal' people? Are they the 'new Swedes', as immigrants are explicitly referred to in the novel at one point (p 44), or the old Sweden that Mankell's middle-aged men recognise as having vanished and that seems to be as much a manufacture of popular culture – in particular, film and television – as the 'new Sweden'?

Challenging neoliberalism's insistence on the individual: the persistence of inequalities

Mankell challenges neoliberalism's insistence on the number one, the 'I' as its key figure. The survival of that 'I' as an individual human being depends upon its social reception, on the manufacture of a culturally acceptable self, of a narrative that will have social resonance and recognition. The refugees' manufacture of different versions of themselves in their efforts to be accepted as refugees in a safe country are emblematic of this. The problematic of this manoeuvre, however, is that it generates social uncertainty as to the veracity of the narratives. One of the key issues, repeatedly explicitly referred to in *The shadow girls*, is the question of the status of the girls' narratives: to what extent are they their own, to what extent are they unique to them, to what extent do they represent quasi-universal dilemmas of refugees? *The shadow girls* itself is somewhat ambivalent about this; questing after 'the truth' of the girls' individual stories, Humlin at one point 'realised that there was no point in asking more questions. Tea-Bag's story was as full of contradictions as Tanya's. He wondered more than ever which story really belonged to whom' (p 195). At another point he recognises that 'The various stories dovetailed into each other' (p 200). Ultimately, it becomes clear that another truth, the truth of need, lies undetected – or detected and rejected – beneath the manufacture of the refugees' narratives. The tension between the ability to engage with the few as 'ones' but not to be overwhelmed by the many arises here. And, in a sense, neither Appadurai nor Mankell offer an answer to this. In neither case is the nation-state seen as capable of responding to these needs, nor are its citizens. The state in that sense has become, and in the narratives remains, bankrupt.

This also pertains to the gender politics of the novels, which imbricate the inequalities between the indigenous population and the migrant communities with gendered inequalities. Mankell conceptualises his narratives in terms of a juxtaposition between his middle-aged men, and women and migrants – in *The shadow girls'* case, explicitly female migrants – thus conjoining race/ethnicity and gender in a structured way. In *Fear of small numbers* (2006) Appadurai distinguishes between what he calls vertebrate and cellular systems of organization, which he sees as in tension with each other. The vertebrate systems are 'organized through the central spinal system of international balances of power, military treaties, economic alliances and institutions of cooperation' (2006, p 129). Such systems operate at macro, that is, global, as well as micro, that is, state and sub-state, levels. But, as he puts it, 'alongside this exists the cellular world, whose parts multiply by association and opportunity rather than by legislation and design' (2006, p 129). Appadurai regards terrorism as the 'dark face' (his formulation) 'of this cellular politics' (2006, p 129), but he suggests that there is potentially also a 'more utopian face', that of, as he puts it, 'international civic society, those networks of activists concerned with human rights, poverty, indigenous rights, emergency aid' and so on (2006, p 131). Mankell portrays this civil society in the form of a church (and churches are also named as such bodies by Appadurai) that gives unquestioning, though illegal, sanctuary to refugees and to which Humlin tries to follow Tea-Bag, and in the form of Törnblom's boxing club, which is constructed as an open social space where people's identities and ethnicities are not interrogated but respected or, rather, let be. This has one important and problematic effect. It leads to the acceptance of all forms of behaviour, most particularly to the acceptance of the policing of women as the 'normal' order of things. It is here that I have my greatest problems both with Appadurai's and with Mankell's work, for in failing to address the question of cultural values other than in terms of old and new orders ('old' Sweden versus 'new' Sweden), that is, as a matter of quasi-linear succession, rather than as a ethical issue, they condone the control of women as a continuing project of the new modernities that, as a woman and as a feminist, I simply cannot accept as 'normal' or in any way appropriate. The same goes for the construction of male patronage as 'normal' that *Shadow girls* promotes. That male patronage never fully ceases, but exhausts itself in its failure to understand the girls' needs (their situation simply appears un-improvable because they are illegal) and in its failure to challenge unacceptable violent forms of coercive control over women as these manifest themselves in the violent attack on an Iranian girl by her family for supposedly violating the family's honour. Thus, ultimately, both the gendered and the ethnic/raced status quo are preserved. We might read this either as a diagnostic of the current situation, as the taking of the measure of the cultural barometer in contemporary Sweden, or as a failure of the imagination to 'think otherwise' (Gunkel 2007). What thinking otherwise there is in *The shadow girls* is the possibility of 'ordinary' citizens lending shelter to the refugee girls, knowingly but illegally, or the possibility of transnational relations as in the romance between Leyla and Torsten, the indigenous carer for Leyla's grandmother.[15]

At the end of *The shadow girls* the situation of the girls is ultimately unchanged. As one refugee says: 'I came to this country to tell my story and now I've done that. No one listened' (p 325). The question raised by this statement is what would it mean 'to listen'? What would it mean to hear this narrative? This is the question that we are left with, the question, I would suggest, that moves us beyond neoliberalism, since it would return us to the question of attending to the other. Listening, however, is only one stage and not enough. We do not simply need to 'hear what you are saying' but to think through the practical implications of hearing what is being said. What do the girls' stories mean for how we conceive of welfare, how we imagine equality, how we translate hearing into supportive practice? These are the questions we need to address.

Afterword

In 2014 I spent repeated periods in Umeå, a town in the north-east of Sweden. The brilliant local *bildmuseet* or university art gallery showed two exhibitions relevant to this chapter while I was there: one, an installation by Pakistani artist Shahzia Sikander entitled 'Parallax' about the fraught history of the Strait of Hormuz (the prominence of the problematics of elsewhere remaining); the other by the Swedish artist Katarina Pirak Sikku entitled 'Nammaláhpán' and concerned with the eugenicist treatment of the indigenous Sami in Sweden in the early to mid-20th century. The distancing devices in place in the exhibitions I had seen in Stockholm in 2008 were still there: elsewhere and in another time things happen/ed ... Simultaneously, I noted two encounters outside the museum: on the streets, for the first time, there were travellers (known as 'romanis' in Sweden) kneeling or sitting, begging. They embodied the limits of the welfare state as this now operates in Sweden, and raised the very same question as Mankell's stories: what would it mean to attend to them – differently? Not to have them beg ... And, at the airport in Umeå, on one occasion when I arrived, there was a group of about ten Somalis, awaiting relatives who had come on the same plane as myself. As we waited in the arrivals hall for our luggage, the Somalis stood quite separately from the rest – us, silently waiting for our baggage. Joyously embracing each other, they were boisterously oblivious – or seemed so – of those around them, who stood in a semi-circle at a distance, just observing ... The feeling for me was one of spatial and communal segregation, akin to the kind of segregation that Andrea Levy's (2004) novel *Small island* foreshadows for London at the end, and that I had also experienced in Stockholm in 2008, where whiteness prevailed in the areas of the city that I spent my time in. Sweden is certainly changing – the arm of the welfare state does not reach as far as the travellers I saw on the streets of cities such as Umeå, Stockholm and Uppsala; the migrant population is much more visible, but at the same time the separation between the indigenous population and the migrants remains in place. Equality remains to be worked at – and for.

Notes

[1] For those like myself in Britain who are not avid crime fiction readers, the Wallander series was effectively popularised in 2008 by the arrival of that series on British television (Tapper, 2009).

[2] See Loftsdóttir and Jensen (2012) for accounts of the 'management' of whiteness in the Nordic region.

[3] Leicester is the first city in Britain expected to have a majority immigrant population by 2016. See P. Gosh (2014) 'The golden mile: could Leicester, the most ethnically diverse place in Britain, become UK's first Asian-majority city?' *International Business Times,* 19 February, at http://www.ibtimes.com/golden-mile-could-leicester-most-ethnically-diverse-place-britain-become-uks-first-asian-majority.

[4] The memorial I refer to here is the Holocaust memorial *Shoes on the Danube Promenade,* created by G. Pauer and C. Togay (2005) in Budapest.

[5] J. Madison Davis (2009) maintains that 'In the United States, Henning Mankell is often said to be a battleship that pulls other Scandinavians in his wake' (p 9).

[6] Mankell practises an ironic reversal through *The shadow girls* with his fictional counterpart Jesper Humlin in that novel who, as a writer of obscure stylised poetry that nobody can understand, is persistently asked throughout the novel to try his hand at crime fiction and who decides to write on immigrant girls 'to write about something real' (Mankell, 2013 [2001], p 72).

[7] See, for example, Charteris-Black (2006).

[8] In an interesting, relevant piece Ekberg (2011) argues that future immigration to Sweden by what are often younger populations will not make it easier to finance the welfare system, as some have suggested.

[9] Interestingly, Ceobanu and Escandell (2010) indicate that research has shown that 'older respondents, men, and those residing in rural areas are more likely to hold negative ATII [attitudes towards immigrants and immigration] than are younger individual, women, and those living in urban areas' (p 320). See also Wilkes et al (2008).

[10] Tham et al (2011) argue that the construction of and emphasis on *victims* of crime in Swedish criminal policy from the 1970s onwards resulted in the homogenisation of those victims in gendered terms as being predominantly women suffering from the violence of men. They link this partly to the rise of equality politics.

[11] Lesser (2004) quotes Mankell as distancing himself from Wallander on the basis that Wallander, inter alia, has 'a strange attitude to women' (p 15).

[12] See Martens (1997) for a discussion of crime rates among immigrants to Sweden.

[13] See, for example, Martens (1997).

[14] The text makes many references to situations that are linked to Dante's *Inferno.*

[15] The notion of interrelations or intermarriage and immigrant integration has been variously explored (see Dribe and Lundh, 2008). It is frequently portrayed as the answer to issues of social cohesion but this ignores the evidence we have from places such as the former Yugoslavia and Rwanda, where intermarriage between ethnic groups came under attack as part of mounting interethnic conflicts ultimately ending in ethnic cleansing and genocide.

References

Ahmed, S. (2009) 'The organisation of hate', in J. Harding and E.D. Pribram (eds) *Emotions: A cultural studies reader*, London: Routledge, pp 251–66.

Appadurai, A. (2006) *Fear of small numbers: An essay on the geography of anger*, Durham, NC: Duke University Press.

Appadurai, A. (2009) 'Fear of small numbers', in J. Harding and E.D. Pribram (eds) *Emotions: A cultural studies reader*, London: Routledge, pp 235–50.

Butler, J. (2004) *Precarious life: The power of mourning and violence*, London: Verso.

Butler, J. (2009) *Frames of war: When is life grievable?* London: Verso.

Ceobanu, A.M. and Escandell, X. (2010) 'Comparative analyses of public attitudes toward immigrants and immigration using multinational survey data: a review of theories and research', *Annual Review of Sociology*, vol 36, pp 309–28.

Charteris-Black, J. (2006) 'Britain as a container: immigration metaphors in the 2005 election campaign', *Discourse and Society*, vol 17, no 5, pp 563–82.

Dribe, M. and Lundh, C. (2008) 'Intermarriage and immigrant integration in Sweden: an exploratory analysis', *Acta Sociologica*, vol 51, no 4, pp 329–54.

Eger, M.A. (2010) 'Even in Sweden: the effect of immigration on support for welfare state spending', *European Sociological Review*, vol 26, no 2, pp 203–17.

Ekberg, J. (2011) 'Will future immigration to Sweden make it easier to finance the welfare system?' *European Journal of Population*, vol 27, pp 103–24.

Essed, P. (1991) *Understanding everyday racism: An interdisciplinary theory*, New York: Sage.

Forshaw, B. (2012) *Death in a cold climate: A guide to Scandinavian crime fiction*, Houndmills: Palgrave Macmillan.

Gunkel, D.J. (2007) 'Thinking otherwise: ethics, technology and other subjects', *Ethics and Information Technology*, vol 9, pp 165–77.

Harding, J. (2009) 'Emotional subjects: language and power in refugee narratives', in J. Harding and E.D. Pribram (eds) *Emotions: A cultural studies reader*, London: Routledge, pp 267–79.

Lesser, W. (2004) 'A detective for our times', *The Threepenny Review*, 96 (Winter): 14–15.

Levy, A. (2004) *Small island*, London: Headline Book Publishing.

Loftsdóttir, K. and Jensen, L. (eds) (2012) *Whiteness and postcolonialism in the Nordic region*, Farnham: Ashgate.

Madison Davis, J. (2009) 'Murder in a cold and peaceful place', *World Literature Today*, vol 83, no 6, pp 9–11.

Mankell, H. (2011 [1991]) *Faceless killers*, London: Vintage Books.

Mankell, H. (2013 [2001]) *The shadow girls*, London: Vintage Books.

Martens, P.L. (1997) 'Immigrants, crime, and criminal justice in Sweden', *Crime and Justice*, vol 21, pp 183–255.

Max, A. (1988) 'Farming town resists immigrants, raising questions of racism: an AP extra', *The Associated Press*, 18 September, International News, at https://www.lexisnexis.com/uk/nexis/results/enhdocview. do?docLinkInd=true&ersKey=23_T19980838456&format=GNBF I&startDocNo=1&resultsUrlKey=0_T19980842245&backKey=20_ T19980842246&csi=304478&docNo=27&scrollToPosition=3760.

Moïsi, D. (2009) *The geopolitics of emotion: How cultures of fear, humiliation and hope are reshaping the world*, London; The Bodley Head.

Nestingen, A.K. and Arvas, P. (2011) *Scandinavian crime fiction*, Lampeter: University of Wales Press.

Nestingen, A.K. (2012) 'Killer research: Scandinavian crime fiction scholarship since 2008', *Journal of Scandanavian Cinema*, vol 2, no 2, pp 153–9.

Rosenberg, G. (1995) 'Sweden and its immigrants: policies versus opinions', *Daedalus*, vol 124, no 3, pp 209–18.

Saarinen, R. (2003) 'The surplus of evil in welfare society: contemporary Scandinavian crime fiction', *Dialog*, vol 42, no 2, pp 131–5.

Sedgwick, E.K. (1985) *Between men: English literature and male homosocial desire*, New York: Columbia University Press.

Tapper, M. (2009) '"More than ABBA and skinny-dipping in mountain lakes": Swedish dystopia, Henning Mankell and the British *Wallander* series,' *Film International*, vol 38, no 7.2, pp 60–9, at www.filmint.nu.

Tham, H., Rönneling, A. and Rytterbro, L.-L. (2011) 'The emergence of the crime victim: Sweden in the Scandinavian context', *Crime and Justice*, vol 40, no 1, pp 555–611.

Westerståhl Stenport, A. (2007) 'Bodies under assault: nation and immigration in Henning Mankell's *Faceless killers*', *Scandinavian Studies*, vol 79, no 1, pp 1–24.

Wilkes, R., Guppy, N. and Farris, L. (2008) '"No thanks, we're full": individual characteristics, national context, and changing attitudes toward immigration', *International Migration Review*, vol 42, no 2, pp 302–29.

FIVE

How is the myth of Swedish gender equality upheld outside Sweden? A case study

Nina Lykke

This chapter looks at Swedish gender-equality models from outside, using mainstream public discourses about Sweden in the neighbouring Scandinavian country of Denmark as a lens for the discussion. Neoliberal ways of breaking down the welfare state and producing new inequalities and racisms have swept across Denmark since the 1990s in some of the same ways as they have in Sweden. Nonetheless, mainstream Danish public discourses regard Denmark as one of the most gender-equal countries in the world, and in this sense the mainstream national self-understanding in Denmark has similarities to the Swedish one. Also very apparent in Denmark are racist and orientalist constructions of a modern, nationalist Danish 'we', as contrasted to the 'backward others out there' who lack the highly praised gender equality that 'we' seem to have in 'our' national(istic) genes. This might lead to the expectation of a certain consensus in the mainstream publics of the two countries regarding equality. But this is definitely not the case. Swedish gender-equality models are generally *not* considered positively in mainstream Denmark, and are certainly *not* seen as ideal models to be adopted. On the contrary, Swedish models are often ridiculed in mainstream public discourses in Denmark; they are considered old fashioned, and negatively connoted as exaggerated political correctness.

Along parallel lines, it should also be noted that from the perspective of the mainstream Danish public Sweden is said to overdo political correctness, in a negative sense, as far as anti-racist politics are concerned. A telling illustration is the ways in which the mainstream Danish media ridicule Swede's banning of racist language and episodes from classic children's books such as Astrid Lindgren's *Pippi Longstocking* (1945). To make the point, let me briefly give an example of how Swedish anti-racist politics figures in the Danish media. When a press release about the deleting of certain phrases from *Pippi Longstocking* was published in Denmark (Ritzau, 2015), Stig Thøgersen, a reporter from the Danish tabloid newspaper *Extrabladet*, invited Mattias Tesfaye, a well-known member of the Danish Social Democratic Party, on a so-called 'racism safari' to a supermarket outside Copenhagen and a library. Tesfaye is well known and high profile in the Danish media for his radical leftist rhetoric on class and manual workers' perspectives. This was evidently one reason for inviting him to the interview. Another reason was probably that he is of Ethiopian descent and therefore supposed to be able to speak about racism from a position of personal experience of being discriminated against. During the 'safari' Tesfaye was interviewed about supermarket items assumed to be considered racist in Sweden, and about children's books in the library that, like *Pippi Longstocking*, had been revised in Sweden in order to exclude racist language. Tesfaye's main point was to dismiss the Swedish 'censoring' of *Pippi Longstocking* and other books as nothing but a totally ridiculous, white Swedish upper-middle-class hysteria. The interview and the 'safari' were filmed and uploaded to *Extrabladet*'s website together with a press release (Ritzau, 2015).

Against the background of a close reading of examples from the Danish press, this chapter takes an external perspective in discussing Sweden's self-image as a world leader in terms of equality and egalitarian values (tolerance, inclusiveness, human rights, anti-racism, anti-sexism, democracy and so on). This self-image appears in official discourses such as the official Swedish website, sweden.se, funded by the Swedish Institute, Business Sweden, VisitSweden and Sweden Government Offices. In agreement with other contributions to this volume, I am critical of mainstream Swedish self-images that gloss over realities that include structural inequalities and power differentials in terms of intersections of gender, racialisation, sexuality, class, dis/ability and so on. It should also be noted that I am equally critical of national Danish mainstream self-images that gloss over structural inequalities and celebrate Denmark as a paradise of equality. Both of these national(istic) self-images are much too self-satisfied. However, in this chapter I want to discuss and question the belief, common to many Swedes, that Swedish equality politics has an unambiguously positive ring in the ears of mainstream publics in other liberal or social democratic countries that celebrate equality and egalitarian values as part of their national identities. I think it is a problem that, no matter whether Sweden's model status is celebrated (as by some Swedish (neo) liberals and social democrats) or criticised as not applying to Swedish 'realities' (as by some more leftist Swedish feminists, socialists and anti-racists), members of both these clusters often subscribe to the claim that Sweden generally has a positive image in the outside world as far as equality and egalitarian values are concerned. I do not deny this international image, sustained for example by the World Economic Forum's *Global Gender Gap Report* (2013). My point is to question the belief that the way in which Sweden appears to the outside world as a world leader in equality is unambiguously positive. Using Danish attitudes toward the Swedish equality models as my example, I shall argue that the image of Sweden outside the country is much more ambiguous than either celebratory or critical Swedish voices seem to imply. I shall use my own situatedness as both an insider (working as a professor of Gender Studies in Sweden) and an outsider (living most of my non-working life in Denmark) to examine these complexities.

I will take as my point of departure the image of Sweden as a world leader in (gender) equality and egalitarian values in two fairly recent cases. One is a Danish media debate focusing on a kindergarten in Stockholm called Egalia. Since 2010 Egalia has applied a policy of what was framed in Denmark as 'gender-neutral' pedagogy,[1] including use of the new, gender-neutral pronoun 'hen' (a merger of the Swedish pronouns 'hon' [she] and 'han' [he]). The other case concerns a debate in the Danish press in 2014 in the wake of Iranian-born poet and journalist Athena Farrokzhad's review (2014) of a Danish poetry collection by poet Yahya Hassan (2013). Hassan had become very famous in the Danish press, due to his blunt exposure of the violence that had been part of his childhood experience in a Palestinian–Danish migrant family. I will use the two cases to examine the discursive mechanisms by which the myth of Swedish (gender) equality is upheld and nourished outside Sweden, even when it is not celebrated or adopted as a model to be followed but, conversely, is ridiculed and presented as being over the top. In order to cut through to more effective strategies for combatting inequalities in Sweden and worldwide, I think it is important to deconstruct the different myths of equality that are embedded in national self-images such as the Swedish one. The overall goal of the chapter is to contribute to such a deconstruction.

The Egalia case: 'stupefying gender madness haunts Sweden'

From its beginnings in 2010, the Egalia kindergarten in Stockholm hit the headlines of news media around the world (for example, Wiseman, 2011; Noack, 2015). Egalia is a kindergarten for children aged 1–6, organised within the municipality in Stockholm. It is based on an anti-discriminatory gender and norm-critical pedagogy, and is LGBTQ-certified by the Swedish Federation for Lesbian, Gay, Bisexual, Transgender and Queer Rights. International broadcasting channels such as CBS News and the BBC, as well as newspapers like the *Daily Mail*, *China Daily* and the *Washington Examiner*, carried the story of Egalia. Danish news media joined in with the sensationalising of Egalia, due to its approach to organising a so-called 'gender-neutral' space. In the summer of 2011, major Danish newspapers, TV channels and blogs reported on Egalia in prominent places, making it into an icon of Swedish gender-equality politics. The news reports described how the pronouns 'she' and 'he' had been replaced by the gender-neutral 'hen', and how the 33 children being taken care of in Egalia learned to refer to each other as 'friends', and not as either 'girls' or 'boys'. Danish journalists also reported how gender-neutral toys were given priority over pink-clad Barbies for the girls and Nintendo warriors for the boys, and how the children's books used in Egalia were chosen in order to portray diversity and non-normative relations. The summary of a story of two male giraffes who wanted to build a family with children and ended up adopting a crocodile egg figured prominently in several Danish newspaper reports. The idea that the children were encouraged to include extra mothers if, in family play, the role of mother was already taken, was also reported by several Danish journalists and bloggers.

Apart from a few moderate and predominantly feminist voices, the overall response in the Danish mainstream media and blogosphere was that the Egalia experiment confirmed suspicions that authoritarian Swedish gender politics prioritised political correctness over the needs and wishes of individuals. Egalia was discursively constructed as a symbol of Swedish gender-political correctness that aimed at erasing sexual difference and, in a quasi-Stalinist vein, forcing children into sameness and crushing creativity and individuality, both of which were constructed as growing out of binary difference. One line of argument, cherished by several participants in the Danish debate, was that to organise a kindergarten along the lines of Egalia would be totally destructive for the boys, who were already enrolled in a female regime due to the statistical fact that the majority of kindergarten teachers are women. Forcing the boys into 'gender-neutral' sameness would deny them their last chance of acting 'boyishly'. The then Danish Minister of Social Affairs, Benedikte Kier (representing the Conservative Party) emphasised, with an unmistakably threatening undertone, that any kindergarten leaders in Denmark who had thoughts of copying the Swedish example should definitely not count on government support or funding through taxpayers' money (Bolander, 2011). To use gender-neutral pronouns and call the children 'friends' instead of referring to binary gender was 'totally wrong'. The minister stated firmly: 'There is something called biology. There are things that boys need more than girls' (Bolander, 2011). Niels Egelund, a professor of pedagogical psychology who is frequently called upon as an expert on pedagogical issues in leading Danish media and governmental commissions, supported the minister's argument. He was interviewed in his capacity as leader of a taskforce established by the Minister of Social Affairs to analyse how Danish kindergartens could be improved so as to better prepare children for the future. In that interview he commented on Egalia and argued that its founders were 'totally off-beam' when they 'reject the psychobiological explanations that we have something that we carry along in our genes which means that boys and girls have different appearances and wishes as far as activities are concerned' (Gjerding, 2011). Anne Sophia Hermansen, a well-established conservative blogger within the framework of the renowned Danish conservative newspaper *Berlingske Tidende*, struck a similar note. She emphasised the image of Egalia as an icon of the ways in which Swedish gender-equality politics had gone awry and turned into a 'stupefying gender madness'. To qualify her statement about this iconic Swedish 'gender madness', Hermansen wrote sarcastically:

> A stupefying gender madness seems, generally, to haunt Sweden. Of course, there are too many lego-men in the boxes. Of course, women should be pushed into management teams and boards. Of course, Little Red Riding Hood should be told that the wolf and the hunter can be women, and of course, it is a trap for women to be full-time housewives, but totally mind-blowing and enriching for the man. And of course, the child should be taken care of in Egalia. – To this, you can only say one thing: poor child. (Hermansen, 2011)

In contrast to this Swedish gender-political mix of madness and quasi-Stalinist feminism, a Danish kindergarten, Triton (in the provincial Danish town of Horsens), was cited as the 'good' alternative. Triton is based on a pedagogy of sexual difference, separating boys and girls into different rooms for part of the day – girls' rooms with Barbie dolls, pink items and pearls and so on, and boys' rooms with Nintendo warriors, cars and guns and so on. Both the minister and the expert professor praised Triton highly as an alternative to Egalia. In particular, they emphasised that here the boys could develop a 'masculine' identity that it was impossible to express in more average Danish kindergartens, which had been 'feminised' over the course of many years.

Gender-conservative and anti-feminist criticisms of Egalia were launched inside Sweden as well. When the Danish blogger Anne Sophie Hermansen wrote of 'stupefying gender madness' in relation to Egalia and to gender politics in Sweden more generally, she was implicitly quoting the conservative and anti-feminist Swedish blogger Tanja Bergkvist. Bergkvist uses the phrases 'gender madness' and 'the stupefying industry' generally in her blog when referring to gender politics, gender studies and feminism in Sweden (see, for example, Bergkvist, 2011, a blog post that includes discussions of Egalia as part of the 'Swedish gender madness'). With regard to Egalia, so-called 'gender-neutral' pedagogy and, in particular, the 'oppression' of boys, there were also outspoken resonances between right-wing, anti-feminist Swedish blogs such as Per Ström's *Genusnytt* and its Danish counterparts such as *Uriasposten* (2011). On the occasion of the Danish debate, Ström and *Genusnytt* took the opportunity to praise the ways in which Egalia's pedagogy had been rejected by authoritative voices in Denmark. A blog post in *Genusnytt* (Ström, 2011) quoted the above-mentioned Danish psychology professor Niels Egelund as well as Gideon Zlotnik, a Danish psychiatrist who is famous for his theories about the 'oppression' of boys' masculinity in 'feminised' kindergartens. Ström's blog post, posted on 24 July 2011, two days after Anders Behring Breivik's terror attack in Norway, also drew attention to this. It asked if there might be a connection between Zlotnik's theories of boys 'becoming restless, aggressive and prone to transgressive anti-social behaviour' and Breivik's terrorist act (Ström, 2011). In other words, links were created between the Egalia pedagogy of 'gender neutrality', boys' being 'hindered' in their masculine development through a feminised/feminist kindergarten regime and Breivik's act of terror. So there was an intense interaction across the Danish–Swedish border when it came to the besmirching of Egalia.

What interests me here is not to discuss these conservative and anti-feminist attacks on the Egalia pedagogy per se, nor to trace Danish–Swedish anti-feminist connections. Rather, my point is to highlight how the gender-conservative Danish participants in the debate constructed Egalia as an expression of *Swedishness*, equating it to exaggerated gender-political correctness. Egalia figured in their discourses not only as an icon of bad gender pedagogy and oppressive feminist ideas; in the Danish debate it was transformed into an icon of *Swedish* gender-equality politics, rendered as a bad mix of quasi-Stalinist feminism and madness.

The Yahya Hassan/Athena Farrokzhad case: 'Swedish in the head'

The Danish media debate about poet and journalist Athena Farrokzhad's (2014) review of Danish poet Yahya Hassan's poetry collection *Yahya Hassan* (2013) took off in January 2014. Drawing strongly on autobiographical elements, Hassan's poetry collection is a description of growing up in a Danish–Palestinian migrant family and, later, in various institutions. Hassan was 19 years old at the time of the collection's publication by the renowned Danish publishing house Gyldendal. In powerful images carried along by passionate anger, he describes a childhood and teenage life pervaded by patriarchal and systemic violence, crime, structural racism and exclusion. From day one of its publication in late 2013, Hassan's book was a huge success. It became a bestseller (very rare for poetry collections), it received enthusiastic reviews in all the mainstream Danish media, it was awarded literary prizes and its author became a media darling. Hassan himself seemed somewhat ambivalent about his success. For example, he cancelled his participation in a literary award ceremony and instead went to the Ukraine to show solidarity with the Ukrainian people's struggle for independence and democracy. In late January of 2014, the discussion of Hassan's book started to resonate in Sweden as well.

First of all, Jes Stein Pedersen, literary editor of the large liberal Danish newspaper *Politiken*, was asked by Daniel Sandström, cultural editor of the liberal Swedish newspaper *Svenska Dagbladet*, to comment on the stir that Hassan's book had caused in Denmark. Pedersen's comment included a critique of Sweden for silencing the problems around violence carried out by 'the Muslim patriarch from the ethnic underclass who has lost his social position' (Pedersen, 2014), while Yahya Hassan was praised for having brought such problems out into the open in Denmark. On account of this and other statements, Elise Karlsson, one of *Svenska Dagbladet*'s freelance journalists, immediately took Pedersen to task, accusing him of racism. She also fiercely attacked *Svenska Dagbladet*'s editorial staff for publishing the comment and for letting a Danish journalist perform as a ventriloquist for the *Svenska Dagbladet*'s editors' own racist attitudes (Karlsson, 2014).

Second, some days later Farrokzhad's review of the book was published in *Aftonbladet* (Farrokzhad, 2014). On the one hand, Farrokzhad praised the book for its strong poetic language. But, on the other hand, she problematised Hassan's act of speaking to a predominantly white audience about childhood memories of his father's violence towards him and his siblings. She did not question his right to do so, nor the authenticity of the pain and rage that motivated him. But she underlined that, even though she had similar experiences as the descendant of an Iranian family who had migrated to Sweden, she would not expose these experiences publicly to the gaze of the white majority, who would read them in a racist manner. To her, the pain of seeing such experiences interpreted through explanations that she 'would combat, would be as destructive as the experiences in themselves' (Farrokzhad, 2014). Having stated the impossibility of establishing a space for dialogue on similarities and differences between Hassan's and her own political and aesthetic projects in a media framed by the white gaze and structural racism, Farrokzhad ended the review with a direct address to Hassan. She suggested entering into a deeper dialogue with him in a face-to-face meeting, away from the surveillance of the white-majority society. But she also ended on a more broadly positive note, expressing the hope that it 'will one day be possible to tell these stories' in a public setting structured on equal terms (Farrokzhad, 2014).

Farrokzhad's review sparked an intense, month-long debate on whiteness and racism in the Danish media, sometimes spiced up with references to the 'scandal' that the literary editor of *Politiken* had been called a racist in the Swedish press. In particular, the debate flourished in the Danish literary milieu, with an epicentre in the blog of poet and literary critic Jørgen Bukdahl, who has a central position in Danish literary circles. The day after the publication of Farrokzhad's review in *Aftonbladet*, Bukdahl commented on it in his blog, and struck two notes that came to frame the debate. One was that Farrokzhad was exerting self-censorship and, by implication, challenging artistic freedom; the other was that she did this because she was 'very Swedish in her head' (Bukdahl, 2014), that is, obsessed with a special kind of Swedish fundamentalism, and was in this sense a negative counterpart to Hassan, who, according to Bukdahl, was totally 'opposite to being Swedish in the head':

> You must be very Swedish in the head in order to censor yourself so forcibly and intensely, very focused on the (most stupid part of the) white majority audience and very little focused on the non-white minority, who could use an intense and honest insider story of patriarchy and violence as a broken mirror.
>
> Yahya Hassan is the opposite of Swedish in the head (which is not Danish, rather Russian perhaps); he sings fearlessly, without compromise, totally indifferent to [the

effects of publishing, NL] all kinds of experiences, including experiences of patriarchy and violence. And this is what he should not be, Farrokzhad says with Swedish emphasis. (Bukdahl, 2014)

A few days later, in an interview for the Danish cultural-radical newspaper *Information*, Bukdahl expanded on the comment about Hassan's being a counterpart to Farrokzhad's Swedish fundamentalism. There he defined Hassan as expressing an 'identity carnivalism' in contradistinction to what he calls Farrokzhad's 'identity fundamentalism' (Hansen, 2014). In Bukdahl's lexicon, the latter implies an identity politics giving special priority to one kind of identity (in this case racial identity), rather than playing around with a multiplicity of different identities. Following on from Bukdahl's statements, a chorus of voices – predominantly white male members of the literary establishment – filled the Danish media, speaking patronisingly and self-righteously about aesthetic freedom versus censorship, praising Hassan's free literary spirit and condemning Farrokzhad's 'fundamentalism' and 'self-censoring' (Hansen, 2014).

Alternative voices came to the fore as well. Some, predominantly feminist and anti-racist voices, took Bukdahl to task, among them researcher Lene Myong (Myong, 2014), writers Kristina Nya Glaffey and Maja Lee Langvad (Glaffey and Langvad, 2014) and writer Mette Moestrup (Moestrup, 2014). They highlighted the ways in which Bukdahl and other detractors of Farrokzhad had totally neglected the ways in which their own positions as privileged white members of the cultural Danish establishment were structurally different from the minoritised positions of both Hassan and Farrokzhad. The utter refusal of Bukdahl and the others to look critically and self-reflexively at this blind spot meant that they were actively contributing to the maintenance of the status quo of structural racism. Myong, Glaffey and Langvad also offered further reflections on Bukdahl's construction of a dichotomy between Hassan and Farrokzhad along the lines of carnival versus fundamentalism. They stressed that, in the context of the discussion of two minoritised voices, both concepts could be read as exoticising labels, inscribed in discourses of structural racism. Moreover, they argued that Bukdahl's discourses constructed the 'carnivalist' Hassan as the 'good' racialised other, while the 'fundamentalist' Farrokzhad was constructed as the 'bad' and perhaps 'dangerous' racialised other. It goes without saying that the epithet 'fundamentalist' is a loaded one in current western discourses. In particular, when linked to people of Middle Eastern descent and/or Muslim background, it is easily associated with 'terrorism' (Glaffey and Langvad, 2014), and Myong,

Glaffey and Langvad certainly have a point when drawing attention to these connections in their sophisticated analyses.

However, in the context of this chapter, there is one more important thing to be noted here, which is briefly touched upon by Glaffey and Langvad (2014). It is that the 'fundamentalist' Farrokzhad is not only constructed as a person of Middle Eastern descent. She is, first and foremost, constructed as *Swedish*. Bukdahl strongly underlines her Swedishness, which is contrasted with the fluid national belonging of Hassan, who, according to Bukdahl, is not confined to the Danish nation-state (see the somewhat strange phrase 'not Danish, rather Russian perhaps' in the above quote, Bukdahl, 2014). In contrast to Hassan, Farrokzhad is, according to Bukdahl, firmly assimilated into the nation-state of Sweden: she is 'Swedish in the head', he claims (Bukdahl, 2014), and he underlines that she speaks with a 'Swedish emphasis' (Bukdahl, 2014). But it is not only Bukdahl who makes this link between Farrokzhad's alleged fundamentalism and her Swedishness. Throughout the many blog posts and media interventions that comment on the Farrokzhad/Hassan debate in Denmark from positions of anti-political correctness, Farrokzhad's incarnation of Swedish values is a recurring theme. Sometimes she is simply referred to as 'the Swedish reviewer' or 'the Swedish woman' (Løwenstein, 2014) who incarnates the attitudes of '"anti-racist" Swedes' who seem to be 'nuts' (Sauer, 2014).

The Swedish gender-equality mantra

I have presented my two cases, and I shall now compare them in order to pursue the question: how is the myth of Swedish (gender) equality upheld and nourished outside Sweden, even in negative anti-Swedish discourses such as the ones examined above? I shall consider both differences and similarities and how they construct intersections between Swedishness, equality, feminism, anti-racism and fundamentalism. I shall also show how, in so doing, in their own way they confirm discourses of Swedish exceptionalism as far as egalitarian values are concerned.

In terms of differences and similarities, I want to note first that the Egalia example is about gender and, more precisely, so-called 'gender neutrality' in kindergarten pedagogy. On the other hand, the pivot of the Hassan/Farrokzhad debate is ethnicity, 'race', racism and whiteness and, in particular, the relationship between ethnically and racially minoritised authors and the white majority that sets the agendas of Scandinavian mediascapes and dominates the literary public. In this sense the cases are different. Nevertheless, in terms of the Swedish equality mantra, that is, the ways in which Sweden is profiled as the most (gender-)equal country in the world, which is being critically scrutinised in this volume, the two cases both touch on related key questions: what is Swedish gender equality? And who can embody its values?

The Danish detractors of Egalia raise the key question of what gender equality actually means, implying that in Sweden it is taken to equate with a socially institutionalised and forced erasure of 'natural' sexual difference. They also claim that an intersection of Swedishness with an exaggerated political correctness, along with a quasi-Stalinist feminist determination to institutionalise this, has led Sweden, in its support for Egalia, to embark upon a dangerous path towards such erasure. Implied in the arguments of these detractors is also an attack on social constructionism, which is discursively constructed as the main theoretical tool to suppress and deny the importance of biological differences between women and men, girls and boys. Moreover, undercurrents of homo-, queer- and transphobia can be detected in the Danish discourses on Egalia and on the so-called erasure of 'natural' sexual difference. The children's story of the two male giraffes adopting a crocodile egg and the family-building play with two or more mothers are mentioned again and again in the Danish news reports and discussions of Egalia's spectacular and 'exotic' features. However, they are rarely contextualised in terms of a discussion of heteronormativity and norm-critical pedagogies. When the expert, Professor Niels Egelund, whom I quoted earlier, emphasises that psychobiology should be taken into account and that boys, in particular, should have space to develop as 'boys', there is no discursive room left for genderqueer boyhood or transgendered experiences.

But even though homo-, queer- and transphobic undercurrents make themselves felt in the passionate rejections of Egalia, these are not the main issue for the Danish detractors. Looming between the lines, and indeed often articulated through pretty openly stated feelings of disgust, is the main target of the Danish detractors: man-hating, fundamentalist feminists, bent on destroying boys' development of 'normal' masculinity by simply erasing their difference.

The aspect of the equality mantra that is touched upon by the Hassan/Farrokzhad case is the construction of a modern, Swedish 'we' who have organised families on an equal basis where violence does not occur. This is contrasted with a 'they' consisting of 'backward' others who are culturally and religiously confined to old-fashioned patriarchal traditions of family building, which per se imply the use of violence. Hassan's poetry, dealing with his specific childhood experiences, is thus taken to represent immigrant families from non-western countries in general, through the trope of 'the mark of the plural'. Anti-colonialist scholar Albert Memmi forcefully pinpoints this as common to colonialist discourses, referring to the ways in which the coloniser never characterises the colonised in an individual manner, but lets the colonised 'drown in an anonymous collectivity' (Memmi, 1991, p 85). Additionally, Farrokzhad's question to Hassan, encouraging a thorough reflection of the strategic relations of minority authors to the white majority public and to the dominant white gaze, is immediately taken to advocate the suppression and silencing of his violent childhood memories. Thus, Farrokzhad is constructed as occupying a position that is claimed to exert fundamentalist violence against cherished western democratic rights to freedom of speech and artistic expression. Moreover, with a patronising claim to knowledge of the 'common good', Farrokzhad's position is also said to do the children of 'their' (read: 'non-western, violent and patriarchal') families a major disservice, because these children most of all need to be 'liberated' and integrated into 'our' modern (read: 'non-violent and equality-loving') Scandinavian nation-state.

This way of representing Farrokzhad occurs frequently in the Danish debate, when Bukdahl and others attack her for wanting to suppress Hassan's freedom of speech and artistic freedom. However, what Bukdahl and other detractors of Farrokzhad in the Danish literary milieu do not address is the epistemology of ignorance (Sullivan and Tuana, 2007), in terms of the effects of the white gaze and the neoliberal beliefs that Danish and Swedish mediascapes are uncontaminated and 'free' of any kind of structural racism. Nor do they reflect on the 'modern we/backward they' figure. It just pops up in their discourses as a taken-for-granted 'fact'. Jes Stein Pedersen, the literary editor of *Politiken*, who was accused of racism after his presentation of the Danish debate around Hassan's poetry, for example, took it as self-evident that Sweden was divided precisely along such 'we/they' lines:

> I can hardly see any parties who are farther away from each other than the modern, free, well-educated and self-confident Swedish woman and the Muslim patriarch from the ethnic underclass who has lost his social position, and who tries to make his existence in the freedom of modernity match his touchy codes of honour and views of women. Yahya Hassan's poetry collection cuts without mercy into the distance between these two parties and says in between

the lines to both of them: Look the truth in the eyes, too many human lives are destroyed, if hypocrisy continues. (Pedersen, 2014)

Farrokzhad may seem to be positioned ambiguously in this discursive landscape. As pointed out by Myong, Glaffey and Langvad, and other Danish feminist anti-racists, she is rendered 'fundamentalist' in the discourses of her Danish detractors, and thus in racist and essentialist ways she becomes associated with her Iranian heritage. However, I shall try to sustain my point that she is also constructed as an incarnation of Swedishness, and argue that one of the discursive mechanisms at stake here is an assimilation of Farrokzhad into the nation-state of Sweden.

To make the point, I shall refer to migration and diaspora studies that discuss constructions of nations and nationalisms in terms of the question: who is counted as belonging/not belonging to the nation? Notably, I shall draw upon queerfeminist and postcolonial scholar Jasbir Puar's discussion of the concept of 'homonationalism', which refers to an assimilation of queer others into the nation-state. Puar (2007, 2013) pinpoints shifts in discourses on homosexuality in liberal mainstream media in the US. During the 1980s and 1990s, Puar argues, the image of homosexuals in the US was linked exclusively in the media to death and contamination (in particularly as part of the unfolding of the HIV and AIDS crisis). This changed, however, in the aftermath of President Bush's introduction of the 'axis of evil' after the 9/11 terrorist attacks. Now, liberal discourses interpellated the figure of the 'good', assimilated homosexual to perform as the marker of the 'progressiveness and tolerance' of the modern western 'we', who, in contradistinction to 'backward' Iranian theocrats, do not torture or kill queer others. This discursive mechanism of assimilation is what Puar defines as 'homonationalism' (2007, 2013). To understand what is happening with the figure of Farrokzhad in the discourses of her Danish detractors, I take as my framework a slightly reworked version of Puar's analysis of assimilation into the nation-state. I suggest reworking Puar's framework and expanding it from a tool to be used only for the analysis of celebratory and self-righteous national self-images to one that can also assist in the understanding of negative and derogatory images projected onto other nations from outside; in this case, contemporary, negative Danish images of Swedish equality models.

Against this background, I suggest that what the mainstream Danish media are doing in the two examples I have discussed is to construct Sweden as being governed by a feminist equality fundamentalism that is prone to erasing the differences between boys and girls (as demonstrated in the Egalia case) and to silencing the experiences of childhood violence in 'backward' Muslim families (as demonstrated in the Hassan/Farrokzhad case) in order to appear as the most egalitarian country in the world. I shall also claim that the ambiguous construction of Farrokzhad as fundamentalist *and* Swedish in this particular context ends up being carried by an *un*ambiguous discursive logic. Interpreted against the backdrop of the suggested expansion of Puar's thinking around assimilation into the nation-state, Farrokzhad becomes a figure who, in the mainstream Danish media discourses, is assimilated into *Swedish fundamentalism*.

To avoid misunderstanding, I want to underline that I am not implying that discursive operations of the racialising othering of Farrokzhad have been erased by her assimilation into Swedishness. I agree with the points made by several Danish anti-racist feminists (Myong, 2014; Glaffey and Langvad, 2014) that the Danish detractors also figure Farrokzhad as a racialised other – a position she also comments upon herself. What I suggest is that the operation of discursive assimilation into Swedish fundamentalism *and* the racialisation as fundamentalist other occur in parallel, as is evident in the heading of Bukdahl's blog post written the day after the publication of Farrokzhad's review of Hassan: 'Swedish non-white girl' (Bukdahl, 2014). My claim is thus that the Danish detractors inscribe Farrokzhad in two mutually reinforcing discourses, one of Swedish fundamentalism and one of Muslim fundamentalism.

Interpellating anti-colonial scholar Homi Bhabha's analysis of 'colonial mimicry' (1994, pp 121f) to make sense of this double inscription, I suggest that Farrokzhad is constructed as 'Swedish, but not quite'. Moreover, along the lines of Bhabha, I suggest that this ambivalent construction is potentially disruptive. It resonates with the position of 'not-quite-ness' of the colonial subject that Bhabha traces in the context of British–Indian colonial history as the difference between being 'Anglicised' and being 'British' (1994, p 128). The disrupting and deconstructive effects that Bhabha sees in this 'not-quite-ness' lie in its '*double* vision, which in disclosing the ambivalence of colonial discourse also disrupts its authority' (Bhabha, 1994, p 126).

Swedish exceptionalism

Negative debates about Swedishness are not new in Denmark. The book *Tilfældet Sverige* [*The case: Sweden*], published by the Danish journalist Mogens Behrendt (1983), testifies to this. In this volume, which was mentioned in relation to both the Egalia debate and the Hassan/Farrokzhad debate (Andersen, 2014), Behrendt coined the pejorative expression 'Prohibition Sweden', referring among other things to the restrictive Swedish alcohol policies. In the context of the Hassan/Farrokzhad debate, this book (now over 30 years old) is cited to characterise Sweden as permeated by 'fundamentalism' – from the question of alcohol policies to political correctness around issues such as gender, equality and 'race'. However, even though the Danish claim that Sweden is obsessed by fundamentalist views is evidently not new, it is interesting to note in the context of this chapter that the focus has shifted. What qualifies Sweden as 'fundamentalist', according to contemporary Danish mainstream media, has changed since the 1990s. As exemplified by my two cases, it has today become equated with 'political correctness' regarding issues of gender, racialisation, equality, feminism and anti-racism.

This change has happened in parallel with gender equality's becoming incorporated into Swedish state identity and Sweden's image as the most gender-equal and egalitarian country in the world taking off internationally. This occurred, among other things, in the wake of the UN conference on women in Beijing in 1995 and Sweden's joining the EU in the same year (Towns, 2002). But gender equality seems definitely not to be the only issue at stake in the construction of Swedish equality fundamentalism. When looking at my cases and considering how Swedishness is portrayed in the Farrokzhad/Hassan debate, and also in the briefly mentioned Danish debates on Swedish revisions of classic children's books such as *Pippi Longstocking*, it seems as though 'anti-racism' is currently being forcefully added to the equation concerning Swedish 'equality fundamentalism'.

Even though my focus in this chapter is on Danish representations of Swedishness, I would like in passing to suggest that this discursive construction of Swedishness as equivalent to 'equality fundamentalism' in terms of both feminism and anti-racism is a broader phenomenon, and not only found in Danish mainstream media. The remark that Sweden is 'the Saudi Arabia of Feminism' (quoted in Sveland, 2013, p 80) was made by Wikileaks founder Julian Assange in connection with the request for his extradition to Sweden due to the court case raised against him in 2012 for sexual offences against two Swedish women. It is an indication of the ways in which discourses of anti-Swedishness, anti-feminism, racism, Islamophobia and anti-political correctness are made to intersect not only in the Danish media, but also on a broader international level.

What interests me in the context of this volume, in terms of the perjorative characterising of Sweden as an 'equality fundamentalist' nation – which has been a noticeable dimension of the Danish debate in recent decades and which can perhaps also be traced as a broader international trend – is that even these negative and anti-Swedish discourses on Swedish equality still confirm Swedish exceptionalism. In these anti-Swedish discourses, Sweden's equality policies and practices are constructed as so *exceptionally* radical that they exceed all limits and transform into madness and fundamentalism.

Seen against the background of the actual inequalities that haunt contemporary Sweden – as demonstrated by many authors (for example, Towns 2002; de los Reyes, Molina and Mulinari, 2003; de los Reyes and Martinsson, 2005), including contributors to this volume, in terms of power differentials regarding gender, 'race', ethnicity, class, sexuality, dis/ability and so on and their intersections – the ways in which celebratory versions of the (gender-)equality mantra gloss over these inequalities are, of course, highly problematic. But I claim that it is just as problematic that the image of Swedish exceptionalism is repeated and confirmed in anti-Swedish discourses such as those I have analysed in this chapter, and that these discourses contribute just as much to the glossing-over of existing inequalities as the celebratory ones do.

Conclusion

In this chapter I have discussed the myth of Sweden as the most (gender-)equal country in the world, seen from the point of view of negative images projected onto Sweden in the mainstream media of neighbouring Denmark, which in some respects may stand for more general international trends. Via two case studies I have discussed how Sweden is depicted as *fundamentalist*, but also *exceptional* in terms of the way in which issues of equality, gender, 'race', feminism and anti-racism are taken up in the country. It is important to unpack these derogatory and anti-Swedish discourses on Swedish 'equality fundamentalism' because they contribute to confirming the myth of Sweden as exceptionally (gender-)equal, while glossing over a diversity of intersecting inequalities and power differentials along the lines of gender, racialisation, sexuality, class, dis/ability and so on in contemporary Sweden.

One more reason for unpacking these derogatory Danish discourses is that, in addition to confirming the myth of Swedish equality, they also nourish and sustain growing anti-feminist and racist discourses in Sweden. As discussed in connection with the Egalia case, there are noticeable overlaps between, for example, anti-feminist Swedish blogs such as those of Per Ström, Pelle Billing and Tanja Bergkvist, and arguments articulated by high-level scientific experts and politicians in

Denmark. The anti-feminist Swedish bloggers support their arguments with references to authoritative Danish voices, and it is politically important to make these links visible.

Finally, I want to suggest that it is important to unpack the complex relations between constructions of Swedishness, equality and fundamentalism in order to expose their in/stability. I have looked at unstable constructions of Swedishness, as seen from outside (in this case, from the perspective of Danish mainstream media debates). Considered from this angle, it seems clear that the image of Sweden has, on the one hand, changed considerably over the last decades and thus appears unstable. On the other hand, 'fundamentalism' has been a cross-cutting dimension, although associated with very different issues, from alcohol politics to political correctness around feminism and anti-racism.

In terms of the issue of the in/stability of nationhood constructions, I want, in particular, to underline the process of assimilation into the white nation of certain racialised others, who might at first glance be expected to be relegated to the margins by the white gaze, independent of their location inside or outside of the nation in question. I suggested that the derogatory Danish-media construction of Farrokzhad as 'Swedish in the head' is an example of such an assimilating move, which makes Farrokzhad into an icon of negatively valued political correctness, that is, fundamentalist Swedishness. Through this assimilation, she becomes ambivalently marked as 'Swedish, but not quite', a position that is in some ways similar to Homi Bhabha's analysis of colonial mimicry (1994, p 126) and can, as such, be located as a place for deconstruction and destabilisation. Against this background, I suggest that the status of 'Swedish, but not quite' exposes a certain instability of discourses on Swedishness and nationhood more generally, perhaps even suggesting that a homogenised image of nationhood is always already impossible, due to the constant operation of intersectionalities, dis/identifications (Lykke, 2014) and assimilating/dissimilating moves.

Note

[1] It should be noted that the term 'gender-neutral pedagogy' that is appearing in the Danish-media presentations of Egalia (for example, Holst, 2011) is not commonly used in Sweden. It is a conflation of the ways in which the term 'gender-neutral' is used to designate the pronoun 'hen', introduced in Sweden to transgress the gender binary options, 'she' [hon] and 'he' [han] and the term 'gender pedagogy' [genuspedagogik]. The latter is used in scholarly, pedagogical and political mainstream circles in Sweden to characterise pedagogies that focus on the building of awareness and deconstruction of gender stereotypes (see, for example, Svaleryd 2003). Another term, used in scholarly,

pedagogical and political discussions of gender-critical pedagogies in Sweden, is 'norm critical pedagogy' [normkritisk pedagogik] (Bromseth and Darj, 2010), which puts focus on gender in its intersections with other power differentials such as sexualities and racialisation.

References

Andersen, O.S. (2014) '"Racist" råber de i Sverige' ['Racist', they shout in Sweden] *BT*, 24 January, http://blogs.bt.dk/olavskaaningandersen/2014/01/24/racist-raber-de-i-sverige/.

Behrendt, M. (1983) *Tilfældet Sverige* [*The Swedish example*], København: Erichsen.

Bergkvist, T. (2011) 'Svensk genusvansinne når utlandsk press' [The Swedish gender insane reach foreign press], 9 July, https://tanjabergkvist.wordpress.com/2011/07/09/svenskgenusvansinne-nar-utlandsk-press/.

Bhabha, H. (1994) *The location of culture*, London: Routledge.

Bolander, R. (2011) 'Socialministeren hylder drenges biologi' [The minister of social affairs celebrates the boys biology], *Avisen.dk*, 1 August, http://www.avisen.dk/socialministeren-hylder-drenges-biologi_149985.aspx.

Bromseth, J. and Darj, F. (eds) (2010) *Normkritisk pedagogik: Makt, lärande och strategier för förändring* [*Norm critical pedagogics: Power, learning, and strategies for change*], Uppsala: Uppsala University.

Bukdahl, L. (2014) 'Swedish non-white girl', *Blogdahl*, 23 January, http://bukdahl.blogspot.dk/2014/01/swedish-non-white-girl.html.

de los Reyes, P. and Martinsson, L. (2005) *Olikhetens paradigm: Intersektionella perspektiv på o(jäm)likhetsskapande* [*The paradigm of difference: Intersectional perspectives on production of (in)equality*], Lund: Studentlitteratur.

de los Reyes, P., Molina, I. and Mulinari, D. (2003) *Maktens (o)lika förklädnader: Kön, klass och etnicitet i det postkoloniala Sverige* [*The different disguises of power: Gender, class and ethnicity in postcolonial Sweden*], Stockholm: Atlas.

Farrokzhad, A. (2014) 'Hans raseri hyllas av danska rasister' [His rage was applauded by Danish racists], *Aftonbladet Kultur*, 22 January, http://www.aftonbladet.se/kultur/bokrecensioner/article18217879.ab.

Gjerding, S. (2011) 'Det har også konsekvenser ikke at gøre noget' [Not doing anything will also have its consequences], *Information*, 15 August, http://www.information.dk/275904.

Glaffey, K.N. and Langvad, M.L. (2014) 'Kære Lars Bukdahl, du taler fra en privilegeret position, racisme og homofobi er ikke en del af din hverdag' [Dear Lars Bukdahl, you speak from a privileged position: racism and homophobia is not part of your everyday life], *Information*, 21 February, http://www.information.dk/488769.

Hansen, A. (2014) 'Skulle Hassan censureret sig selv?'[Should Hassan have censured himself?] *Information*, 29 January, http://www.information.dk/486218.

Hassan, Y. (2013) *Yahya Hassan*, København: Gyldendal.

Hermansen, A.S. (2011) '… her i vores nyfeministiske kønsløse sammenhold' […here in our new feminist gender-lacking context], *Blog: ASH*, 2 July, http://annesophia.blogs.berlingske. dk/2011/07/02/vi-har-det-herligt-i-vores-nyfeministiske-og-k%C3%B8nsl%C3%B8se-sammenhold/.

Holst, N. (2011) 'Svensk børnehave afskaffer drenge og piger' [Swedish day nursery abolishes boys and girls], *Politiken*, http://politiken. dk/udland/ECE1318417/svensk-boernehave-afskaffer-drenge-og-piger/.

Karlsson, E. (2014) 'Rasistiska åsikter drar ner debatten' [Racist opinions impair the debate], *SvD Kultur*, 14 January.

Lindgren, A. (1945) *Pippi Långstrump* [*Pippi Longstocking*], Stockholm: Rabén & Sjögren.

Løwenstein, K. (2014) 'Comment on Hansen, A. (2014) 'Skulle Hassan have censureret sig selv?' [Should Hassan have censured himself?], *Information*, 29 January, http://www.information.dk/486218.

Lykke, N. (2014) 'Passionate disidentifications as an intersectional writing strategy', in N. Lykke *Writing academic texts differently: Intersectional feminist methodologies and the playful art of writing*, New York: Routledge, pp 30–47.

Memmi, A. (1991) *The colonizer and the colonized*, expanded edition, Boston, MA: Beacon Press.

Moestrup, M. (2014) 'Hvidhedskritik i det danske litteraturmiljø' [Critique of whiteness in the Danish literature milieu], *Information*, 2 May, http://www.information.dk/496018.

Myong, L. (2014) 'Værdien af et vidnesbyrd' [The value of a testimony], *Modkraft*, 6 February, http://modkraft.dk/artikel/verdien-af-et-vidnesbyrd.

Noack, R. (2015) 'Sweden is about to add a gender-neutral pronoun to its official dictionary', *Washington Post*, 1 April, http://www. washingtonpost.com/blogs/worldviews/wp/2015/04/01/sweden-is-about-to-add-a-gender-neutral-pronoun-to-its-official-dictionary/.

Pedersen, J.S. (2014) 'Litteraturredaktør: Efter svensk Yahya-artikel bliver jeg nu kaldt racist' [Literature editor: After Swedish Yahya article I am called racist], *Politiken*, 18 January, http://politiken.dk/kultur/boger/ECE2185694/litteraturredaktoer-efter-svensk-yahya-artikel-bliver-jeg-nu-kaldt-racist/.

Puar, J. (2007) *Terrorist assemblages: Homonationalism in queer times*, Durham, NC: Duke University Press.

Puar, J. (2013) 'Rethinking homonationalism', *International Journal for Middle East Studies*, vol 45, pp 336–9.

Ritzau (2015) '"Negerkonge" tages ud af nye udgaver af Pippi' ['Negroking' is now removed from new editions], *Extrabladet*, 14 February, http://ekstrabladet.dk/nyheder/samfund/negerkongetagesud-af-nye-udgaver-af-pippi/5442092.

Sauer, N.C. (2014) Comment to: Hansen, A. 2014. 'Skulle Hassan censureret sig selv?'[Should Hassan have censured himself?], *Information*, 29 January, http://www.information.dk/486218.

Ström, P. (2011) 'Forskare kräver mera manlighet på dagis' [Researchers demand more manliness at the day nursery], *Genusnytt*, 24 July, https://genusnytt.wordpress.com/page/68/.

Sullivan, S. and Tuana, N. (2007) *Race and the epistemology of ignorance*, New York: State University of New York Press.

Svaleryd, K. (2003) *Genuspedagogik* [*Gender pedagogics*], Stockholm: Liber.

Sveland, M. (2013) *Hatet: En bok om antifeminism* [*Hate: A book on anti-feminism*], Stockholm: Leopard.

Towns, A. (2002) 'Paradoxes of (in)equality: something is rotten in the gender-equal state of Sweden', *Cooperation and Conflict: Journal of the Nordic International Studies Association*, vol 37, no 2, pp 157–79.

Uriasposten (2011) 'Feminiseringen starter i børnehaven' [Effeminisation starts in day nursery], 22 July, http://www.uriasposten.net/archives/27087.

Wiseman, E. (2011) 'A change of perspective', *Guardian*, 10 July, http://www.theguardian.com/lifeandstyle/2011/jul/10/gender-differences-exhaustion-evawiseman.

World Economic Forum (2013) *Global gender gap report*, World Economic Forum.

SIX

Gender equality under threat? Exploring the paradoxes of an ethno-nationalist political party

Diana Mulinari

Introduction

Right-wing xenophobic movements and related political parties have been gaining ground in many European countries, among them, Sweden (Wodak, Khosravinik and Mral, 2013; EXPO, 2014). Their success has brought to the fore questions about their agenda regarding women's rights and gender equality. Extreme right-wing xenophobia is of course not a new phenomenon in Sweden. However, during the most part of the post-Second World War era, support for organisations with nationalist and racist discourses has been marginal in the political and public arenas. But, starting in the late 1980s, an increase in the public visibility of neo-Nazi activities was followed by the emergence of New Democracy, a populist anti-migrant party, and the creation and establishment of the Sweden Democrats. In the 2014 elections, the Sweden Democrats, with nearly 13% of votes, doubled the electoral support they had received in the 2010 general election, and gained a presence in almost all municipalities and counties (Crouch, 2014).

Scholarship on the Sweden Democrats identifies the party's historical roots in fascism and neo-Nazi political circles, conceptualising the ideology of the party as both value-conservative and ethno-pluralist (Fennema, 1997; Hellström and Nilsson, 2010; Ekman, 2010). While racism is the key through which both value-conservatism and ethno-pluralism are understood, gender poses difficult challenges for the party, as gender-equality policies are a central feature of the social and economic organisation of the Scandinavian countries. The scholarship on this and similar parties is well established; the role of gender in general (Blee, 2012), and of gender-equality discourses in particular, for the racist articulation of these parties' agendas generates new research concerns.

The establishment of right-wing xenophobic parties has gone hand in hand with politicians' (especially from right-wing parties, but at times also from the social-democratic party) arguing for policies aimed at connecting citizenship rights with assimilation, sometimes linking migrants with welfare 'cheating', criminality and failing to identify with 'western values' (Razack, 2004; Bredström, 2009; Hübinette and Lundström, 2011). Sweden has long been known internationally as a model multicultural welfare state that has extended substantial citizenship, welfare and labour rights to everyone within its borders (Schierup, Hansen and Castles, 2006). However, under the twin pressures of neoliberalism and a commitment to 'managed migration', this Swedish exceptionalism has been and continues to be substantially eroded (Schierup and Ålund, 2011; Sager, 2011). Thus, when the chairman of the Sweden Democrats identified Islam and Muslims as the biggest threat to Sweden since the Second World War (Åkesson, 2009), it was in a context in which Islamophobia (Gardell 2010) had been present to different degrees in mainstream public discourse since the beginning of the 1990s (Mulinari and Neergaard, 2012). A central aspect of the so-called new assimilation policies is a strong emphasis on gender equality as a national cultural symbol, an essential aspect of 'Swedishness' that is portrayed as conflicting with migrants' attitudes, especially those of migrants with Muslim backgrounds (de los Reyes, Molina and Mulinari, 2002; Gullestad, 2002; Keskinen, 2012).

The aim of this chapter is to explore, through a critical dialogue with feminist scholarship on nationalism and racism, how and through what strategies gender equality is mobilised by the Sweden Democrats (SD) party, conceptualised as right-wing populist (Rydgren, 2007), cultural-racist (Mulinari and Neergaard, 2012) or fascist (Arnstad, 2013). My analysis is based on a qualitative study – involving text analysis, participant observation at municipal meetings, in-depth interviews and a personal anecdote – of women and migrants in the SD. The empirical material was collected between 2008 and 2014. Twenty interviews were done between 2010 and 2011. The informants were female municipal representatives of the SD, including those with migrant backgrounds, selected from the total population of women in city councils. I also draw on official documents of the party available on the web, and the party newspaper *SD-kuriren* (previously available on the web, now closed). This is supplemented with online newspaper items.

I shall briefly introduce the Swedish societal context in which feminist debates regarding gender equality have evolved, with a special focus on shifts in economic and migration policies. I shall explore the SD's visions of gender equality through the analysis of four paradoxes in their thinking, in order to suggest that the parliamentary success of the SD creates new challenges for feminist activists and scholars regarding what it means to be equal and who will have the power to define what gender equality is.

Swedish gender equality at the cross-roads

Sweden, in conjunction with Norway and Denmark, that is, in terms of a 'Scandinavian' or Nordic model, is frequently discussed not only in relation to its social democratic welfare regime with comparatively small class differences, but also, and often together with Norway, as a relatively gender-equal country based on a political project of state feminism (Borchorst and Siim, 2008). Childcare provision and maternity leave (Lundqvist, 2011) as well as the high level of women's participation in the labour market, education and the political sphere are, despite the model's shortcomings, vital achievements from a feminist perspective. Already in the 1990s, and as a response to the financial crisis, social democratic governments introduced measures that decreased both social benefits and resource allocation in public welfare institutions. These measures had serious impacts on the lives of women and men in general and on gender equality in particular (Boréus, 1997; Selberg, 2013).

Gender equality has been a contested issue among Swedish feminist scholars and activists. Central to my understanding of the concept is the critical challenge that feminist researchers have provided to the ideology – and here I use the concept of ideology in the traditional Marxist sense as mystification – of gender equality (Rönnblom et al, 1998). Scholars have not only identified the tensions between the rhetoric of gender equality and the lives of women and men, but also illuminated and problematised how a specific model of the heterosexual couple responding to the needs of the labour market is at the core of gender-equality policies (Siim, 1994; Dahl, 2004). Scholars have also analysed gender equality as a marker of nationhood and state identity (Towns, 2002; Hobson and Hellgren, 2008), aiming to represent Sweden as a global role model regarding women's rights. The connection often made inside Sweden between gender equality and Swedish national belonging poses the topic of migration, racism and the right as belonging at the core of societal and academic debates.

Racism and the field of the political

Central to anti-racist/postcolonial frameworks is an emphasis on the diverse forms of racist ideology and its structuration in specific historical circumstances (Gilroy, 1982; Balibar, 2008). Political philosopher David Theo Goldberg (2006) underlines the centrality of race in the construction of modern Europe and argues that, despite differences, it is possible to grasp basic similarities, developing the notion of 'racial Europeanization' at the intersection between anti-Semitism, the Holocaust and the colonial experience.

In Sweden there are still lacunae in the history of the Swedish racialised regime (see Chapter One in this volume), but racisms and processes of racialisation are much older than the SD (Keskinen et al, 2009). Studies show that ethnic discrimination and everyday racism are widespread phenomena in Swedish society (de los Reyes, 2006). Exploitative racism, represented in many established political parties, focuses on racialised practices through classification systems that create migrants as over-exploited labour. Exploitative racism may be seen as a practice that is ideologically framed in European and Swedish policies of managed migration (Fekete, 2001; Lentin and Titley, 2011). It is basically shaped by an idea of getting access to cheap labour through processes of racialisation and curtailed rights.

In contrast, exclusionary racism is often linked to different forms of crisis and frequently, in its extreme form, to exceptional situations where exclusion may take the form of annihilation. However, the dominant form of exclusionary racism focuses on everyday forms of separation and exclusion, as in the cultural-racist form of the SD. Here it is ideologically framed through ethno-pluralism based on 'ethnic autonomy' via practices of separation, blocking in-migration and expulsion strategies.

Gender is at the core of the construction of both exploitative and exclusionary racism (Lewis, 2005), but in different ways. Whereas in exploitative racism racialised men have an ambivalent role in which they are seen both as a possibly highly educated labour force and as problematic in employment, racialised women are moulded through colonial racist fantasies that position them as a subservient labour force in the expanding low-wage, private-service sector (Gavanas, 2010). In contrast, exclusionary racism, with its focus of migrants as a threat to the nation, has quite different gendered conceptions. Aiming at the expulsion of the racialised 'other' from the national body, in the extreme it portrays migrant men both metaphorically and literally as rapists of the national body. Racialised women are conceptualised both as parasites, reproducing the racialised other and annihilating the national body, and also as threatened by their patriarchal cultures. Given the ways in which understandings of ethnicity and nationalism are rooted in gendered relationships, attention to gender should be at the forefront of the analysis of cultural-racist parties.

Gender and cultural-racist parties

Since the mid-1970s the role of gender and sexuality in ethno/racist nationalism has attracted increasing scholarly attention (Bacchetta and Power, 2002; Puar, 2007). According to Blee (2012), the study of gender and the far Right has developed not because of the discovery of 'facts' regarding the role of women in these movements, but due to a shift from mainstream social theory towards a feminist understanding of the role of women as political subjects. Feminist theoretical interventions that challenge the private/public distinction provide an alternative and original frame for exploring women's role in the field of the political.

Feminist scholars have argued that women play a central role in the symbolic construction of the nation and its boundaries and are central actors in the construction of narratives of exclusionary belonging (Bulbeck, 1997; Kaplan et al, 1999; Yuval-Davis, 2011). Women, these scholars assert, play a central role in nationalist, conservative and racist movements that promote patriarchal values. What attracts women to far-right movements that appear to denigrate their rights? Feminist historian Claudia Koonz's (1987) work on Nazi women and on women's support of Nazism provides an interpretation focusing on the process of empowerment that women's participation in these movements implied. Nazi women's central role in the creation of the nation and the people opened public/political spaces to them. The connection between empowerment and women's participation is also at the core of the explanation that sociologist Kathleen Blee (2007) provides, based on her study of women of the Ku-Klux-Klan. The author argues that women members of contemporary US racist groups reconcile the male-oriented agendas of organised racism with understandings of themselves and their gendered self-interests, situating the political action of women racists in rational (if deplorable) understandings of self and society (Blee, 2007).

Maarten van Ginderachter (2005) develops a similar argument in his study of the extreme Right and the Flemish nationalist women's organisation in interwar Belgium. The author suggests that these movements were not uniformly anti-feminist, citing a 'relational' tradition to justify women's public and political participation. Women were attracted to these organisations that appeared to denigrate their rights because they were actively engaged in the production of a nationalist discourse of their own, feeling empowered with new opportunities for agency (see also Kevin, 2003; Gottlieb, 2004).

However, one of the clearest boundaries regarding support for cultural-racist parties in Europe is gender (Norris, 2005; Norocel, 2013), with men supporting these parties to a much higher degree, although women leaders in parliamentary successful parties are relatively common.[1] Betz (1994, p 142) provides several reasons for this gap: labour-force participation, religiosity, age and occupational stratification. Women, Betz argues, are less likely to support racist parties because of their different position from men within the labour force, as well as within the welfare state. Betz suggests that women do not experience the same level of insecurity, working as they do in the public sector, and are less vulnerable to neoliberal transformations. However, extensive evidence regarding women's labour conditions in neoliberal Europe tends to challenge explanations that depart from the binary opposition between women as stable and men as suffering from high levels of uncertainty (Givens, 2004).

In their critical review of these explanations of the role of gender in right-wing populist parties, Gidengil et al (2005) assert that one of the most serious shortcomings of mainstream explanations in political science and sociology is their focus on the category of women when explaining women's lack of identification with racist parties. The authors argue that if the focus shifts towards men, the gender gap could be explained as a male response to the success of second-wave feminism, a feminist backlash. They further suggest that women's dis-identification from these parties is, to a certain extent, based on the centrality of gender equality for most women across the political spectrum. However, not all racist parties are conservative on moral issues, such as the shift of the Norwegian Fremskrittspartiet (Akkerman and Hagelund, 2007) towards what could be considered 'feminist' values regarding family and sexuality, a shift that has improved the rate of support from women voters.

Women in the Sweden Democrats

While the SD has a membership of over 9,000, only about 20% are women. Furthermore, women account for only 15% of the SD's national parliamentarians (the second-lowest representation of women is in the Centre Party, with about one third); in regional and local municipalities the representation is slightly higher (17% and 19%, respectively). Opinion polls estimate the female vote for the SD to be around a quarter to a third, and this is not increasing. This is in line with voting patterns in other European countries (Mudde, 2007; Rydgren, 2007).

Many of the SD women whose narratives underpin the analysis developed in this chapter claim that there is a big challenge in being a representative for the SD. They can be ostracised by the other political parties, and be called racists by the media, neighbours and friends. Family members may consider their political choices objectionable or even mistaken. Yet these women choose to represent a racist party (although they do not see themselves or the party as racist). Who are these women? What inspires them? What visions of gender emerge from their world-view?

The women in the study differ in their paths to political involvement. While some have had long-term experience in politics in other established political parties, others have been active in far-right populist parties at the municipal level or within extreme-right racist organisations and a third group have never been in parliamentary politics (Linden and Klandermans, 2007). Stories that explain membership in the party through identification with others, especially husbands, are common. Mia, who was very defensive during the interview, said: 'I am here because of him,' and often thought her husband would have better answers to our questions. With two exceptions (a young girl with a background in neo-Nazi activism and a middle-aged woman with an academic career), all the women we spoke to were irregularly and part-time employed, unemployed, on sick leave or dependent on welfare because of their sporadic employment patterns.

'And it began with my husband – he joined from the beginning. And he thought, well, I needed something to do; because I'm on sick leave and can't really do anything but stay at home.' (Åsa)

'I needed to come out and meet people. No money. The Soc [a reference to the Welfare Board and its policy regarding state allowances] controlling what you eat. I've never been politically involved before.' (Annahi)

'It's hard. I almost wouldn't have coped if I'd had a job. But as I'm unemployed, then it is easier.' (Monika)

The women who represent the SD seemed unable to cope with the demands that a gender-equality regime inspired to a certain extent by second-wave feminism (Bergqvist, Olsson Blandy and Sainsbury, 2007) imposes.

'It is impossible. Impossible. Only feminists believe in this. All these young women, with small children and a career. Of course they get sick. That is why I do not have a career. Or rather I had a career as a mother.' (Annika)

'I tried to work and take care of my two children, but all the demands at work. It turns to be impossible. I am on sick leave now.' (Marianne)

It is a model that has decreased some forms of men's power within the family and workplace, while empowering – but also making difficult demands of – women as citizens, workers and mothers. There are tensions between the (gendered) self and society, tensions that are intensified by neoliberalism and that this group has chosen to resolve through an identification (Holmes, 2000; Lee, 1997) with a racist world-view.

Neoliberalism, gender and support for racist parties

Sunday night. Waiting in Accident and Emergency (A&E). Two 'Swedish' women in their late seventies are sitting nearby. One of them does not stop talking (or maybe I am only tired and irritable). She asks me where I come from and happily celebrates the coincidence (her own words) that her neighbours who drove her to A&E also come from Latin America. I ask the two women if they would fancy something to drink. The talkative woman says no; the other one would like a cup of tea. We have waited for three hours already.

Suddenly increased movement in the nearby rooms. Not so much shouting but people running around. After a while a (stressed) young nurse who wears a headscarf communicates with us as if we were in school: 'A traffic accident, many injured, we are forced to prioritise.' Mumbling in the room, many sighs. The – until recently – silent woman looks straight into the air and asserts: 'They always take them first.' I do not understand what she is saying. Or do I not want to understand? A 'fucking bitch', clearly articulated by a young man who speaks Farsi with his father, forces me to realise what is happening. The woman had a particular interpretation of the word 'first'. In her world-view first translates into taking 'migrants' before 'Swedes'. 'They do what they must do', says a well-dressed middle-aged man almost in a whisper, defending the medical staff. I move myself and my cup of tea. Turn extremely chatty and comment on the knitting project the other woman is working on ... I write 'Stop feeling sorry for her.' But I cannot help it. She's so alone with her hatred. (Author's personal notebook, October 2012)

I had just begun to analyse the interviews when the above event took place. In my notes of the event no connection is made to the SD. I did not know then and do not know today what the woman's voting preferences were. But similar arguments, based on entitlement fantasies where 'Swedes' (as white, European and Christian) are discriminated against and marginalised in favour of migrants emerged in the interviews with the SD women.

And I still remember the colour of the knitting of the woman who could not stop talking. I wear the colour of the gloves she was working on, and her eternal talking about her amazing Latino neighbours was a reminder that most citizens, and especially most women, had chosen other ways to interpret the long wait in the emergency room. Would an explanation of the rules governing priority in emergency care change the other woman's world-view? Or perhaps a statistic on the number of people with migrant backgrounds who make Swedish healthcare at all possible? Or would a list help that showed that the SD voted in a budget and tax profile that strongly decreases public health resources? I am not so sure. The woman had made up her mind. Migrants should be blamed for the time she was forced to wait. Sara, one of the SD women in the study, developed similar arguments:

'With the SD's policies we will be getting back some of what we've lost in healthcare. Ten to fifteen years ago it was much easier to get access to a doctor and it is quite clear that it is because we have so many migrants. I have been in hospital a lot because I've been sick, very sick. And I can assure you that we could have excellent healthcare if the migrants were not there, using our hospitals, our doctors, our time.'

The term 'our' is very present in all the interviews. The sense of (private) property covers both welfare state institutions and family relations. Citizenship is not only expressed through essentialist notions of culture and belonging, but also mediated through an understanding of capitalist-inspired notions of ownership. 'Our elderly' is at the core of a number of the SD's interventions, such as the election advert where an elderly woman with a walker painfully tries to approach what looks like an insurance office, and many women dressed in burkas with many children, violently force her to move away, to stand in line. In most of the interviews the category of migrant was juxtaposed with the category of retired, elderly people. Many other categories could serve as binary oppositions, but the focus on migrants versus the elderly captures the lived experiences of female SD politicians and the SD's generation profile; elderly voters are central to the success of the party.[2]

While informants often argued that women should have the right to choose whether they wanted to stay at home with their 'own' or invest in a career, they themselves never considered staying at home with elderly parents as an option. State institutions were expected to take responsibility; they shifted responsibility from 'their own' towards what they experience as their 'own' welfare state. In Karina's narrative, an unattended old mother is juxtaposed with a luxury Mercedes:

> 'They say that we are racist. That is not true. This has nothing to do with racism. I live in xxxx and we see every day how the services for the elderly are being eroded. When somebody has his old mother getting a shower once a week and then see migrants getting all this support, taking all the money, driving around with their shining Mercedes … I'm not saying that this is so for everybody, but that is not the point. It is so unfair.'

Karina does not explain how and why she associates migrants with the lack of welfare provision. This connection is taken for granted, despite extensive scholarship and public debates that highlight the effects of neoliberal policies on elderly care. The informant herself points out that it is very possible that this is not so, or rather, that what she is saying is an awkward generalisation; but as she herself says, it does not matter.

Lena moves from the resources supposedly invested in migrants to the dignity of ageing working people, with a 'they' getting all the resources:

> 'All this money for migrants takes away the dignity of our elderly people. They have worked all their lives and for

what? To be left alone, abandoned in a nursing home. They get all the money. They come here with all these wars, this hate, this racism. And our old people are alone.'

Note the projection process through which migrants end up as solely responsible for the financial crisis. Note also that racism is understood as a problem migrants carry with them from their countries of birth. It is their fault that elderly people are alone; racism is constructed as a cultural product that migrants import to Sweden.

What emerges from the interviewees' narratives is the political significance of gender, an area conventionally ignored or located as private and apolitical. What emerges also is the centrality of what Adrienne Rich defined as forms of female racism (1979). Any feminist analysis that explains the participation of women in racist parties only as a product of their marginalisation in the context of neoliberal transformation is problematic. Women's investment in racist selves must also be understood through the historical continuity between forms of white (Christian) femininity and European racism.

Four paradoxes: a feminist reading of the Sweden Democrats

Gender equality (*jämställdhet*) is a difficult issue for culturally racist parties in the Nordic countries in general, and in particular for the SD. Gender equality is not given a specific place in the SD's key policy documents. Nor is gender given a separate section in its 2012 municipality programme. However, in its county programme (regional issues concerning health, transport and so on) the party argues for what it defines as formal equality between men and women.[3] I shall now explore four paradoxes at the core of the SD's understanding of gender equality.

Similarity versus difference

The Sweden Democrats view the nation as the most important, oldest and most natural human community after the family ... National affinity binds the nation's members across time and space and creates links between the dead, the living and the unborn generations and between young and old, different social classes, political camps and geographic regions ... The Sweden Democrats define the Swedish nation in terms of loyalty, shared identity, a common language and common culture. Membership of the Swedish nation can in our view be achieved either by being born into it or by, in later life, actively choosing to join it. (Sverigedemokraterna, 2011, p 11)[4]

it is the SD's understanding that there are innate differences between most men and most women that go beyond what can be observed with the naked eye. It is also our opinion that the masculine and feminine qualities in many contexts complement each other, and because of this we believe that children must have the right to both a mother and a father in their lives. (Sverigedemokraterna, n.d.[3])

Here the being together in the nation is grounded in 'cultural similarity', or rather, cultural similarity is understood to be a precondition of the possibility of being together, but families should be composed of a woman (mother) and a man (father), defined through difference. In the SD's world-view, children need difference and a particular form of heterosexual difference to be able to develop, while citizens need similarity in order to be able to identify with one another. The notion that similarity is central for solidarity within the nation but difference is fundamental for the complementary within the family at first glance seems to be at the core of one of SD's driving paradoxes. The natural hierarchies within the family, with the authority of a loving father towards a subordinated (but protected) wife and children, are fundamental in legitimating colonial forms of social organisation (McClintock, 1995). This model is moved from the family towards the public legitimisation of hierarchies among societal groups. It is in this sense a repoliticisation of the private as a model for the public.

Patricia Hill Collins (1998) argues that the idealised traditional family combines a seemingly natural hierarchy with a feeling of unity among its members. Another characteristic of the traditional family, the author suggests, is its location in discourses of belonging through genetic links that are blood ties. If the nation is understood in terms of family bonds, the control of women's sexuality for the 'purity of the race' becomes central, and blood ties enter into the conceptualisation of the nation. Demands for restricted immigration, closed borders and assimilation are a logical consequence of this line of thought.

Hate versus love

Through the politicisation of the private, the emergent model of a family that cares for 'their own' provides legitimacy for the notion of a human essence that identifies only with 'their own'. The SD's racist agenda is transformed into an agenda of care. Sara Ahmed (2003) provides an analysis of the shift within racist organisations from discourses of hate to discourses of love. Ahmed suggests that it has become very common among racist organisations to rename themselves as organisations of love and to claim that they act out of love for their own. While the women I met did not speak about love, they often returned to their political engagement as based on care. Contrary to the view of the SD as racist, the women saw themselves as generous, engaged and caring. In the words of Åsa:

> 'I could not understand, I will never understand until she apologises for this. She, my best friend, well my former best friend, she does not speak to me anymore. Does not answer the phone. Does not answer my emails. The days and nights that she went about laughing at migrant ways in her job. But now she says what is different. That she is not a racist. And then I wonder, I told her in my last letter. If to be a racist is to care that your elderly mother gets a shower every day, then, well. Don't you think that it is a strange country where to care for others is called to be a racist?'

A central tenet in Scandinavian feminist research has been the link between the welfare state and women's reproductive and care work. This scholarship has focused on unpaid, privately paid and publicly paid reproductive/care work. The linkage between various forms of care work and what has been called 'care politics' has also been theorised (Hernes, 1988). An often taken-for-granted aspect here has been the normative 'good' in care, while avoiding the issue of (over-) exploitation in care work. In the interviews with the female activists of the SD, care became an important theme. However, it was care mediated through a culturally racist prism. The concept of caring racism (Mulinari and Neergaard, 2014) describes the political articulation of racism with particular forms of (racist) femininity in the Swedish context. Social anthropologist Uma Narayan (1995) has argued that while contemporary care discourses focus on acknowledging human needs and relationships, there is also a need to identify a colonial care discourse that enables colonisers to construct themselves as superior.

Narayan asserts that thinking about care discourse in the colonial context illuminates the roles it has historically played in legitimating relations of power.

Choice versus biology

A central characteristic of the women politicians in this study was that they rarely spoke about male dominance and, when they did, they never described it as something negative, as Swedish female politicians often do. SD women enter parliamentary politics as a reaction against the Swedish women's movement and its demands for gender equality, as a challenge to the parliamentary dominance of gender equality policies – a dominance that, according to them, 'has gone too far' (informant's words).

Gender entered the SD women's narratives in different ways. The first was through a before/now dichotomy in their description of the changes that have occurred within Sweden, where feminism often functions as a code word for social problems and undesirable changes. In Lina's words:

> 'Things were different before. Divorce is okay. I am divorced. But people divorce … well, like abortion. They do not take things seriously. And those feminists have parties when they divorce.'

The second way that gender entered the SD women's discourse was through the silence/speech metaphor, a metaphor often used by the SD. When asked about gender-equality issues, the informants tended to follow the SD's political propaganda that is based on the equation 'We, the SD, say what people think and feel (but dare not say).' The same argument was used in relation to gender equality, as Maja's words illustrate:

> 'In this country if you say you want to marry and stay at home and be a good mum, feminists would destroy you. Who would have the courage to say such a thing? But we [the SD] know that many women would like to have these choices. But nobody dares to speak up.'

The argument that people/women do not dare to challenge the authoritarian gender norms established by the SD but 'invented' by feminists (the silence argument) is strongly related to the conviction that the party voices the opinions of those who do not dare speak out. In the propaganda film that the SD women created during the EU campaign 2014, a young (blonde) woman in a tiny bikini, posing near the sea, in the genre of men's magazines, was portrayed. The SD women explained that they consciously chose this image to challenge the extremism of Swedish feminism that, in their world-view, opposes women's representation as sexual objects. According to them, the image of the nearly naked woman clearly showed that women could make other choices.[5] The term 'choice' is recurrent in the arguments. Swedish women (oppressed by feminism) should make other choices, it is argued, particularly other forms of doing gender and femininity, just like the one provided in the propaganda film. Central to the SD is an invitation to Swedish women to make other choices.

However, it seems that choice is clearly narrowed through biologically given frames for both men and women, as one of the leaders of the Sweden Democrats argued:

> Since the dawn of history, humanity has survived thanks to the fact that men and women depend on each other. Not just for the need of procreation, but to survive in everyday life. Men knew how to hunt, how to defend the group. Women gave birth, took care of men and children and cooked the food. Men have an easier time solving technical and logical problems, women are more likely to teach children the language and give them social skills. (Sara-Lena Bjälkö, 2014, Almedalen)[6]

This follows the SD's party programme, which underlines: 'We argue for formal gender equality where neither women nor men are discriminated against. If this leads to women and men not doing things in the same way, then by the same extension we do not consider this a problem.'[7] However, while individual choice is underlined with regard to the position of women in society, state intervention is demanded with regard to women's role as reproducers of the nation, particularly in the regulation of abortion rights and in the prohibition of insemination for lesbians. State intervention is also demanded with regard to the rights of ('Swedish') men in issues such as custody.

Gender equality versus feminism

The third and most important way in which gender equality enters into the narratives is in relation to migrants and migration. In the following quotes, gender equality is linked to what the majority of the informants believe is the key political issue for the SD: migration.

> 'Yes, partly because we had achieved gender equality here. But now, especially here in town when you're out, a lot of women feel unsafe when they go out, and ... not all men are like Swedish men, you know.' (Sara)

> 'And to those who come here, they learn that here in Sweden men respect women, they are not doormats. They must accept our culture.' (Åsa)

> 'That's fine with equality but not when it goes too far. As feminists who have parties when they divorce and then cry because not all migrants can stay. Everyone knows how it is. Girls are girls and boys will be boys. There is nothing strange about it.' (Marianne)

> 'Women, girls are vulnerable. We used to have equality and respect in this country but we are now in danger of women being raped and abused. And afterwards they receive no punishment. Or get a sentence and we taxpayers pay for their pleasant time in Swedish prisons.' (Selma)

Sara, Åsa, Marianne and Selma have a split relation to gender equality. On the one hand, gender equality is perceived as 'Swedish' in the context of racist beliefs about other cultures. On the other hand, gender equality should not be 'exaggerated', but it must be based on what is perceived as 'natural' gender differences. Discourses based on the need to protect 'Swedish' women create an arena where the agenda of law and order that the SD argues for can be established. Finally, feminists are identified as responsible for the crisis, not only of the family but also of the nation, because of their support for a multicultural agenda.

On 8 March 2012 the SD women's network presented a film that aimed to put the topic of 'honour killing' on the public agenda. The first scene of the film showed a female body brutally beaten; in the second scene a blonde young woman cleans up the blood, accompanied by a speaker's voice saying: 'Think that culture can kill.' The SD women active in Almedalen before the 2014 Swedish elections systematically linked rape to migration, asserting that the courses offered to refugees seem unable to teach them Swedish cultural values regarding women. 'The Alliance has introduced community education classes for asylum seekers, but apparently without success … Look at the increasing number of honour crimes and the exploding figures regarding rape.'[8]

Although there is little evidence to suggest that similar ideological points inform the arguments of some groups within the Swedish women's movement, there is a clear overlap in the description of migrant (Muslim) women who are culturally oppressed by dangerous Muslim men. Sara Farris (2011) uses the concept of femonationalism to describe the discursive formation that creates a shared space for heterogeneous anti-Islam and anti-(male) migrant concerns and sections of the women's movement under the idea of gender equality.

The SD is strongly anti-feminist. It frequently criticises various aspects of gender-equality policy, arguing that it violates 'human nature' and weakens 'normal' family cohesion (Towns et al, 2014, p 237). But in the construction of Swedishness, and against immigrants, especially Muslim 'others', the SD identifies the positive aspects of equality on the grounds that (a soft version of) equality is culturally Swedish and can thus be contrasted with the position of (Muslim) immigrants. In other words, gender equality is highlighted the most when the SD talks about 'the other'.

Journalist Anna Ekström (2011) has interviewed Stellan Bojerud, one of the candidates for the position of leader of the SD party after Jimmy Åkesson. The party programme uses the phrase 'open Swedishness' to identify the characteristics that make a person Swedish. Swedes 'have a strong work ethic' (*arbetsvillig och pålitilig*), are clean (*håller jämförelsevis rent omkring sig*) and are secularised, the product of a gender-equality culture. He also argued that Swedes like animals, especially dogs – an animal that is dirty within Islam. Swedes (following Nazi-inspired romanticism of nature) are powerfully linked with nature. This argument, Ekström contends, expands the classification system: that not all Swedish-born people develop in a Swedish way; Muslim qualities, according to the party, may be embodied in Swedish people also. The argument that not all Swedish-born people develop in 'Swedish ways' is central to a political agenda in which those classified as Swedish and who challenge the SD's world-view are defined as traitors to the nation.

The journalist concludes her article by drawing a parallel between the SD's new party programme and the Nordic Family Year Book of 1920 and what she calls 'folkloristic taxonomies'. A central and powerful continuity in this classification system is the reinforcement of a Swedish whiteness frame (Sawyer 2002) where those categorised as non-white are excluded from the right to belong to the nation.

Conclusions

Sweden is a leading OECD member in terms of its rapidly increasing inequalities of various kinds, albeit from a low starting point (OECD, 2011). State intervention seems to have prioritised and promoted profit over citizens' needs, in a context of the growing political articulation of racism. The SD, with its historical roots in Nazi and fascist organisations, is strongly anti-feminist. The issue of gender equality is present in its agenda only when targeting migrants or in debates about multiculturalism. However, in the construction of Swedishness and its stance against migrants, the SD at times ends up highlighting positive aspects of gender equality, arguing that (a soft version of) gender equality is culturally Swedish and thus antithetical to migrants. It is in this sense that the SD is forced to balance its (racist) understanding of gender equality as a Swedish cultural value with its anti-feminism. In its world-view, 'Swedish' women are oppressed by feminism; an ideology that challenges what is natural in terms of gender roles forces women into the labour force separating them from their children and creating and supporting policies that destroy the family.

Blee (1996) suggests that during the process of modernisation of the Ku Klux Klan in the late 1920s the Klan provided a political rhetoric that departed from respect for women's rights at the same time as its policies (and values) aimed at relocating women within the private sphere. The same could be said regarding the SD. Despite its recognition of gender equality, both in its programme and in members' individual values, ideas of what a woman and a family is or should be are linked to notions of a 'good society' within, on the one hand, a strong neo-conservative profile and, on the other hand, a solid racist frame.

However, the relationship between the SD and Swedish mainstream feminism has been transformed by the former's parliamentary success. The participation of the Norwegian Gender Equality Minister, member of a racist party, in the concluding panel of the Nordic Forum 2014 (see Chapter Eight in this volume), one of the largest gatherings of the Scandinavian women's movement, created confusion, anger and criticism among many feminists.

While there is little evidence to suppose that, when hegemonic Swedish feminists and the SD argue in similar ways regarding the oppression of migrant women, their arguments are based on similar ideological positions, some serious overlaps can be traced in their shared understanding of both the (cultural) superiority of the Swedish model and their understanding of migrant men as dangerous and patriarchal.

Both the SD and hegemonic Swedish feminism define the veil as a social problem, and religion (or, rather, Islam) as a threat to women's rights.[9]

What I, an anti-racist feminist of migrant background, and many others – outside the 'we' – learned from the debate that followed the forms of hegemonic feminism that the Nordic Forum embodied was that privileged forms of femininity, despite their identification with the Swedish women's movement, have in recent years reinforced an emotional regime of banal nationalism that is shaped by both amnesia and denial of European racial formations. Needless to say, for most of us (queer, anti-racist feminists, social justice activists), our communities endangered by these parties, the agenda is one of both survival and resistance. Inspired by Latin American feminists, we will go for more (*vamos por mas*). From the location of our migrant communities attacked by these racist parties, from the location of those living clandestinely in the shadow of Fortress Europe, debates about gender equality must be radically transformed to name, include and even depart from our (without quotations marks) understanding of social justice. We want bread, but roses too.

Notes

[1] In Denmark there is Pia Kjærsgaard (Danish People's Party); in France, Marine Le Pen (National Front); in Italy, Alessandra Mussolini (Social Alternative); and in Norway, Siv Jensen (Progress Party).

[2] SD politiker mest lika sina väljare. [Sweden Democrats politicians are very similar to their electorate] http://www.scb.se/sv_/Hitta-statistik/Artiklar/SD-politikerna-mest-lika-sina-valjare, accessed 10/02/2015.

[3] Sverigedemokraterna (n.d.) *Sverigedemokraterna, familjen och jämställdheten* [Sweden Democrats, family and gender equality], https://sverigedemokraterna.se/var-politik/familjen/, accessed 22 April 2014.

[4] https://sd.se/wp-content/uploads/2013/08/principprogrammet2014_webb.pdf (accessed 1 December 2015) and https://sd.se/var-politik/var-politik-a-till-o/ (accessed 1 December 2015).

[5] http://www.dagensmedia.se/nyheter/kampanjer/article3828524.ece, accessed 24 May 2014.

[6] Almedalen is the location of one of Sweden's *most* important political events. It takes place in the summer and gathers politicians, the media and civil society organisations.

[7] Sverigedemokraterna (2003/2005) Sverigedemokraternas principprogram, http://www.sverigedemokraterna.net/asikt_text.php?action=fullnewsandid=317, accessed 10 September 2009.

[8] https://thereseborg.wordpress.com/2010/08/30/problem-maste-belysas-for-att-kunna-losas-2/, accessed 10 February 2015.

[9] http://sverigeskvinnolobby.se/blog/radslan-att-kallas-rasist-hindrar-kampen-mot-hedersfortryck.

References

Ahmed, S. (2003) 'In the name of love', *Borderlands*, vol 2, pp 1–41.

Åkesson, J. (2009) 'Muslimerna är vårt största utländska hot' ['Muslims are our biggest foreign threat'], *Aftonbladet*, http://www.aftonbladet.se/debatt/debattamnen/politik/article12049791.ab, (accessed 13 July 2014).

Akkerman, T. and Hagelund, A. (2007) 'Women and children first! Anti-immigration parties and gender in Norway and the Netherlands', *Patterns of Prejudice*, vol 41, no 2, pp 197–214.

Arnstad, H. (2013) *Älskade Fascism: De svartbrunna rörelsernas ideology och historia* [*Loved Fascism: The blackbrown movement ideology and history*], Stockholm: Nordsteds.

Bacchetta, P. and Power, M. (eds) (2002) *Right-wing women: From conservatives to extremists around the world*, New York: Routledge.

Balibar, É. (2008) 'Racism revisited: sources, relevance, and aporias of a modern concept', *PMLA*, vol 123, no 5, pp 1630–9.

Bergqvist, C., Olsson Blandy, T. and Sainsbury, D. (2007) 'Swedish state feminism: continuity and change', in J. Outshoorn and J. Kantola (eds) *Changing state feminism*, Basingstoke: Palgrave Macmillan, pp 224–45.

Betz, H.-G. (1994) *Radical right-wing populism in western Europe*, Houndmills: Macmillan.

Blee, K. (1996) 'Becoming a racist: women in contemporary Ku Klux Klan and neo-Nazi groups', *Gender and Society*, vol 10, no 6, pp 680–702.

Blee, K.M. (2007) 'Ethnographies of the far right', *Journal of Contemporary Ethnography*, vol 36, no 2, pp 119–28.

Blee, K.M. (2012) 'Does gender matter in the United States far-right? Politics, ideology and religion', *Politics, Religion and Ideology. Special Issue: Women, Fascism and the Far Right, 1918–2010*, vol 13, no 2, pp 253–65.

Borchorst, A. and Siim, B. (2008) 'Woman-friendly policies and state feminism: theorizing Scandinavian gender equality', *Feminist Theory*, vol 9, no 26, pp 207–24.

Boréus, K. (1997) 'The shift to the right: neo-liberalism in argumentation and language in the Swedish public debate since 1969', *European Journal of Political Research*, vol 31, pp 257–86.

Bredström, A. (2009) 'Sweden: HIV/AIDS policy and the "crisis" of multiculturalism', *Race and Class*, vol 50, no 4, pp 57–68.

Bulbeck, C. (1997) *Reorienting western feminisms: Women's diversity in a postcolonial world*, Cambridge: Cambridge University Press.

Crouch, D. (2014) 'Swedish far-right leader: Jews must abandon religious identity to be Swedes', *Guardian* 17 December, http://www. theguardian.com/world/2014/dec/17/swedish-far-right-leader-jews-swedes (accessed 4 June 2015).

Dahl, U. (2004) *Progressive women, traditional men: The politics of knowledge and gender stories of 'development' in the northern periphery of the EU*, Santa Cruz: University of California Press.

de los Reyes, P. (ed) (2006) *Arbetets (o)synliga murar: Utredningen om makt, integration och strukturell diskriminering* [*The invisible boundaries of working life: Official government inquiry into power, integration and structural discrimination*], Stockholm: Statens Offentliga Utredningar, vol 59.

de los Reyes, P., Molina, I. and Mulinari, D. (eds) (2002) *Maktens (o) lika förklädnader. Kön, klass och etnicitet i det postkoloniala Sverige* [*The diverse disguise of power: Gender, class and ethnicity in the postcolonial Sweden*], Stockholm: Atlas.

Ekman, P. (2010) *Ut ur skuggan: En kritisk granskning av Sverige Demokrater* [*Out of the shadows: A critical analysis of the Sweden Democrats*], Stockholm: Natur och Kultur.

Ekström, A. (2011) 'Vem är svensk nog för SD?' [Who is Swedish enough for the SD?], *Sydsvenskan*, http://www.sydsvenskan.se/ opinion/aktuella-fragor/vem-ar-svensk-nog-for-sd/, 111030 (accessed 13 February 2012).

EXPO (2014) 'Patriotism and patriarchy: The impact of nationalism on gender equality', Expo Research Publications, M. Ekerstedt (ed), Stockholm: The Kvinna till Kvinna Foundation.

Farris, S. (2011) 'The political economy of femonationalism', *Feministische Studien*, vol 29, no 2, pp 379–80.

Fekete, L. (2001) 'The emergence of xeno-racism', *Race and Class*, vol 43, no 23, pp 23–40.

Fennema, M. (1997) 'Some conceptual issues and problems in the comparison of anti immigrant parties in western Europe', *Party Politics*, vol 3, no 4, pp 473–92.

Gardell, M. (2010) *Islamofobi* [*Islamophobia*], Stockholm: Leopard.

Gavanas, A. (2010) *Who cleans the welfare state? Migration, informalization, social exclusion and domestic services in Stockholm*, Stockholm: Institute for Futures Studies.

Gidengil, E., Hennigar, M., Blais, A. and Nevitte, N. (2005) 'Explaining the gender gap in support for the new right: the case of Canada', *Comparative Political Studies*, vol 38, no 10, pp 1171–95.

Gilroy, P. (1982) 'Police and thieves', in Centre for Contemporary Cultural Studies (ed) *The empire strikes back: Race and racism in 70s Britain*, London: Hutchinson, pp 143–82.

Givens, T.E. (2004) 'The radical right gender gap', *Comparative Political Studies*, vol 37, pp 30–54.

Goldberg, D. (2006) 'Racial Europeanization', *Ethnic and Racial Studies*, vol 9, no 2, pp 331–64.

Gottlieb, J. (2004) 'Women and British fascism revisited: gender, the far-right, and resistance', *Journal of Women's History*, vol 16, no 3, pp 108–23.

Gullestad, M. (2002) 'Invisible fences: egalitarianism, nationalism and racism', *The Journal of the Royal Anthropological Institute*, vol 8, no 1, pp 45–63.

Hellström, A. and Nilsson, T. (2010) '"We are the good guys": ideological positioning of the nationalist party Sverigedemokraterna in contemporary Swedish politics', *Ethnicities*, vol 1, no 10, pp 55–76.

Hernes, H. (1988) *Welfare state and women power: Essays in state feminism*, Oslo: Norwegian University Press.

Hill Collins, P. (1998) '"It's all in the family": intersections of gender, race and family', *Hypatia*, vol 13, no 3, pp 62–82.

Hobson, B. and Hellgren, Z. (2008) 'Cultural dialogues in the good society: the case of honour killings in Sweden', *Ethnicities*, vol 8, no 3, pp 385–404.

Holmes, D.R. (2000) *Integral Europe: Fast-capitalism, multiculturalism, neofascism*, Princeton, NJ: Princeton University Press.

Hübinette, T. and Lundström, C. (2011) 'Sweden after the recent election: the double binding power of Swedish whiteness through the mourning of the loss of "old Sweden" and the passing of "good Sweden"', *NORA: Nordic Journal of Feminist and Gender Research*, vol 19, no 1, pp 42–52.

Kaplan, C., Alarcón, N. and Moallem, M. (eds) (1999) *Between woman and nation: Nationalism, transnational feminisms and the state*, Durham, NC: Duke University Press.

Keskinen, S. (2012) 'Limits to speech? The racialised politics of gendered violence in Denmark and Finland', *Journal of Intercultural Studies*, vol 33, no 3, pp 261–74.

Keskinen, S., Irni, S., Tuori, S. and Mulinari D. (2009) 'Introduction: Postcolonialism and the Nordic Models of Welfare and Gender', in S. Tuori, S. Irni, S. Keskinen, and D. Mulinari (eds) *Complying with colonialism: Gender, race and ethnicity in the Nordic region*, Farnham: Ashgate, pp 1–16.

Kevin, P. (2003) *Women, gender and fascism in Europe 1919–45*, New Brunswick, NJ: Rutgers University Press.

Koonz, C. (1987) *Mothers in the fatherland: Women, the family, and Nazi politics*, New York: St. Martin's Press.

Lentin, A. and Titley, G. (2011) *The crises of multiculturalism: Racism in a neoliberal age*, London: Zed Books.

Lewis, G. (2005) 'Welcome to the margins: diversity, tolerance and policies of exclusion', *Ethnic and Racial Studies*, vol 28, no 3, pp 536–58.

Linden, A. and Klandermans, B. (2007) 'Revolutionaries, wanderers, converts, and compliants: life histories of extreme right activists', *Journal of Contemporary Ethnography*, vol 36, no 2, pp 184–201.

Lundqvist, Å. (2011) *Family policy paradoxes: Gender equality and labour market regulation in Sweden, 1930–2010*, Bristol: Policy Press.

McClintock, A. (1995) *Imperial leather: Race, gender, and sexuality in the colonial context*, London: Routledge.

Mudde, C. (2007) *Populist radical right parties in Europe*, Cambridge: Cambridge University Press.

Mulinari, D. and Neergaard, A. (2012) 'The Sweden Democrats, racisms and the construction of the Muslim threat', in G. Morgan. and S. Poynting, (eds) *Global Islamophobia: Muslims and moral panic in the West*, Farnham: Ashgate, pp 67–82.

Mulinari, D. and Neergaard, A. (2014) '"We are Sweden Democrats because we care for others": exploring racisms in the Swedish extreme right', *European Journal of Women's Studies*, vol 21, no 1, pp 43–56.

Mulinari, D., Keskinen, S., Tuori, S. and Irni, S. (eds) (2009) *Complying with colonialism: Gender, race and ethnicity in the Nordic region*, Farnham: Ashgate.

Narayan, U. (1995) 'Colonialism and its others: considerations on rights and care discourses', *Hypatia*, vol 10, no 2, pp 133–40.

Norocel, O.C. (2013) '"Give us back Sweden!" A feminist reading of the (re)interpretations of the folkhem conceptual metaphor in Swedish radical right populist discourse', *NORA: Nordic Journal of Feminist and Gender Studies*, vol 21, no 1, pp 4–20.

Norris, P. (2005) *Radical Right: Voters and parties in the regulated market*, Cambridge: Cambridge University Press.

OECD (2011) *Recruiting immigrant workers, Sweden*, Paris: OECD Publishing.

Puar, J. (2007) *Terrorist assemblages: Homonationalism in queer times*, Durham, NC: Duke University Press.

Razack, S.H. (2004) 'Imperilled Muslim women, dangerous Muslim men and civilised Europeans: legal and social responses to forced marriages', *Feminist Legal Studies*, vol 12, no 2, pp 129–74.

Rich, A. (1979) *On lies, secrets, and silence: selected prose 1966–1978*, New York: W.W. Norton & Company.

Rönnblom, M., Tollin, K. and Mattsson, A. (1998) *Jämställdhet – retorik som praktik?* [*Gender equality. Rhetoric or practice?*], Länsstyrelsen i Västerbotten: meddelande 8.

Rydgren, J. (2007) 'The sociology of the radical right', *Annual Review of Sociology*, vol 33, pp 241–62.

Sager, M. (2011) *Everyday clandestinity: Experiences on the margins of citizenship and migration policies*, Lund: Lund University Press.

Sawyer, L. (2002) 'Routings: race, African diasporas, and Swedish belonging', *Transforming Anthropology*, vol 11, no 1, pp 13–35.

Schierup, C.-U. and Ålund, A. (2011) 'The end of Swedish exceptionalism? Citizenship, neoliberalism and the politics of exclusion', *Race and Class*, vol 53, no 1, pp 45–64.

Schierup, C.-U., Hansen, P. and Castles, S. (2006) *Migration, citizenship, and the European welfare state: A European dilemma*, Oxford: Oxford University Press.

Selberg, R. (2013) 'Nursing in times of neoliberal change: an ethnographic study of nurses' experiences of work intensification', *Nordic Journal of Working Life Studies*, vol 3, no 2, pp 9–35.

Siim, B. (1994) 'Engendering democracy: social citizenship and political participation for women in Scandinavia', *Social Politics: International Studies in Gender, State and Society*, vol 1, no 3, pp 286–305.

Towns, A. (2002) 'Paradoxes of (in) equality: something is rotten in the gender equal state of Sweden', *Cooperation and Conflict: Journal of The Nordic International Studies Association*, vol 37, no 2, pp 157–79.

Towns, A., Karlsson, E. and Eyre, J. (2014) 'The equality conundrum: gender and nation in the ideology of the Sweden Democrats', *Party Politics*, vol 20, no 2, pp 237–47.

van Ginderachter, M. (2005) 'Gender, the extreme right and Flemish nationalist women's organisations in interwar Belgium', *Journal of the Association for the Study of Ethnicity and Nationalism*, vol 11, no 3, pp 265–84.

Wodak, R., Khosravinik, M. and Mral, B. (eds) (2013) *Right-wing populism in Europe: Politics and discourse*, London: Bloomsbury Academic.

Yuval-Davis, N. (2011) *The politics of belonging: Intersectional contestations*, London: Sage.

SEVEN

'What should we do instead?' Gender-equality projects and feminist critique

Angelika Sjöstedt Landén and Gunilla Olofsdotter

Introduction

As the editors of this volume have already noted, the equality mantra in Sweden has led the Swedish government to produce policies that grant women and men certain opportunities related to, for example, work–life balance and childcare provision, and so on. At the same time, the realities of the 'equality situation' are messy and often quite difficult to pinpoint and conceptualise. An important part of the gender-equality discourse in Sweden is the desire for a gender-equal labour market. However, one of the great conundrums related to work life is that although women take part in paid work to nearly the same extent as men (SCB, 2014; SOU, 2014b), women's sick-leave rates are much higher than those of men (Angelov et al, 2011; SCB, 2014; SOU, 2014a). This has been framed as one of the big problems in terms of public spending (Michailakis, 2008; Olofsdotter Stensöta, 2009a; Johnson, 2010) and the organisation of work in and the recruitment of personnel to the welfare sector, because women are often found in care work (Arbetsmiljöverket, 2014b).

In this chapter, we draw on empirical work from a government project aimed at changing this pattern. This was a project that came to harbour a lot of hope for change. While researching this project, we became increasingly interested in unfolding the meanings of these hopes. The aim of our chapter is to explore what promises gender-equality work – commonly conceptualised as gender mainstreaming – makes to the governance of 'gender equality', regarded as a 'national treasure'. In our research during the project we continually met participants who asked for advice on how to perform gender-equality work in the 'right way' and often expected us to deliver answers. We therefore found that the promises of gender mainstreaming seemed to stick to us as gender scholars in particular ways. As we got caught up in the fantasy of Swedish gender equality, we also needed to explore what this stickiness of gender-equality politics might mean for presenting a feminist critique of how gender mainstreaming is done. The persistent posing of questions about how to perform gender-equality work and the question 'What should we do instead?' in this chapter are our analytical entry point for exploring what the promises of gender mainstreaming do.

We elaborate on the imaginary dimensions of gender mainstreaming in two stages of analysis: we begin by sketching some of the features of gender-mainstreaming policy that carry the promise of putting Sweden on the geopolitical map as a champion of gender equality. For example, this is done through specific ways of relating to 'others' who 'have not come as far' as Sweden in developing gender-mainstreaming policy at a national level. Our description will be brief, because our primary analysis is not focused on policy itself, but on the planning and implementing of a gender-mainstreaming intervention that we researched more closely.

The empirical material is drawn from a nationwide project tasked with integrating new working practices at a Swedish government agency responsible for ensuring that all Swedish employers observe the health-and-safety-at-work legislation. We followed the implementation of the related new working practices between 2012 and 2014. The project was guided by the aim that all practices should include a 'gender perspective' on working environments in order to improve women's working life (Arbetsmiljöverket, 2015). It included educating all staff at the agency in elementary knowledge about gender, providing information about the role of gender in the workplace to a large number of employers and other actors with labour market interests (politicians, HR managers, civil servants, union representatives and so on) and carrying out inspections of the working environment at workplaces throughout the country.

The agency also decided to include research as part of the project. A call was sent out to a number of university departments in the country that had a gender-research profile. After sending in a tender, we were chosen to do the research. This kind of research requires an interactive approach, and in our case this meant drawing on ethnographic methods and action research. The set-up differed from action research in that the responsibility for organisational change lay solely with those working within the organisation (see Callerstig and Lindholm, 2011, p 86). This meant, for example, that we took on the task of giving feedback to the project managers and participants as the project went along, but we left it to the project managers to decide how to act (or not act) upon it.

Through this set-up we came face to face with idealised images of feminist intentions and interventions. Our points of departure were constantly challenged throughout the project because we were not only asked to give feedback and identify problems in the performance of the project, we were also continually confronted by project participants with the question 'What should we do instead?' We use the persistent posing of this question here to explore the promises of gender mainstreaming. The question might be read as a sign of longing for expert-approved norms for doing gender equality 'the right way' and wanting expert opinions to lean on in a messy situation, especially at a time when everything should be 'evidence-based' (Olsson, 2014, p 100). The question also urged us, as researchers and feminists, to explore how we imagined our own boundaries and what we stand for in our research. We will illustrate some of the instances of being confronted with having to answer the question of what we thought should be done. In the final section of this chapter, we discuss what could happen if we consider this question from another perspective: could it, for example, hold other promises that might unsettle the ties between gender equality and nationality?

The promises of gender mainstreaming: background and theoretical points of departure

The overarching idea of gender mainstreaming is that it should be a strategy for implementing gender equality (see, for example Madsen, 2011, p 27; Calvo, 2013), although it is not exactly clear what such implementation should entail. There is no consensus as to what gender-mainstreaming practices include or how they should be defined. Looking at some of the original policy documents from the late 1990s, it is clear that gender mainstreaming was thought to consist of 'tools', such as statistics and research, for mapping gender relations; it could also entail training and awareness raising, which required experts. There also seemed to be an ambition to spread the knowledge to others, which involved hearings, conferences and other kinds of meetings (Verloo, 2005, p 351). All of these features were present in the project we researched. Since the 1990s, gender mainstreaming has become a powerful feature of public policy and has been taken up globally in politics, policy and social organisations (Sainsbury and Bergquist, 2009; Zalewski, 2010; Calvo, 2013). As a nation, Sweden has been one of many actors in this geopolitical development, but it has also taken on a particular position as a forerunner for gender equality as well as gender-mainstreaming policy (see, for example, Sainsbury and Bergquist, 2009). Since gender mainstreaming has become a widespread idea, it has also been well researched (see, for example Bacchi and Eveline, 2010c; Lavena and Riccucci, 2012; Ritterhofer and Gatrell, 2012). The overall impression gained from reading current literature on gender mainstreaming is that it lacks the transformative potential to make the changes to relations and institutions that are needed in order to destabilise the foundations of gender regimes, although 'gender mainstreaming claims to address and redress the genderedness of systems and processes' and thereby stands out as 'transformative' (Verloo, 2005, p 347).[1] This imaginary aspect of gender mainstreaming might be seen as misleading and promising more than it can live up to, but nevertheless, the imagining of gender mainstreaming as transformative *does* something. For example, research done in the Swedish context concludes that gender mainstreaming has become a depoliticising practice that turns gender-equality work into an administrative task that disables its political potential (Rönnblom, 2009; Calvo, 2013) and that the very fantasy of gender mainstreaming as transformative contributes to its 'automatisation' and settles it as a purely administrative process in the Swedish system of governance.

One criticism of the research done to date, which suggests that gender regimes are not displaced by gender mainstreaming, is that much of the work on gender mainstreaming has been done on the discourses of policy, whereas research on what actually happens during different processes of trying to 'do' gender mainstreaming might provide a more nuanced picture of where transformation at the micro-level might be possible. It is also suggested that the 'failure of gender mainstreaming' possibly lies in a lack of conceptualisation of what gender means, and implies that its political and transformative dimension is disregarded (Calvo, 2013, p 259). The everyday doings of gender-mainstreaming projects have not been that well researched in the Swedish context (but see Dahl, 2004; Olofsdotter Stensöta, 2009b; Sainsbury and Bergquist, 2009; Gunnarsson, 2011; Callerstig, 2014; Olofsdotter and Sjöstedt Landén, 2014a). This critical research, however, also concludes that although the actors involved in practical gender-equality work often aim at transformation, they do not tend to define what transformation means to them too clearly. This means that particular framings of 'gender knowledge' may thus reproduce inequality and hierarchical distinctions, intentionally or not (Olofsdotter and Sjöstedt Landén, 2014a). The idea seems to be that transformation automatically comes with implementing gender-mainstreaming practices. This too suggests that the very promise of gender mainstreaming as a transformatory practice may be what promotes the status quo. Exploring the imaginary dimensions of gender mainstreaming enables us to understand something about what keeps the status quo in place, through understanding how the dis/connections of gender equality, nationality and feminism interrelate.

Theorising the doing of gender-equality projects

Bacchi and Eveline (2010c, p 111) have noted that 'specific policy proposals "imagine" "problems" in particular ways that have real and meaningful effects'. We argue that gender mainstreaming has imaginative dimensions, not only in terms of the ways in which problems are defined, but also in terms of the expectations that this brings to how Sweden as a nation is imagined. Gender mainstreaming can therefore be conceptualised as a fantasy that nurtures certain desires concerning the construction of a modern and democratic nation that is 'nice' and 'good' to its citizens (Verloo and van der Vlauten, 2009).

Gender mainstreaming should not be understood as a given, but as open for signification as well as contestation. This means that we study signifying work: how gender mainstreaming is imagined and embodied in particular ways and articulated in certain practices. We draw on the notion of ideological fantasy to explore what kind of work bears the promise of fulfilling certain ideal images (of the gender-equal nation) that are thought to be legitimate and desirable (Glynos, 2008). As a social phenomenon, this fantasy does not only go on in individual minds. Instead, a fantasy is something shared that is laden with normative force. It functions to conceal contingency (Glynos and Howarth, 2007). For example, if gender mainstreaming is seen as an empty concept, open to signification, gender-mainstreaming practices could (in theory) be constructed in a myriad of ways, but instead the concept tends to 'stick' to or attach itself to certain ways of doing and being. The role of fantasy, however, is not to set up an illusion, 'a false picture of the world', but to keep contingency at bay (Glynos and Howarth, 2007, p 145). The concept of fantasy also draws attention to the gripping forces of a particular practice and how a certain ideology exerts its hold over us (Glynos, 2001).

Researching the ways in which Swedish state policy becomes practice and vice versa, Sjöstedt Landén (2012) conjoins the concept of fantasy with Sara Ahmed's queer-phenomenological approach to the notion of affect. Ahmed (2004, p 90) uses the metaphor of 'stickiness' to describe how something that gets repeated in social life accumulates affective value. Ahmed argues that when a sign or object becomes sticky it can function to block the movement (of other things or signs) and to bind (other things or signs) together (Ahmed, 2004, p 91). The concept of stickiness helps to explore how the binding effect of words and other practices can also block shifts in meaning (Ahmed, 2004, p 92). Ahmed uses the concept of stickiness to address the performativity of disgust and how this holds racist structures in different societal contexts in place. We use Ahmed's work to explore how gender mainstreaming and national identity are mobilised to create blockages and bindings. Olsson (2014, p 100) concludes that in Sweden gender equality has taken specific 'Swedish' forms, such that gender mainstreaming is about the 'most familiar women and men, heterosexuality, modernity, rationality but also about the nation-state, and particularly Sweden as a national state, welfare state and collective project' (our translation). This is related to the fact that the Swedish concept of gender equality has its historical roots in the concept of the bourgeois white, Christian nuclear family. Consequently, critiquing this image and pointing to inequalities is potentially a sensitive and undesired topic in Sweden and across the Nordic area more generally (for example, Tienari et al, 2005). We think that the kinds of 'blockages' and 'bindings' that such views articulate help us to clarify the conditions for a feminist critique of – and within – gender-mainstreaming practices.

We have analysed the kinds of promises gender mainstreaming makes to the governance of the national treasure of 'gender equality' and how the promises seem to 'stick' to us as gender scholars in particular ways in the empirical setting of a project aimed at improving women's work environment. This project was guided by a gender perspective. We took an interactive approach and drew on a multiplicity of empirical sources. We followed the project from 2012 to 2014. The project activities were divided into different aspects: staff training, information activities and inspections of workplaces. Policy documents and documents setting out decisions are the kind of binding project documents that are very difficult to bypass in project work (by researchers as well as by the participants involved). We therefore took an interest in how the problems that the project was supposed to solve were defined in the key documents. We also gathered rich material from observations at meetings with project managers and from the everyday practices of the civil servants. We drew on email correspondence, which constitutes part of the everyday practice for all categories of project workers. These different sources were given equal analytical status in our research. Documents are interesting because project practices are guided by them. They also present ideal images of the expected outcomes in equality work (see Ahmed, 2012). Furthermore, documents are important in relation to how the problem to be solved by the project is constructed in the first place and how the construction of the problem is itself an act of power (Bacchi and Eveline, 2010a, 2010b).

A core part of the gathering of data during the project was sitting in on meetings. When we observed larger gatherings, such as a gender training day for all the staff, or conferences, we were very clear that we were attending merely as observers. We did not participate in any of the activities, but made notes of the practices. In other situations, such as project meetings, we often had our own agenda item so that we could present reflective comments on project activities and could also ask questions or give feedback. We therefore took on what Lather (2001) refers to as a within/against position (see also Olofsdotter and Sjöstedt Landén, 2014b). This also meant that reflexivity became inherent in our analysis and that we needed to include our own doings and positions in the analysis of the fantasy of gender mainstreaming.

We will address the fantasy of gender mainstreaming in two stages. First, we will zoom out from the project that we researched and provide an outline of how gender mainstreaming has become constructed in the policy context. Here, we are especially interested in how 'Sweden' and 'Swedishness' become signifiers for the fantasy of gender mainstreaming. Second, we discuss how the work in the project we observed was organised and the ways in which this was made sense of by the project participants. We explore further how assumptions about gender relations were reproduced in a situation that in the first instance was said to be transformative of the same.

Images of Swedish gender mainstreaming

It is very often underscored in official documentation that gender mainstreaming has been the official strategy for reaching the gender-equality goals in Sweden since 1994 (Proposition, 1993/94), and that this occurred before the EU and the UN did the same (SOU, 2007, p 19). Europe is commonly invoked as a site for comparison that can promote Sweden as a good example. One such image of Sweden is found on the website of the European Institute for Gender Equality (EIGE).

The image on the EIGE website[2] represents a view of Sweden that is very common. It shows a small country with a big profile in the European community and suggests that Swedish gender-equality policy is something that can be exported in the global context (Towns, 2002). Verloo and van der Vlauten (2009) stress that the discursive politics of ranking and benchmarking as a way of constituting a gender-equality discourse are very powerful bearers of values in policy and politics. In particular, this process contributes to the construction of a nation's good or bad 'reputation' (Verloo and van der Vlauten, 2009, p 169ff). Swedish national identity is heavily invested in maintaining a reputation for being 'good at' gender equality and, consequently, gender mainstreaming. Reputation could be seen as playing on imaginative strings, because it is all about presenting the right kind of data that can communicate the image to be promoted (see Verloo and van der Vlauten, 2009).

On a government website (regeringen.se) that disseminates basic information about Sweden, gender equality is presented as a long Swedish tradition. The aim of gender-equality policy is, 'on the one hand, to combat and change systems that preserve the gender-based distribution of power and resources at societal level, and on the other, to create the conditions for women and men to enjoy the same power and opportunities to influence their own lives'.[3] Moreover, it is noted that women and men participate in paid work to the same extent in Sweden, but that in academia, the church and the private sector men hold the majority of leading positions. The state, however, is promoted as a good role model since Parliament is made up of 45% women and 55% men.[4] The state is constructed as already good at gender equality because of the even distribution of men and women in Parliament. This is understood to be a good example that others should follow.

On the one hand, there is a discourse about how Sweden is already very gender equal, but on the other, a number of government commissions have been created since the beginning of the twenty-first century to map inequalities in different sectors; for example, the Commission for Gender Equality in Higher Education,[5] the Commission for Gender Equality in Schools[6] and the Commission for Gender Equality in Work Life.[7] There have also been a number of targeted gender-equality programmes in which the government has given government agencies the task of implementing gender equality. In 2013, the Swedish government initiated a development programme[8] with the aim of strengthening and further developing gender mainstreaming in government agencies so that their activities will contribute even more effectively to achieving gender-equality policy goals. Eighteen agencies were tasked with drawing up a plan for gender mainstreaming to be implemented in 2014.[9] Selected agencies were to showcase good practice and illustrate lessons learned about how gender mainstreaming in central government operates and how it can be conducted in a more effective and sustainable manner. The Swedish

Secretariat for Gender Research at the University of Gothenburg was tasked with supporting the agencies and disseminating lessons learned to other agencies via the portal www.includegender.org.[10]

One issue suggested in this brief overview of how gender mainstreaming is currently articulated in the Swedish context is the fantasy of the Swedish state as 'better than' (other countries, other sectors in society) and that new actors are constantly urged to showcase good examples. With this in mind, we now go on to explore the fantasy of gender mainstreaming in the context of a particular project.

Women's work: a mainstreaming project

Our study was set in one of the 18 government agencies targeted by the extensive gender-mainstreaming programmes mentioned above. The project we followed was itself not initially part of the big gender-mainstreaming programme, but was set up following a special instruction from the government to the agency to prevent women from being excluded from work life because of problems in the working environment. The project was called Women's Work and was carried out between 2012 and 2014. While the gender-mainstreaming project of the 18 agencies was directed at mainstreaming the internal steering processes of the agencies themselves, the project we studied was directed more towards external actors: public and private employers, policy and decision makers, especially in municipalities, county councils and meta-organisations such as trade unions, and private sector representatives. The two projects, however, partly merged in 2014.

The project we followed was instituted by the Swedish government in relation to the agency responsible for issues to do with the working environment, the Swedish Work Environment Agency (SWEA). The principal aim of the agency is to 'protect the right to a healthy and safe working environment'[11] in workplaces throughout the whole country. Generally, the agency is meant to strive to 'improve the working environment in a holistic way' and to 'realize the public policy objective of a good and developmental working environment for all'.[12] In order to accomplish this goal in different parts of Sweden, the agency is divided into several regional districts and local offices staffed by inspectors with diverse specialisms. In the project at hand, both public and private organisations were inspected in two main sub-projects.

One sub-project focused on the working environment in the departments of home-help services and elderly care and technical services in 59 municipalities. Approximately 250 inspectors participated, carrying out 900 inspections and talking to more than

2,000 employees and 500 managers. The other sub-project addressed ergonomics in industries with a predominantly female workforce, public and private medical treatment and elderly care. Around 700 inspections were conducted (Arbetsmiljöverket, 2014a, 2014b). The sub-projects overlapped, and an overarching programme management group was created in order to coordinate and manage their mutual goal. A programme manager was operationally responsible for the whole programme and was expected to take part in both project groups' activities, to manage the external reference group and to be responsible for reporting to a steering group made up of the department managers at the agency and the programme owner. An administrator, a lawyer and a communicator were appointed to the programme management. Each sub-project consisted of a project manager, a communications officer, and project members from different districts, mostly inspectors (Arbetsmiljöverket, 2012).

The managers responsible for the project did not explicitly state that they were doing gender mainstreaming, but the project included features that commonly occur in gender-mainstreaming projects, such as educating staff and disseminating information about gender inequality in the workplace, and so on. Moreover, the project gradually became more explicitly linked to the simultaneous process of gender mainstreaming the whole agency.

Wearing gender spectacles

The efforts in the project were directed at reducing sick leave generally in the country by developing new 'gender-sensitive' working practices. The project outline stated that 'The focus on women's work will consist of the acquisition of knowledge, information, seminars, training of inspectors and national inspection efforts' (Arbetsmiljöverket, 2011, p 1). In practice, the project involved a wide range of actors. We followed the extensive efforts of those trying different methods of inspecting workplaces; we went with inspectors to different workplaces and sat in on sub-project meetings all over the country; and we followed the work of the programme management group. We discuss these aspects in other publications (Olofsdotter and Sjöstedt Landén, 2014b, 2014a). For this analysis of the fantasmatic dimensions of gender mainstreaming, we have specifically chosen instances in which the work done in the project was to be communicated to other actors, because these moments revealed how contingencies were covered up and how the subjects were gripped by the fantasy of gender mainstreaming. One example of this occurred in the final year of the project when the management group was discussing how to proceed after the end of the project, retold here in field notes from a meeting with the project group:

> 'How should we proceed with the gender spectacles and so on?' the project manager asks. The project group had to write proposals for the planning process, the management functions: the finance department and communications have attended a one-day course on 'gender-equal planning'. (Notes from a telephone meeting, April 2014)

The (imaginary) gender spectacles were an object of debate throughout the project. For example, they were used as a way of imaging the ways in which the agency staff's view of the world should be altered as an effect of a one-day gender training course in the middle year of the project. The notion of gender spectacles struck people in different ways. For many, these spectacles were evidence that the project had had an impact on the daily work at the agency. For others, they were a source of resentment and a prompt to resist gender-mainstreaming practices. The gender spectacles accumulated different kinds of affective quality and impacted on people in different ways. Ahmed explores the relation between disgust and stickiness and 'how "stickiness" becomes an affective quality of objects' (Ahmed, 2004, p 84). Although the word 'disgusting' was not specifically used about gender spectacles (at least not as far as we are aware), we could observe a certain affective intensification as this object was brought up. Sometimes gender spectacles were talked about in a joking but positive manner, sometimes we could hear resentful muttering at the back of a room when the concept was brought up. For example, we heard inspectors say, 'Can't we just skip the gender spectacles now?' The image of gender spectacles places gender-mainstreaming practices 'in people's face'. Ahmed argues that it might be that 'stickiness becomes disgusting only when the skin surface is at stake such as what is sticky threatens to stick to us' (Ahmed, 2004, p 90). Not knowing what it means to put on gender spectacles can have the effect of wanting to throw them off instead of becoming curious about their potential powers.

The resistance to taking an interest in what gender-mainstreaming work might entail could be spotted at all levels of the organisational hierarchy. This was noted by the programme management group and there was an ongoing discussion throughout the project about how the project practices might gain legitimacy in the organisation more generally so that the insights from the project would live on after it had ended. One of the strange things about projects in general is that they usually become located at the middle levels of organisations. It then becomes the task of the project workers to legitimise their work in relation to the top-level management (Johansson et al, 2007). This was also the case in the project we followed and studied, although that very project was initiated by the Swedish government itself and it was therefore not for the top management to decide whether to prioritise it or not. The project group was worried that they had done all the project work in vain. The project manager concluded that gender-equality work 'is not so incorporated in the regular processes that it happens automatically'. Nevertheless, it was always possible to counteract these kinds of contingencies in the fantasy of the achievements of gender-mainstreaming projects and to integrate them into a narrative of success.

When the project was almost finished, one of the top managers at the agency that was part of setting up and initiating Women's Work argued that there were 'more mature discussions when it comes to gender' at the agency, that 'knowledge about gender in work environment issues had increased in the organisation' and that 'it was also visible in the management group'. The coming into existence of the gender-mainstreaming subject (at the different levels of the organisation) was articulated through acquiring 'gender spectacles' and doing 'gender-conscious' work. Interestingly, increased gender awareness was viewed as particularly 'sticking to' project members. They were seen as imbued with a higher level of gender knowledge, as compared to other agency staff outside the project group, who were regarded as less competent in gender issues. The project group was constructed as 'better than' them, the ultimate confirmation of the fantasy of gender mainstreaming.

Numbers that count

One key measure of being better than others is figures. In the project, numbers defined success and failure in particular ways and thereby made other, non-measurable aspects of the project work not really 'count'. In the following, this is manifested in notes from a telephone meeting with the programme management group:

> Apparently, representatives from the Ministry of Employment are going to pay a visit to the agency and they want to be informed about the present state of the project. The project manager comments, 'They like statistics; they like it when we are out there producing.' The project assistant in turn mentions the importance of summarising and making

visible that the funding of the project will run out soon and that there is no economic resource to continue. 'Can you fix this too?' says the programme manager to one of the sub-project managers, laughing. He continues, 'But what I really need is the statistics.' (Notes from a telephone meeting, April 2014)

Critically minded researchers have questioned the efficacy and consequences of applying a rationalistic, functionalistic and instrumental view to projects and project management (Cicmil and Hodgson, 2006; Lindgren and Packendorff, 2006; Sage et al, 2010). Qualitative results do not legitimise project work in the same way as numbers do. This has implications for what kind of change is seen as important and successful. There is a complexity to what is often referred to as 'qualitative values' that is not so easily translated into quantifiable terms. This was especially apparent in the project we followed, where quantity in terms of a large number of nationwide inspections somehow took precedence over more in-depth analyses of work environments. As the programme came to an end, we listened to the sub-managers reflecting on why they had had to do so many inspections, especially at the beginning of the project when they did not even know how to do them. In just one of the two sub-projects, they had talked to as many as 2,000 employees and 500 managers in municipalities all over the country. One of the sub-managers noted, 'We could have taken time to do more pilot work and had a less frantic start.' But the reason why the project activities were set up in this way was to make sure that the work was 'good enough'. The fantasy of gender mainstreaming stuck to quantifiable terms as desirable and as a marker for doing good work. The quantifiable and measurable is seen as the concrete and precise (Olsson 2014, p 100) and thereby accorded a taken-for-granted legitimacy. This also makes it possible to spread a certain kind of knowledge and to market that knowledge in particular ways. All this goes very well with the idea of audit, which seems to enter new realms. This has been described as 'audit culture', where 'calculative practices of measurement and ranking have become institutionalised, extended and above all, *financialised*', constructing a 'governing by numbers' (Shore and Wright, 2015, p 24).

Gender mainstreaming on the market

One of the practices that required a lot of effort by the programme management group during the final year of the project was organising the final conferences that took place in different cities in the country. One imaginary dimension of doing gender mainstreaming included the desire to influence actors that were seen as important for transforming gender relations, in order to pass something on.

> The final conferences are getting more important the more we talk. We call them 'relay conferences' because it has gradually become clearer that we believe we have something to pass on to decision makers, managers and politicians and employers. (Email from communications officer, December 2013)

It was seen as natural that the project needed to be legitimised, not least externally, in relation to its 'customers'. In the following excerpt, the project management starts to plan how to 'sell' the project on the conference market:

> We understand that we are not supposed to use the words gender, gender equality and suchlike in headlines or marketing. But we need your good advice about how to think, plan and act in order to reach this group that is hard to please in relation to these issues. What should we think about? What should we avoid? Best practices? Traps? We have to get them to pay 2,000 SEK for our conference! (Email from project manager at the agency, December 2013)

The experiences from the project and the gender knowledge that the project participants had acquired were seen as something to disseminate to others, in the organisation and nationwide through these conferences. However, as the planning went on, the project management group hesitated whether to put forward the gender perspective or do the opposite, which was to create a more 'gender-neutral' programme. Their inside position in the project had given them knowledge that they thought might be considered somewhat provocative for prospective conference participants.

When we received the email just mentioned, we wondered whether the focus of the project had got lost. Should the focus be more on what kind of message the project wanted to impart, rather than on directing energy at how they needed to adapt it to the market? Moreover, we did not think that our task was to provide advice on how to manipulate markets. Instead, we saw our task as questioning the influence of the market on the projectification of the welfare sector. Abrahamsson and

Agevall (2009, p 39) write that 'parallel to the traditional administration a new legitimizing administration develops that is externally directed to the surrounding society in order to show that the work that is done is important and is managed in a "modern" way'. The fantasy of gender mainstreaming as a way of installing modernity (by conforming to market logics) also contributes to covering over the contingency of resources allocated to gender-equality work. The greater the uncertainty over resource allocation in a project, the stronger the tendency to set up the project in line with the resources allocated (see Abrahamsson and Agevall, 2009, p 38).

As the planning of the conferences progressed, the project management group presented a poster promoting the conference. In this poster, any mention of concepts such as 'gender' or 'gender equality' had been removed from the headlines. Instead, these were replaced by concepts such as 'organising for sustainability', 'efficiency' and 'quality'. Economic incentives became opposed to gender equality, which was not imagined as profitable from an economic viewpoint. Concepts such as 'gender equality' did not appear to attach to market economics. We were struck by the logic that downplaying concepts such as 'gender' and 'gender equality' could be viewed as the proper way of performing a gender-mainstreaming project even though it seemed to contradict the very aim of the project, since the conferences were arranged by a project that was set up specifically to address the impact of gender and gender inequality in workplace settings. When we raised this we were assured by the management group that as soon as they had got people to pay the conference fee and got them into the room, they would start to talk about issues of gender and gender equality.

The fantasy of gender mainstreaming was assembled in a particular way: *economism*, *knowledge about gender as a transformative force*, and *gender research* constructed a certain chain of meaning. The national discourse of 'better than' that is often used in international contexts when talking about gender equality as particularly 'Swedish' also seemed to surface in the project we researched. The discourse of being 'better than' contributes to framing gender mainstreaming in terms of the development of the modern welfare state, where Sweden is often constructed as the model of success in terms of integrating gender-mainstreaming practices in the whole state apparatus (see, for example Daly, 2005). In that context, a discourse about being 'better than' became a way of making the project exceptional within a wider organisational and national context while at the same time keeping at bay (feminist) criticisms of how gender equality was done.

Conclusions: gender mainstreaming and feminist critique

> In challenging ideas about gender, feminists have already offered challenges to how happiness is defined, and by whom. This struggle over happiness forms the political horizon in which feminist claims are made. (Ahmed, 2010, p 580)

At a meeting towards the end of the project at SWEA, one of the civil servants who had participated in the reflective dialogue about the outcome of the project suddenly said, 'We're talking about gender here, but are there any statistics about foreign-born people?' Potential intersections of gender, national identity and ethnicity had not been explicitly articulated within the project before and now they were met with silence. The question of how aspects of being born in another country than Sweden could matter in the context of work-life discrimination quickly slipped off the surface of the gender-mainstreaming project. It seemed to be more difficult to articulate and acknowledge such intersections than to acknowledge the inconvenience of the concept of gender in relation to the conference market in the example mentioned before. This is true for many organisational contexts in Sweden: the discourse of gender equality has a language for addressing gender inequalities, while racial discrimination is often made impossible to address (Mulinari, 2014). This silence illustrates a core issue for feminist critique, namely, what is made visible through 'gender spectacles' and what remain blind spots, and what is seen as ruining the happiness of the mainstream (see de los Reyes, 2002; Ahmed, 2010) and the reputation of the gender-equal nation. Because gender equality has become so strongly connected with national identity, criticisms directed at how the concept is assembled and that focus on differences between men and women, and not on those within groups of men and women, or on how these categories are produced, or that raise the question of what we can see when we cross-section gender and national identity, may also be understood as critiquing 'the Swedish'. Feminist scholars who critique certain definitions of gender equality thus become a threat to the image of Sweden as gender equal (Fahlgren and Sjöstedt Landén, 2014). The inspector posing the question about statistics concerning those born abroad became, in Ahmed's terms, a 'killjoy' who revealed the contingent nature of gender mainstreaming, that is, revealed that gender mainstreaming practices might be assembled in other ways. This moment of contingency was covered over by keeping to the investment in a fantasy of gender mainstreaming in which being born in a country other than Sweden was insignificant for the analysis. One might argue that in an international gender-mainstreaming context, Sweden is lagging behind in not including the concept of intersectionality in gender-mainstreaming work (see Yuval-Davis, 2006).

When we were researching the project at SWEA, we could not be critical about what was going on without also always being confronted with the question 'What should we do instead?' Critique was not legitimate without a normative sentence about how to do things in a different way. Of course, we had, in a sense, agreed to this when signing the contract for the research project. We thus became vested in the fantasy of gender mainstreaming, although our position was a position of dis-identification with the traits of what made up the fantasy. The fantasy of gender mainstreaming desires a connection between gender research and gender-equality work. When the call for researchers to participate in the project was published, it was sent to institutions that were known to do gender research. This builds on the notion of a taken-for-granted connection between gender-equality work and gender scholars that has proved to be quite problematic. For example, at an early stage of the project we were asked to be 'just critical enough' (*sv. lagom kritiska*) (see also Olofsdotter and Sjöstedt Landén, 2014b).

Sara Ahmed's definition of a feminist killjoy is that she 'spoils the happiness of others; she is a spoilsport because she refuses to convene, to assemble, or to meet up over happiness' (Ahmed, 2010, p 581). We were the spoilsports in this project for many reasons. Bringing critique in terms of diversity and intersectionality ruins the happy face of gender mainstreaming, especially in national contexts where gender equality has been especially about what is often called women's issues (Olsson, 2014, p 99, with reference to Squires, 2009). Moreover, our ontological view of gender as contingent and discursive was viewed as strange in an organisational context in which biological perspectives on sex and gender were hegemonic. We considered knowledge to be co-produced between researchers and project participants. This often clashed with the bureaucratic notion that 'the gender experts' would deliver answers and 'the right ways' of doing gender mainstreaming and thus be part of the modern narrative about experts. We were convinced that the concept of gender equality itself needed to be problematised, rather than just the separate (working) conditions for men and women.

The question 'What should we do instead?' was very closely connected with the fantasy of what researchers should do in a gender-mainstreaming project. This question was difficult for us to respond to, partly because it was constantly posed from perspectives that presupposed that we were the experts in gender mainstreaming. Instead, one of our missions was to promote the actors of the project as the experts in their organisation and in what they had done. There was something radical about suggesting this, and we never really convinced the programme management group that it should pay attention to the knowledge of the inspectors. Could we bring the question of what we should do instead back into the discussion from another angle: what *could* we do instead of acting as if the promises of gender mainstreaming were going to be realised and instead of suppressing feminist agendas and critique?

The fact that gender mainstreaming started to stick to us in a way that made us want to rub it off must also be regarded as an affective mode that was accumulated in relation to the fantasy of gender mainstreaming. Could we think about gender mainstreaming as something that might give feminists hope – not in a way that made us need to convince ourselves and others that gender mainstreaming is going to offer solutions for a better world, or that it is at all compatible with feminist agendas, but as a site for presenting feminist critique to a field of politics that has been described as depoliticised? Ahmed (2012, p 592) notes that 'revolutionary forms of political consciousness involve heightening our awareness of what there is to be unhappy about'. The fantasy of gender mainstreaming is intended to close off critiques of institutionalised practices and to maintain the reputation of Sweden as a champion of mainstreaming gender equality. As researchers, we have the privilege of sticking with the messiness of relations that this fantasy evokes.

Notes

[1] There are, however, different versions of how this body of research should be interpreted. Walby (2011, p 80), for example, complies with the notion that '[d]oing gender mainstreaming in a way that is successful is a major challenge for feminism' while influential Swedish researchers of gender mainstreaming policy argue that a totally new and different politics is needed (Edenheim and Rönnblom, 2012).

[2] http://eige.europa.eu/about/gender-mainstreaming/sweden, accessed 20 November 2014.

[3] http://www.government.se/sb/d/4096/a/26327, accessed 2 February 2015.

[4] http://www.regeringen.se/sb/d/17973/a/226845, accessed 1 February 2015.

[5] http://www.regeringen.se/sb/d/108/a/120104, accessed 1 February 2015.

[6] http://www.regeringen.se/sb/d/108/a/107667, accessed 1 February 2015.

[7] http://www.regeringen.se/sb/d/108/a/177544, accessed 1 February 2015.

[8] http://www.regeringen.se/content/1/c6/20/89/71/69b29fbb.pdf, accessed 2 March 2015.

[9] http://www.includegender.org/about-us/about-the-assignment/, accessed 1 February 2015.

[10] http://www.government.se/sb/d/4096/a/125215, accessed 1 February 2015.

[11] http://av.se/inenglish/, accessed 1 February 2015.

[12] http://av.se/inenglish/, accessed 1 February 2015.

References

Abrahamsson, A. and Agevall, L. (2009) 'Välfärdssektorns projektifiering: kortsiktiga lösningar av långsiktiga probem?' [The projectification of the welfare sector: short-term solutions for long-term problems?], *Kommunal ekonomi och politik*, vol 113, no 4, pp 35–60.

Ahmed, S. (2004) *The cultural politics of emotion*, Edinburgh: Edinburgh University Press.

Ahmed, S. (2010) 'Killing joy: feminism and the history of happiness', *Signs*, vol 35, no 3, pp 571–94.

Ahmed, S. (2012) *On being included: Racism and diversity in institutional life*, Durham, NC: Duke University Press.

Angelov, N., Johansson, P., Lindahl, E. and Lindström, E.Y. (2011) *Kvinnors och mäns sjukfrånvaro* [Women's and men's sick leave], Uppsala: IFAU (Institute for Evaluation of Labour Market and Education Policy) 2011, p 2.

Arbetsmiljöverket (2011) 'Projektdirektiv för regeringsuppdraget om kvinnors arbetsmiljö' [Project directives for the government assignment on women's work environment], pp 1–7, Stockholm: Arbetsmiljöverket [Swedish Work Environment Agency].

Arbetsmiljöverket (2012) 'Övergripande plan för programledning av regeringsuppdraget om kvinnors arbetsmiljö' [Plan for the programme management of the government commission on women's work environment], Stockholm: Arbetsmiljöverket [Swedish Work Environment Agency].

Arbetsmiljöverket (2014a) 'Ergonomi i kvinnors arbetsmiljö: Inspektioner med fokus på riskbedömning vid personförflyttning inom vård och omsorg' [Ergonomics in women's work environment: inspections with a focus on risk assessment in the transportation of persons in care], *Rapport 2014:5*, Stockholm: Arbetsmiljöverket [Swedish Work Environment Agency].

Arbetsmiljöverket (2014b) Projektrapport. Inspektioner av kvinno- och mansdominerad kommunal verksamhet, hemtjänst och teknisk förvaltning [Project report: Inspections of the female- and male-dominated municipal sector, home-help services and technical administration], *Rapport 2014:3*, Stockholm: Arbetsmiljöverket [Swedish Work Environment Agency].

Arbetsmiljöverket (2015) Kvinnors arbetsmiljö 2011–2014 – Slutrapport [Women's work environment 2011–2014: final report], *Rapport 2015:6*, Stockholm: Arbetsmiljöverket [Swedish Work Environment Agency].

Bacchi, C. and Eveline, J. (2010a) 'Approaches to gender mainstreaming: what's the problem represented to be?' in C. Bacchi and J. Eveline (eds) *Mainstreaming politics: Gendering practices and feminist theory*, Adelaide: University of Adelaide Press, pp 111–38.

Bacchi, C. and Eveline, J. (2010b) 'Mainstreaming and neoliberalism: a contested relationship', in C. Bacchi and E. Joan (eds) *Mainstreaming politics: Gendering practices and feminist theory*, Adelaide: University of Adelaide Press, pp 39–60.

Bacchi, C. and Eveline, J. (2010c) *Mainstreaming politics: Gendering practices and feminist theory*, Adelaide: University of Adelaide Press.

Callerstig, A.-C. (2014) 'Making equality work: ambiguities, conflicts and change agents in the implementation of equality policies in public sector organizations', PhD thesis, Linköping University.

Callerstig, A.-C. and Lindholm, K. (2011) 'Det motsägelsefulla arbetet med jämställdhetsintegrering' [The contradictory work with gender mainstreaming], *Tidskrift för genusvetenskap*, vol 2–3, pp 80–96.

Calvo, D. (2013) 'What is the problem of gender? Mainstreaming gender in migration and development policies in the European Union' (Gothenburg Studies in Sociology No 51), PhD thesis, University of Gothenburg.

Cicmil, S.,and Hodgson, D. (2006) 'Making projects critical: an introduction', in D. Hodgson and S. Cicmil (eds) *Making projects critical*, Basingstoke: Palgrave Macmillan, pp 1–25.

Dahl, U. (2004) 'Progressive women, traditional men: the politics of 'knowledge' and gendered stories of 'development' in the northern periphery of the EU', PhD thesis, University of California Santa Cruz.

Daly, M. (2005) 'Gender mainstreaming in theory and practice', *Social Politics: International Studies in Gender, State & Society*, vol 12, no 3, pp 433–50.

de los Reyes, P. (2002) 'Det problematiska systerskapet. Om svenskhet och invandrarskap inom svensk genushistorisk forskning' [The problematic sisterhood: of Swedishness and immigrantship in Swedish research on the history of gender], in P. de los Reyes, I. Molina and D. Mulinari (eds) *Maktens (o)lika förklädnader: Kön, klass och etnicitet i det postkoloniala Sverige* [*The different disguises of power: Gender, class and ethnicity in postcolonial Sweden*], Stockholm: Bokförlaget Atlas.

Edenheim, S. and Rönnblom, M. (2012) 'Avskaffa jämställdhetspolitiken!' [Abolish gender equality politics!] in M. Eduards, M. Jansson, M. Wendt and C. Åse (eds) *Det heter feminism! 20 anspråksfulla förslag för att förändra världen* [*It's called feminism! 20 demanding suggestions for changing the world*]. Stockholm: Hallongrottan, pp. 22–7.

Fahlgren, S. and Sjöstedt Landén, A. (2014) 'When gender research becomes a threat to gender equality: a discourse analysis of an opinion piece', *Tidskrift för genusvetenskap*, vol 35, no 1, pp 7–26.

Glynos, J. (2001) 'The grip of ideology: a Lacanian approach to the theory of ideology', *Journal of Political Ideologies*, vol 6, no 2, pp 191–214.

Glynos, J. (2008) 'Ideological fantasy at work', *Journal of Political Ideologies*, vol 13, no 3, pp 275–96.

Glynos, J. and Howarth, D. (2007) *Logics of critical explanation in social and political theory*, London: Routledge.

Gunnarsson, E. (2011) 'Gemensam handling för hållbar förändring: tillämpad genusforskning i ett innovationssystem' [Joint action for sustainable change: applied gender research in an innovation system], *Arbetsmarknad & Arbetsliv*, vol 17, no 2, pp 45–57.

Johansson, S., Löfström, M. and Ohlsson, Ö. (2007) 'Separation or integration? A dilemma when organizing development projects', *International Journal of Project Management*, vol 25, no 5, pp 457–64.

Johnson, B. (2010) *Kampen om sjukfrånvaron* [*The struggle about sick leave*], Lund: Arkiv Förlag.

Lather, P. (2001) 'Postbook: working the ruins of feminist ethnograph', *Signs*, vol 27, no 1, pp 199–227.

Lavena, C. and Riccucci, N.M. (2012) 'Exploring gender mainstreaming in the European Union', *International Journal of Public Administration*, vol 35, no 2, pp 122–36.

Lindgren, M. and Packendorff, J. (2006) 'What's new in new forms of organizing? On the construction of gender in project-based work', *Journal of Management Studies*, vol 43, no 4, pp 841–66.

Madsen, H.D. (2011) 'Getting the institutions right for gender mainstreaming', *Kvinder, Kön & Forskning*, vol 1, pp 25–35.

Michailakis, D. (2008) *Sjukdom och sjukskrivning: En sociologisk observation* [*Illness and sick leave: A sociological observation*], Malmö: Gleerups Utbildning AB.

Mulinari, P. (2014) 'Tystnad och osynlighet: hur hanteras diskriminering inom organisationer?' [Silence and invisibility: how is discrimination handled in organisations?], in P. de los Reyes (ed) *Inte bara jämställdhet: Intersektionella perspektiv på hinder och möjligheter i arbetslivet* [*Not only gender equality: Intersectional perspectives on obstacles and possibilities in working life*], Stockholm: SOU No 34, pp 223–46.

Olofsdotter, G. and Sjöstedt Landén, A. (2014a) 'Gender as headline and subtext: problematizing the gender perspective in an occupational health project', *Vulnerable Groups & Inclusion*, vol 5, pp 1–24.

Olofsdotter, G. and Sjöstedt Landén, A. (2014b). *Lost in transformation: Following projects in the Swedish welfare sector*, paper presented at the Making Project Critical 7 Workshop, Stockholm.

Olofsdotter Stensöta, H. (2009a) *Sjukskrivningarna och välfärdens infriare: en studie av svensk sjukvårdsbyråkrati* [*Sick leave and the fulfillmen of welfare: A study of Swedish healthcare bureaucracy*], Stockholm: Hjarlmarson and Högberg Bokförlag.

Olofsdotter Stensöta, H. (2009b). *Jämställdhetsintegrering i statliga myndigheters verksamhet: Hur långt har myndigheterna nått? Vad beror det på? Hur kan arbetet utvecklas vidare?* [*Gender mainstreaming in govenment authorities activities: How far have the authorities reached? What does it depend on? How can this work develop further?*], Göteborg: Nationella sekretariatet för genusforskning.

Olsson, A. (2014) 'Arbetslivets villkorade jämställdhet: varför jänställdhetsarbete och intersektionalitet hör ihop' [The circumscribed gender equality of working life: why gender equality work and intersectionality belong together], in P. de los Reyes, ed. *Inte bara jämställdhet: Intersektionella perspektiv på hinder och möjligheter i arbetslivet* [*Not only gender equality: Intersectional perspectives on obstacles and possibilities in working life*], Stockholm: SOU No 34, pp 87–114.

Proposition, R. (1993/94) Jämställdhetspolitiken: delad makt – delat ansvar [The politics of gender equality: shared power – shared responisbility], http://data.riksdagen.se/fil/EDCAFA56-8FC6-4C54-B6E3-BE3B5001646C (accessed 9 March 2015).

Ritterhofer, I. and Gatrell, C. (2012) 'Gender mainstreaming and employment in the European Union: a review and analysis of theoretical and policy literature', *International Journal of Management Reviews*, vol 14, pp 201–16.

Rönnblom, M. (2009) 'Bending towards growth: discursive constructions for gender equality in an era of governance and neoliberalism', in E. Lombardo, P. Meier and M. Verloo (eds) *The discursive politics of gender equality: Stretching, bending and policy making*, London: Routledge, pp 105–20.

Sage, D., Dainty, A. and Brookes, N. (2010) 'A consideration of reflexive practice within the critical projects movement', *International Journal of Project Management*, vol 28, no 6, pp 539–46.

Sainsbury, D. and Bergquist, C. (2009) 'The promise and pitfalls of gender mainstreaming', *International Feminist Journal of Politics*, vol 2, pp 216–34.

SCB (2014) *På tal om kvinnor och män: Liten lathund om jämställdhet 2014* [*Speaking of women and men: A crib sheet on gender equality*], Stockholm: Statisktiska Centralbyrån [Statistics Sweden].

Shore, C. and Wright, S. (2015) 'Governing by numbers: audit culture, rankings and the new world order', *Social Anthropology/Anthropologie Sociale*, vol 23, no 1, pp 22–8.

Sjöstedt Landén, A. (2012) 'Moved by relocation: professional identification in the decentralization of public sector jobs in Sweden', PhD thesis, Umeå University.

Squires, J. (2009) 'Intersecting inequalities', *International Feminist Journal of Politics*, vol 11, no 4, pp 496–512.

SOU (Statens Offentliga Utredningar) [Official state report] (2007) 'Stöd för framtiden: förutsättningar för jämställdhetsintegrering' [Support for the future: opportunities for gender mainstreaming], *States offentliga utredningar* [*Official state report*] No 15, Stockholm: The Swedish Government.

SOU [Official state report] (2014a) 'Jämställdhet i socialförsäkringen? Forskningsrapport till Delegationen för jämställdhet i arbetslivet' [Gender equality in social insurance? Research report to the Delegation for gender equality in working life], *Statens offentliga utredningar* [*Official state report*] No 74, Stockholm: The Swedish Government.

SOU [Official state report] (2014b) 'Jämställt arbete? Organisatoriska ramar och villkor i arbetslivet' [Gender equal work? Organisational settings and conditions in working life], *Statens Offentliga Utredningar* [*Official state report*] No 30, Stockholm: The Swedish Government.

Tienari, J., Söderberg, A.-M., Holgersson, C. and Vaara, E. (2005) 'Gender and national identity constructions in cross-border merger context', *Gender Work and Organization*, vol 12, no 3, pp 217–41.

Towns, A. (2002) 'Paradoxes of (in)equality: something is rotten in the gender equal state of Sweden', *Cooperation and Conflict*, vol 37, no 2, pp 157–79.

Verloo, M. (2005) 'Displacement and empowerment: reflections on the concept and practice of the Council of Europe approach to gender mainstreaming and gender equality', *Social Politics: International Studies in Gender, State and Society*, vol 12, no 3, pp 344–65.

Verloo, M. and van der Vlauten, J.M. (2009) 'The discursive logic of ranking and benchmarking: understanding gender equality measures in the European Union', in E. Lombardo, P. Meier and M. Verloo, eds. *The discursive politics of gender equality stretching, bending and policymaking*, London: Routledge, pp 169–87.

Walby, S. (2011) *The future of feminism*, Cambridge: Polity Press.

Yuval-Davis, N. (2006) 'Intersectionality and feminist politics', *European Journal of Women's Studies*, vol 13, no 3, pp 193–209.

Zalewski, M. (2010) '"I don't even know what gender is": a discussion of the connection between gender, gender mainstreaming and feminist theory', *Review of International Studies*, vol 36, no 1, pp 3–27.

EIGHT

Frictions and figurations: gender-equality norms meet activism

Lena Martinsson

A feminist event

The Feminist Nordic Forum in Sweden in 2014[1] was dominated by a modernist, radical state feminism, which has been of importance for how Swedish gender-equality norms have emerged. One of the main ambitions of the forum was to 'formulate requirements and specific proposals for the Nordic governments and politicians linked to future gender policy'.[2] The state was thereby given considerable importance in the feminist struggle for, and in promoting, gender equality. This importance was also emphasised through the attendance of all the Nordic countries' ministers for gender equality at the final plenary session of the Forum.

One consequence of this set-up was that Solveig Horne, representing the Norwegian culturally racist party Fremskrittspartiet, was invited. Not only is she famous for her racist political work, but she also has expressed and been criticised for trans- as well as homophobic views.[3] When she gave her speech during the final session, many people in the audience got up and left the hall in protest. At this moment a critique of Swedish and Nordic state feminism became very clear. When a state or government is racist and transphobic, as in Norway, collaboration with it means collaboration with those who openly and intentionally take part in political processes that are racialising and, thereby, othering people, as well as threatening LGBQT-bodies. It is a sort of violence that also denaturalises the state as a unit for *all* people living in the country. It creates an outside inside (see Butler, 1997; Trinh, 2011), in this case in Norway.

The critique of Horne and the Nordic Forum was predictable. Although the work for gender equality is recognised as important and has been partly successful, activists and researchers have critiqued not only Swedish welfare state policies and their modernist, linear gender-equality politics, but also how the gender-equality norm is performed in everyday life, working life, the judicial system and the care system. Gender-equality policies and norms have been criticised for becoming neoliberal and thereby depoliticising the gender-equality issue and privileging middle-class women's needs. They have been criticised for being racist and postcolonial because of their nationalist iterations and, with their focus on the heterosexual couple, for being heteronormative and incapable of problematising trans★[4] issues (de los Reyes, 2001, 2014; Martinsson, 2001, 2006; Mulinari and Nergaard, 2004; Dahl, 2005; Mattsson, 2010; Wasshede, 2010; Bremer, 2011; Fahlgren, Johansson and Mulinari, 2011; Rönnblom, 2011; Wottle and Blomberg, 2011; Harrison and Engdahl, 2013). Nonetheless, as the final session of the Nordic Forum clearly showed, the gender-equality norm remains a powerful force, even if it is challenged in many ways. It is also significant that the protest, according to the media, was not recognised by the head of the steering committee, Gertrud Åström.[5] She dismissed the protest, saying that the people who left 'had a train to catch'.

While Åström, through this stance, became a symbol for a certain kind of stabilising force in how to understand 'equality' by demonstrating a will to continue as usual – which is quite common – activists, researchers from various fields and people taking part in an everyday non-organised movement are trying to challenge and change problematic norms reiterated in feminist and gender-equality strategies and rhetoric (Wasshede, 2010; Ambjörnsson and Bromseth, 2013). These activists, and these movements, which can be described as part of a diversely constituted and challenging outside (Butler, 2004) of the gender-equality norm and modernist feminism, need to be recognised as an aspect of the current Swedish political landscape around gender issues. Through these movements the gender-equality norm is challenged and many frictions, denials and emotions are produced, and privileged positions that also emerge through the gender-equality norm are questioned (Ahmed, 2004). In this chapter I will investigate these frictions and emotions as well as the challenges arising out of them, and also the insight of inhabiting privileged positions even as an activist, and as a researcher, and what that could mean for possible new understandings of gender politics beyond the gender-equality norm. What new norms, strategies, subjectivities, visions or figurations might emerge in this space of necessary conflicts?

This chapter draws on the extensive theoretical and empirical work of de los Reyes, Molina and Mulinari (2002), who, together with other researchers, challenged and partly also changed the normalised Nordic gender-equality discourse in their volume *The different (dis)guises of power*

(*Maktens (o)lika förklädnader*). They critique the ongoing production of Swedish nationality and an imagined Swedish exceptionalism (Habel, 2012) through postcolonial and post-structural perspectives. They show how the Swedish nation has been re-established, constructing a 'we and them' through an ongoing process of othering in policies, research, media, education and working life. An imagined 'Swedish White We' is produced over and over again. Their work is part of an important field of research that explores how racism, ableism or hetero-/cis-normativity are produced and reproduced in the Swedish welfare system (Tesfahuney, 1998; Mattsson, 2001; Barron, 2004; Dahl, 2005; Khamali and Sawyer, 2006; Hübinette et al, 2012; Bayatti, 2014; Reimers, 2014). This critique is not only important for researchers. It has also had an impact on the growing feminist anti-racist movement in Sweden. The critique has been heard at many demonstrations, in media, in feminist magazines and in panels.[6]

With the work of these researchers as my starting point, I also use researchers such as Trinh T. Minha-ha (2011), Judith Butler (2004; 2005), Saba Mahmood (2012), Sara Ahmed (2004; 2012), Elspeth Probyn (2010) and Rosi Braidotti (2006) in order to understand normative frictions and emotions and their outcomes in the feminist and activist landscape. I understand this landscape as an assemblage of changing norms and normative materialities such as bodies, economies, emotions, but also houses, architecture and so on, which connect and disconnect through affective events in a way that is far from predictable and quite messy (Braidotti, 2006). New norms emerge through these different (dis)connections, and normative materialities as well as positions possible or impossible to identify with (see Butler, 2004). This messiness may produce situations of disorientations, of not knowing, moments of bodily frictions and possible changes (Probyn, 2010), and, in line with Saba Mahmood (2012), I want to stress the importance of these forms of frictions and disorientations for how political projects change and emerge. In order to understand the complexity of these positions and to be able to identify with different, sometimes contradictory, positions, I also draw on Trinh T. Minh-ha's work on borders and her discussion of how a position – such as 'immigrant' – is placed both inside and outside society. In the present chapter I discuss the possibility for political subjectivities to emerge through these frictions, in other words, the possibility of becoming aware of political conflicts through affects and frictions that might cause displacements and wanting to make a difference and struggle for change (Spindler, 2013).

In this context I use the notion of figurations to describe politically produced positions. Figurations refer to historical and normative positions that become part of orienting political practices. Braidotti (2006, p 90) writes: 'a figuration is the expression of one's specific positioning in both space and time'. She also states that a figuration 'marks certain territorial or geopolitical coordinates, but it also points out one's sense of genealogy or of historical inscription' (Braidotti, 2006, p 90). Of special importance for this chapter is her argument that figurations 'deterritorialize and destabilize the narratives of self and others' (Braidotti, 2006, p 90). Figurations, as I understand them, emerge in different spheres, activist as well as academic, and in the cross-roads between them, intentionally as well as unintentionally. Many of the figurations used by Swedish activists could be described as anti-figurations, such as 'the white heterosexual cis-man', the 'privileged', 'the white cis-feminist'. They point out the norm, the problem, that needs to be subverted, thereby creating another political 'we', outside the many norms. I will come back to these anti-figurations later in the chapter.

This chapter draws on different sorts of material collected in relation to two research projects[7] in which I am involved. One is on activism and the gender-equality norm and the other on gender and sexuality in a changing global civil society. As a feminist researcher, a teacher at the university in Gothenburg and an activist outside academia in a country on Europe's margins, I have been affected by this research both intellectually and emotionally. These emotions and frictions are not understood as my own, but as part of normative, national as well as transnational conflicts, and I have therefore also conducted auto-ethnography. Those experiences are augmented by my observations as a participant in several feminist, LGBTQ and anti-racist events during 2013–14, such as 1 May 2014, 8 March 2013 and 2014 and West Pride 2014. I followed the big event Nordic Forum over the internet and through traditional and social media in May 2014. I have conducted other forms of net-ethnography, focusing on different movements, discussions and presentations on the web and in social as well as in traditional media. While collecting this material I came into contact with people whom I subsequently interviewed in person. In this chapter I will make use of interviews with three of them.

A field of political struggle

The political field challenging the hegemonic gender-equality norm can be described as diverse in many ways. To exemplify: the way the economy is understood differs between the groups and activists. During the decline of the welfare state, neoliberal normativity gained influence among certain activists while simultaneously being highly criticised by others. Some organisations, even quite radical ones like the trans and anti-racist organisation Interfem,[8] teach people to become entrepreneurs for change. Some activist entrepreneurs describe their work as a position 'full of frictions'. Others are very critical and totally dismissive (Martinsson, 2016). The trans, anti-racist and queer movements, and a growing movement concerned with issues of ableism as well as ageism, are important in this field of political struggle. The same is true for a growing feminist Muslim movement. Communities such as Voice of Hijabis challenge dominant notions of how a feminist could act, and criticise the notion of secularity as the only vantage point for critique (Asad et al, 2009).[9] All these groupings are part of a diverse and rather messy assemblage of activism. Even if this activism is diverse, or precisely because of its diversity, these groups have changed or affected the Swedish feminist landscape. They interrupt the heteronormative gender-equality norm, the white Swedish self-image of being the most gender-equal country in the world, and put pressure on gender-equality state feminism and what it means to identify oneself as a feminist. These groupings also challenge, question and radicalise each other and, as I will discuss later in this chapter, sometimes also reflect on their own positions, trying to be aware of how they, themselves, reiterate norms (Mouffe, 2005; Johansson and Lilja, 2013).

Two Swedish political parties, Feminist Initiative (F!) and Sverigedemokraternas or the Sweden Democrats (SD), have for different reasons become important in this political field as well. F! could be understood as influenced by, or having emerged from, the different groupings described above, but it is also strongly influenced by state feminism, as it wants to take part in Parliament. During the spring of 2014 F!, with a steering committee that has experienced racism, homophobic violence, patriarchy and has an intersectional perspective, became politically prominent and got massive support. Its public demonstrations in different cities both on 8 March and on 1 May 2014 gathered large groups of people. F! gained a seat in the European Parliament, with a representative who herself became a sort of figuration for possible new connections between different movements. As a Romany woman, Soraya Post has extensive experiences of racism and of being discriminated against. F! became an alliance of different feminisms, LGBTQ concerns and anti-racism. However, even this party has been criticised for locating the problem of racism in the right-wing racist party the SD. F! has been criticised for not focusing enough on everyday racism, racism in societal structures and racism repeated in and by the feminist movement itself. In the autumn of 2014, the SD got nearly 13% of the votes in the general election. They advocate a conservative gender model and want immigrants to assimilate – or leave (see Chapter Six in this volume).

To summarise, there are many different struggles going on and different kinds of political 'we's and 'them's emerging. It is therefore somewhat paradoxical that the struggle for gender equality is usually talked about as a non-political issue in Sweden. A soft liberal consensus is said to reign (Rönnblom, 2011; Tollin, 2011). However, that has been true only at the parliamentary level. And in 2015, with Sverigedemokraternas' increased influence, it is no longer true.

Frictions

I have long been one of the critical voices referred to above who challenge gender-equality norms as nationalist, heteronormative and so on. I have also critiqued social-diversity management and its neoliberal imperatives in business life and in education. I have analysed how class works and how economic inequalities are naturalised (for example, Martinsson, 2006; 2014). Through this work I have problematised norms that often, but not always, position me in privileged sites. To do such research and at the same time take part in my colleagues' work has meant that I have felt shame, guilt, anger, frustration and a lot of nervousness (Probyn, 2010). I can see how these feelings are a combination of ambivalent norms and my body, norms that make it possible for me to be a subject, giving me privileges and power, and norms according to which these privileges are wrong to inhabit. The self becomes a problem and there is no way to go. The self is turned against itself. These impersonal as well as highly personal normative frictions and clashes create bodily sensations, displacements and disorientation. The body is always part of something else, something that transcends the personal. The body is also in this sense political (Ahmed, 2004; Bertelsen and Murphy, 2010; Probyn, 2010; Spindler, 2013).

Having said this, I also want to emphasise that I do not think that I am alone in feeling all these frictions. People have privileged positions, and repeat problematic norms that give them power and possibilities to situate themselves in specific ways. This could be described as a condition of existence. At the same time, the norms according to which one should not take part in discriminatory practices and so on are quite strong, and of importance for how it is possible to understand oneself and the way one should act. It is therefore not possible to think about oneself as either good or utterly bad, as the victim or as the oppressor (Eriksson, 2013). However, even if I claim that the experience of having privileged positions, recognised or not, is unavoidable, some inhabit, or identify with, such privileged positions more than others do (Butler, 2005; Mahmood, 2012). And some, like Åström and the steering group, might not be responsive to these frictions or understand them as relevant at all. It is not predictable what will happen with these assemblages of principles when different groups or individuals are affected by and articulate them.

I want to discuss the affects these frictions cause and how they could be used, or be part of another sort of political awareness regarding political conflicts. I understand these frictions as messy spaces where there is a potential for both transformation and conservatism. Even though I hope that these frictions could be a place or a source for the emergence of a deeper understanding of political conflicts and for a changing political subjectivity, I am also aware that these mixed feelings can lead to conservative and reactionary strategies. In Sweden, there are many who feel 'wronged' by these discussions, and react against any work for gender equality, anti-racism and so on (Lindeborg, 2013). In line with what I have just said, and in line with Mia Eriksson's (2013) discussion on this topic, I am not interested in this group or in taking part in reconstructing figurations common in Sweden, such as 'the heterosexual man' or 'the white heterosexual middle-class woman', which are used to point out a problematic normality. These figurations have their role in the political field just described, and they are certainly part of de-territorialising the norm by making these highly normative and hegemonic positions into a problem. However, the problem is that in these sorts of figurations some bodies are constructed as a problem, rather than the norms being repeated and stabilised across many other bodies, materialities and situations. There is also a risk with these figurations that some people become defined as good and others as problematic (Braidotti, 2006; Eriksson, 2013).

8 March: Women's Day

Let me now change place and context in order to describe certain frictions experienced by others as well as by myself. Women's Day, on 8 March, is a day of many public events and discussions in Sweden. At the 8 March public demonstration in Gothenburg in 2014, anti-racist movements, LGBTQ groups, F!, anti-patriarchal organisations that problematise both masculinity and identifying yourself as a man were represented and there were many thousands of participants. The demonstration ended in the large square, Götaplatsen, in central Gothenburg. After listening to speeches by famous activists many participants went to the Museum of World Culture a few blocks away, to listen to and take part in panel discussions, seminars and workshops. The afternoon started with a panel session titled 'Feminist Starting Points: Strategies and Visions'. During the presentations one of the panellists, Alex Snäckerström, who represented Mötesplats Simone, a separatist trans and queer organisation, criticised the composition of the panel. No one on the panel was, as Alex described it, 'racialised'. The panel consisted of the white norm. One person on the panel, very well known for her extensive work on feminist and lesbian and gay rights, said that she also spoke for the elderly and not only as a lesbian, woman or feminist. She reminded the audience and the panel that age was also a category often forgotten. This was an important statement. Ageism needs to be discussed and problematised. For the purposes of this chapter it is important to note that she talked about a norm that situated her in a non-privileged position. Alex, whom I will come back to in this chapter, on the other hand, talked about those not represented at all on the panel: the people on the panel were not haunted by racialising processes but privileged by them. Alex thus questioned the panel members' own positions, reminding them of their privilege.

I cannot say much about what took place in the big hall, what others thought about the situation that arose when Alex criticised the composition of the panel, but I presume many felt as I did: bothered, frustrated and maybe also a bit ashamed about not having thought about how the panel was composed. Maybe we also felt bad about our own limitations as activists and researchers. However, for some in the audience the composition of the panel could have been a quite violent reminder of racialising processes they were constantly exposed to. The organisers ended up feeling distressed and worried, Alex told me later. At the same time my feelings were quite ambivalent, thinking that they, the panel participants, nearly all represented non-privileged positions. They had experiences of struggling against discrimination and most of them also had significant experiences of not having a voice or not being recognised. Now one of them had taken on the responsibility of problematising their ongoing production of whiteness. At the same time, this was a reminder that there are no entirely non-privileged places or bodies. It was also a possible learning moment for those who, like myself, had not reflected on the composition of the panel. If we were prepared to take a risk by subverting our own subjectivities, our own normalised positions as 'white', we could learn something.

Some months later I visited Alex and also met Mario, who works at the same separatist trans and queer organisation as Alex. I wanted to ask about the 8 March event and the feelings Alex had had when they[10] questioned the composition of the panel:

> AS: I felt bad, I should have checked, I checked it afterwards and then they told me that they did not know where to look, where to find any, I could have told them.

> LM: But, at the same time, you represented people who are also excluded? Did you feel you had to be responsible for this as well?

> AS: As political activists, we have to take that responsibility, and we have to take it right now, (…) It should have been cis-persons, cis-men, who just breeze through life. But I as a white person must be responsible. I made a mistake. I know. I also breeze through a lot because I am white.

> LM: Breeze?

> AS: Yes, breeze, if you write a list of norms it becomes obvious that I breeze, I get privileges all the time.

The concept 'breeze through' describes a situation free from frictions, without any obstacles. It is an example of how Alex understood these positions, even though they were questioned. It is a situation of the self being recognised as the norm, not having been made into the Other in relation to the norm. Alex felt bad about the situation with the panel; the experience of breezing was full of frictions, guilt and shame. Alex's recognition of the situation was also an example of how 'breezing through life' is shameful; you become part of an oppressive norm, a norm that displaces, excludes and others people, and you feel ashamed that you do not live up to your standards (Probyn, 2010).

Alex and Mario are both sensitive to other sorts of exclusions. They get some limited support for their work from the municipality, which means that they can work supporting vulnerable youth. I asked them if they, as some have done in the movements, had thought about starting a business, selling lectures and so on to the municipality or to other organisations. Both of them dismissed this entrepreneurial option.

Their experience is that the events, meetings or courses created by social companies often become very expensive, thus making it difficult for small organisations and young, exposed people to take part. They also told me that they had changed the location of the organisation because their previous place had been accessible only for people who lived in line with the norm for abled bodies. In changing buildings to accommodate others, they had been accountable for their positions and practised an intersectional activism.

Alex's criticism of the panel composition reminded me of 8 March the year before, 2013, when I took part in an event organised by the university in Gothenburg. I was on a podium in the main hall of the university in a white, middle-aged, cis-normative, able-bodied panel, which was typical for the whole arrangement. It was the order of the day, one panel after another – repetitive as in a play or popular song. Some of us felt more and more uncomfortable. We talked to each other about the composition of the panels and we discussed it with the organisers. We felt worried and reflected upon what this said about our university and about ourselves. It was quite obvious to us that this non-representativeness was a performative setup. Through different processes of othering, the expectation of who could be listened to, who could represent the university, was stabilised. It thus became a process of the ongoing production of privileged positions, possible for some to inhabit and recognise and not for others – the normative side of an ongoing discrimination. We contributed to a process of exclusions as well as being an effect of these processes and took part in the rematerialisation of an unequal society. We were experiencing this day as privileged people, whereas many others experienced it through being excluded, again. We, or at least some of us on the panels, knew that what we did, sitting there, was wrong, but we did not act. Not one of us raised the issue of the composition during the panel discussions as Alex did one year later, in order to open up certain frictions, let more people feel our uncomfortable feelings and then openly question our own positions, our own responsibilities, without merely blaming the organisers. But, sitting there, ashamed and feeling guilty for not having reacted beforehand, was also an example of the need to challenge our own subjectivities as feminists, as researchers, as individuals who take part in the work for gender equality, as we also do.

Saba Mahmood (2012, p xiii) writes that 'political projects are not only the result of coalitional organizing, ideological mobilization and critical deliberation', they are also 'predicated upon affective, ethical and sensible capacities that are often ignored as consequential to the analyses of the political'. Maybe our disorientation on 8 March expressed a situation where we, once more – it was absolutely not the first time – were affected by the unequal order and the threatening insight into our own privileged positions, an insight that could destabilise our subjectivities and might be part of another emerging way of being. Mahmood also writes that to move from one political position to another, or in our case to seriously question our positions, identities and subjectivities, necessitates a whole series of affective and emotional reorientations; new spaces need to be developed and people need to teach themselves to inhabit a different kind of body (2012, p xiii). Change is necessary, and Mahmood emphasises deep change, which not only challenges the assemblage of norms and normative materialities that constitute different subjectivities but also the people who inhabit those constituted subjectivities. During the event in the hall, our *bodies talked*, and transcended the idea of mind and body as separate, but we needed to change more, to inhabit, in Mahmood's words, a different kind of body. It is therefore important not to treat this issue of representation as one that has a simple answer, such as 'find someone', and not letting it change anything else, anyone's subjectivity. If that becomes the only strategy for those who inhabit privileged positions the panels just risk becoming what Trinh T. Minh-ha calls someone's private zoo (Trinh, 1989), a zoo where the ones who are privileged, as we were in the panel that day, or the institution, do not need to change or be challenged. A discussion that just focuses on representation on panels or on other symbolic set-ups runs the risk of merely constructing alibis. However, it is also important to recognise the problem of non-representation as especially Alex – but also we – did, in order to see the conflict and to recognise the problem of the performativity of absence, and the performativity of presence.

On not understanding the problem

On 8 March 2013 I understood, again, how I was reiterating, among others, racist and cis-normative principles. I was interrupted, again. At other times, however, I have had a lot of problems understanding that different kinds of critique also embrace myself and my work. In Sweden, as well as in many other countries, women with trans-experience have said that they feel unsafe in certain feminist circles. One example of this is a feminist event called Love Party that took place on 8 March 2014 (it is a day full of conflicts, and it is important as such) in Stockholm. For some time some feminist groups in Stockholm have been criticised for excluding women with trans-experiences. At the Love Party a famous radical feminist who has expressed transphobic views had been invited to speak. And even though the organisers were strongly criticised by a large group of feminists for inviting this radical feminist to speak in the first place, and for not inviting a woman with trans-experience to do the same, they refused to change the programme. Another party, announced as a Love Party For All, was planned instead[11] and a woman with trans-experiences prepared a speech[12] for this second party, in which she broke with the feminist movement.

I remember how angry I felt about this. I did not want to be a feminist if that meant excluding persons with trans-experiences or who identified themselves as trans★. Some of my friends felt the same way and organised a seminar in order to discuss this particular situation, and the role of, and problems within, feminism in general. During the seminar I said that I was very critical of the sort of excluding feminism practised by the organisers of Love Party. If that was feminism, I did not want to be a feminist. I tried to say that feminism could be something else. I was not that sort of feminist. I am quite convinced that I shared this self-image of being a good feminist with many of those cis-feminists who were critical of the Love Party. We all wanted to be allied with women with trans-experience. But were we?

Several months later I read an article by the trans-activist Maria Ramnehill in the Swedish feminist magazine *Bang* in which she, with reference to what had happened in relation to the Love Party, talked about people like me and other cis-feminists:

> When I talk about the existence of cis-normativity inside feminism, I often get the question, 'But what feminism do you mean? There are many feminisms.' I know that. The answer is that I mean all feminisms: all the feminist rooms I am in, irrespective of whether they are digital rooms or in the world of meat (Köttvärlden). In feminist everyday life the cis-norm is obvious: when trans experience does not exist or is regarded as supplementary and nothing to take notice of.

She writes that the feminist movements lack trans-experience:

> There is an unconscious resistance to letting trans-women exist on the same terms in every feminist room, to recognizing our lives and experiences as legitimate and as valid women's experiences. It means that feminism treats trans-issues as supplementary, that it never touches

trans-issues without prejudice or without ignorance. A trustworthy feminist movement needs trans-feminism, because a feminism which does not engage with the most marginalised women is hardly trustworthy.[13]

Maria Ramnehill recognises a worried group of cis-feminists who do not want to identify with transphobic movements, who do not want to admit their part in the problem – but it could be a group who might want to change. Ramnehill does not try to comfort this group. Instead she continues to put pressure on it, showing what it still lacks. It needs to take a new step, to become something else, in order to become trustworthy. It needs to be aware of, and affected by, the political conflicts traditional feminism and a traditional struggle for gender equality reiterate and take part in. She criticised feminists for placing the cis-normative problem somewhere else, precisely as I had done, instead of challenging their owns subjectivities and self-images. Her critique could be understood as part of an ongoing radicalisation of movements that Chantal Mouffe too has discussed as an important necessity for building alliances (Mouffe, 2005). Ramnehill's critique is an example of how new spaces and reorientations need to be developed among feminists (Mahmood, 2012).

Separatist spaces

> 'Interfem is my favourite organisation, I really like what they are doing and I am trying to learn from them but I can't take part in their organisation because I am white.' [Adrian, an activist and writer who fights for gender equality and trans issues]

In light of the ongoing exclusion of people and the persistent reproduction of privileged positions described earlier in this chapter, it is easy to understand the need for different separatist movements. In this section I focus on the affects that are created when people, like Adrian, are stopped, not allowed to take part.[14] Adrian understands, entirely, Interfem's need for separatism and does not question it at all, even if he feels a desire to take part.

However, before I continue to discuss what it could mean to be stopped, I will start with a reminder from Alex about the importance of separatist rooms and spaces and what these do for both those who are inside and those who are outside. I asked Alex if separatist spaces have any political importance, if they change anything and whether their organisation is a place to recover, to seek comfort for those who experience discomfort in a hostile and threatening world:

> AS: We have been here for 15 years, we are part of trans-history, and we are self-organised. The people who come here are those who, according to the suicide figures, have the strongest suicidal tendencies. To strengthen those who are the most vulnerable is so damn political. There are so many other ways to live, to be seen, role models and friends and it is heavenly important to show that one exists in society. Society will be broadened if we are able to live, then we will be seen in norm-society.

Even if my question was rhetorical, it was as stupid and insulting as it is common. It contains a critique, a questioning of separatist movements' possibility to be political. 'Could it be political without "us"?' 'Without society?' 'Without struggling with normative processes?' 'Could it be political on its own?' It is obvious that the question comes from someone outside the separatist space, someone who maybe feels a little bit lost at the same time as she places herself in the middle of the world. On the other hand, the answer shows, in a painful way, the effects of the violence coming from hegemonic 'norm-society'. It also describes the political role that the possibility to live at all might have, how some lives, given the opportunity, can change course, eventually open up other possible societies. This is far beyond a normative understanding of separatist space as 'revenge'. Rather, the answer contains an understanding of the effects, which the presence as well as the absence of certain bodies has in the assemblage of norms and bodies called society. To be alive becomes political (Stryker, 2013).

Alex's explanation is a way to understand the effect separatist rooms may have on societies; they can make other lives possible. The introductory quote by Adrian is also an indication that separatist rooms are affective; they give some the experience of being stopped, of not being allowed to take part. Adrian understands this. I want to give three further examples of separatist spaces. This might seem repetitive, but it is intentional. The repetitiveness in a sense mirrors not only the often violent situation that the people who construct these rooms or spaces are exposed to. It also mirrors, and this is important to point out, the experience of being stopped from entering the separatist spaces. The participants in the platform Voice of Hijabis separate themselves from a feminism that does not respect Islam and their right to wear hijabs, and are now constructing their own picture of themselves. In

April 2015, in an op-ed article published in the Swedish newspaper *Expressen*, the newly formed group wrote:

> We don't need the feminism that teaches us that equality is equal to similarity. They say that they are struggling for equal rights and equal values. But we as Muslim women got our rights 1400 years ago. Thanks to Islam we were not seen as a burden or as a problem [...]
>
> We want to own the picture of our selves and not be a project for white western feminism [...] We are women, Muslims and feminists and free to make our own choices, with our own voices. (*Expressen*, 8 April 2015)

In the Swedish secular hegemony, where religion, especially Islam, has become a reiterated sign of the oppression of women and therefore marked as very 'un-Swedish', the critique raised by Voice of Hijabis and Ramla Abdullahi, Noor Behrooz, Aiman Kayani and Sagal Yusuf, who signed the article, would be quite easy to understand. However, Voice of Hijabis was strongly criticised by the leader writer Malin Lernfeldt in one of Sweden's largest newspapers, *GP* (*GP*, 9 April 2015). Lernfeldt claimed that Voice of Hijabis was an expression of 'navel-gazing' and 'race-biology', and that those who seriously wanted freedom for women should try to obtain a broad discussion with different perspectives instead. Lernfeldt was also critical of the newly formed group for criticising the western women's struggle, which has been going on for a century, and which, she said, made it possible for the group to express their opinions in one of Sweden's largest newspapers. In other words, Lernfeldt did not like being stopped. The suggestion to obtain a broad discussion also shows that she did not recognise the inequalities between different feminists. It was these inequalities that Abdullah, Behrooz, Kayani and Yusuf tried to make the readers aware of. Through her article, Lernfeldt reinforced a Swedish 'we' and 'them'. The long Swedish struggle for gender equality should be something to respect and be grateful for. Lernfeldt's article became a significant example of the reproduction of the notion of Swedish exceptionalism.

There are many discursive similarities between Voice of Hijabis and the next example, called The Room (Rummet). It is a platform for discussions and analyses in social media as well as in real life, created by and for those who usually become racialised as Others. Through The Room this process of othering is temporarily changed and white bodies are excluded. The Room writes about their position as outsiders within:

It eats away at you, always being a conditional part of the societal we. It is destructive always being on sufferance. It makes us tired and dispirited but also suspicious and aggressive. It makes us anxious. Therefore we build another we: through shutting the white bodies out. We turn, for the first time, to each other.[15]

'We build another we: through shutting the white bodies out.' The creation of a separatist room is the creation of a space that one can also close, a room with another outside, and another inside than the hegemonic one; white bodies are locked out, stopped.

A third example of locking white bodies out comes from a Facebook post in the group 'Why do monkeys not wear pink dresses?' ('Varför bär inte apor rosa klänningar?', 6 August 2014) – and I want to stress that I got permission from the initiator of the thread to cite this text. The text contains an open request to those with white bodies, a request about taking a step back and not taking up space:

This thread is intended to be a separatist thread. It means that I will now ask all whites to stand back and not take up space. Read and listen to what is written, send a PM if you absolutely have to ask something, but let the thread be! White = persons who belong to the norm regarding culture and appearance. If you've never had to reflect about your skin or origin before now, you are with 99.99% certainty white.

To 'stand back' is a very clear critique of a person's subjectivity and this critique becomes even clearer when they, those with white bodies, are asked not to take up space. White people are here stopped in a physical way, by not being allowed to click the 'like'-button or write comments. Their possible desire to take part is hindered. What they think and do is not relevant. At the same time white people are openly racialised, but this time as the problem, not as the usual norm. They are displaced. The author gives example after example of how racism is part of everyday life, how she becomes excluded from the nation and even distanced from her adoptive parents. Racism is everywhere. The writer asks others for strategies and tactics to deal with racism. At the end she makes the following request:

I ask you again, here at the end: all whites, please do not comment, and please don't 'like' the comments, which contain stories from our lives. [I] understand that it is an act of good faith but it becomes a judgement of what we share. 'Like' by all means my TS, but let it rest at that. Thank you for showing respect.

In this example a space of one's own is created as a thread on Facebook. Don't comment. 'Don't judge our lives.' But also, as in the earlier examples above, the whites are not an invisible normalised group of individuals; rather, they are talked to as a problematic group.

What eventually emerges in affective situations of being stopped, of interruption, a hindrance in the habit to stretch out, when you inhabit positions that usually urge you to act and take part, and being asked to stand back, is of course difficult to embrace (Ahmed, 2004). I will refer to a theoretical art work by the artist-researcher Annica Karlsson Rixon, in order to describe the affect produced when one is not allowed to take part. Karlsson Rixon has long worked with the concepts of distance and position. Influenced by artists and theorists like Trinh T. Minh-ha, Karlsson Rixon's art opens up possible understandings of affective situations like the ones above – where one is stopped at the same time as there is a desire to participate. In one of Karlsson Rixon's artworks, a lesbian summer camp is photographed at a distance. The title of the work is *Vid tiden för den tredje läsningen/ At the time of the third reading/Во время третего чтения*. The title refers to the fact that the photographs were taken at the same time that the Bill about the prohibition of homosexual propaganda in Russia was finally passed.[16] The work shows the participants at the camp speaking to each other, eating and working. However, as an observer or as a reader of this performative piece of art, I want to come closer, and with all my messy baggage I walk up close to the image, but get physically stopped by it, of course. It is not possible to get into it, to come really close. I squint to see the image better, but this does not help. At this moment this insurmountable distance also tells me something about my desire to come closer. The walking into the image, an effect the artist has also discussed in her writing about her work (Karlsson Rixon, forthcoming), makes me understand something about the will to connect, to be part of whatever is happening over there. The feeling of distance is frustrating. As a desiring observer, the position given to me, the me who is not just me, also tells this me that I am not really needed, not asked for. The image does not interpellate me, but it affects me. It keeps me at a distance and it is this distance that one can grasp, embrace. The will to connect, to take part, and then being stopped, can be a moment where it might be possible for those who, in one way or another, inhabit positions produced by dominant norms to be aware of a political conflict. It produces the possibility to take a risk, to understand the need for change, to understand one's own problematic subjectivity in another way.

Body talks

In a programme on Swedish television in December 2014,[17] Irene Molina, professor in human geography and one of those who have challenged the gender-equality norm for its nationalistic content, said that 'white' Swedish society should not be too quick to give itself credit for the advanced anti-racist discussions going on in Sweden. Rather, the many people with a background in other countries and who have struggled for change in Sweden should be recognised for their work. To be, as Trinh T. Minh-ha might have expressed it, outside at the same time as one is inside, is also a way to understand Molina's point (Trinh, 2011). Maria Ramnehill's critique is another example of the important challenging of an unavoidable dominant normativity when one is inside as a woman, and at the same time placed outside through cis-norms. Ramla Abdullahi, Noor Behrooz, Aiman Kayani and Sagal Yusuf and the organisation Voice of Hijabis is a third example. Hetero- and cis-normativity, class-divides, ageism, the normative secular/religious divide, patriarchal norms, just to mention a few, are challenged by many of those who exist and are subjectified in different in-betweens (for example, Butler, 1993; Trinh, 2011).

Privileged positions, produced in line with hegemonic norms, are of course also inhabited by those who are challenged, exploited and excluded by other norms. Alex's description of both being excluded and breezing through life is one such example. Another contradiction, discussed in the present chapter, that could affect the understanding of one's subjectivity is when those usually interpellated as unquestioned subjects oriented to act are stopped, hindered from taking part. This messiness, produced through complex normative processes and political interventions, creates feelings of friction, shame and guilt, frustration, refusals as well as agency. What sorts of subjectivities will emerge in this messiness is of course not predictable. They could be conservative as well as transformative. But it is possible to think about this messiness as a condition for political subjectivity to be produced. Mötesplats Simone as well as Alex and Mario are examples of political subjects emerged in a field of frictions. To understand the role of the body, the frictions and emotions as a possibility for political subjectivity to emerge can offer hope, and turn insecurities into something important. And, again, political projects are not only the result of coalitional organising. There is, as Mahmood states, a need of a whole series of affective and emotional reorientations. And people need to teach themselves to inhabit a different kind of body. Deep change is necessary (Mahmood, 2012, p xiii).

Another political possibility, in connection to the need of separatist spaces, is described by the gender researcher Evelina Johansson (2015). She suggests that there is an ongoing emergence of counter-spaces, spaces that challenge the hegemonic understanding of what is politically possible. A counter-space shows that what may be dismissed as utopian by others is actually working here and now. The text makes me think, again, about Alex and Mario and their organisation, which could be understood as one such counter-space in which it is possible to live lives that are not possible to live otherwise. Both perform what Johansson calls 'ethical practices'. Their meeting place was changed in order to open it to those who do not live in line with the able-bodied norm. They do not want to work as entrepreneurs and sell expensive courses. Instead they struggle with a small budget in order to make it possible for poor, vulnerable youths to take part and so on. Their meeting place becomes a counter-space connected to necessary fantasies about the future (Johansson, 2015).

Alex's and Mario's work also differs, which is especially important for this chapter, from the work for change urged on and conditioned by the gender-equality norm and the modernist figuration 'the Swedish gender equal couple', so connected to the national fantasy about the future. As briefly mentioned in the Introduction, as well as in Chapter Seven in this volume, with the gender equality norm, a linear developmental way of working and understanding the problem dominates. There is one way to go, and it seems rational and easy. While Alex and Mario are open to changes, incorporation of other issues such as struggle against racism, it is very problematic when the modern work for gender equality is reiterated (Grip, 2013). The gender-equality norm seems incapable of changing, of being intersectional. Some are maybe melancholic over this possible loss of a meta-strategy, but what is happening now is promising. Many movements and activists, as well as researchers today, but also people hired to work with gender equality and diversity, are struggling with necessary interruptions, with scarcity and insecurities about how to orient oneself. Not being sure about where to go could be a necessary risk. It is a way of trying to be responsible for the many existing, and emerging, political conflicts. It is maybe the only possibility to use and tread new paths in quite rhizomic and unpredictable ways in order to create new spaces, and new bodies.

Notes

[1] http://nf2014.org/2014/06/17/svar-pa-kritik/.

[2] http://nf2014.org/wp-content/uploads/2014/06/FEMINISTISKA-%C3%96VERENSKOMMELSER-OCH-KRAV_slutdokument.pdf .

[3] http://www.aftonbladet.se/debatt/article19066919.ab, http://www.dagbladet.no/2013/10/17/nyheter/innenriks/politikk/erna_solberg/solveig_horne/29829331/.

[4] Trans★ is an umbrella term that refers to all of the identities within the gender-identity spectrum.

[5] http://www.friatidningen.se/artikel/114669.

[6] https://www.youtube.com/watch?v=j1vg34zuooU.

[7] Activism and Gender Equality and Futures of Gender and Sexualities [Swedish Research Council].

[8] www.interfem.se.

[9] http://www.expressen.se/debatt/att-bara-hijab-ger-oss-frihet/.

[10] This is Alex's preferred pronoun.

[11] http://sverigeskvinnolobby.se/blog/det-feministiska-manifestet-en-karleksfest http://eventviva.com/event/1420660931512829.

[12] https://themegabitch.wordpress.com/2014/03/03/transkvinnorna-gor-slut/.

[13] http://www.bang.se/feminismen-behandlar-transfragor-som-en-plusmeny/.

[14] Interfem, a platform for feminist and anti-racist change. For racialized women and trans-persons.

[15] http://www.bang.se/vi-vander-oss-for-forsta-gangen-till-varandra/.

[16] Refers to when a Bill is read for approval for the third time in order to get final approval by a legislative body.

[17] SVT, 14 December 2014, Runda Bordet.

References

Ahmed, S. (2004) *The cultural politics of emotion*, Edinburgh: Edinburgh University Press.

Ahmed, S. (2012) *On being included*, Durham, NC: Duke University Press.

Ambjörnsson, F. and Bromseth, J. (2013) 'Aktivism' [Activism], *lambda nordica*, vol 1, pp 11–31.

Asad, T., Brown, W., Butler, J. and Mahmood, S. (2009) *Is critique secular?* Berkeley: University of California Berkeley, Townsend Papers in the Humanities.

Barron, K. (2004) *Genus och funktionshinder* [*Gender and disability*], Lund: Studentlitteratur.

Bayatti, 2014 *'Den Andre' i lärarutbildningen* [*'The other' in teacher education*], Göteborg: Acta.

Bertelsen, L. and Murphy, A. (2010) 'An ethics of everyday infinities and powers', in M. Gregg and G.J. Seigworth (eds) *The affect theory reader*, London: Duke University Press, pp 138–57.

Braidotti, R. (2006) *Transpositions*, Cambridge: Polity Press.

Bremer, S. (2011) *Kroppslinjer* [*Body lines*], Göteborg: Makadam.

Butler, J. (1993) *Bodies that matter: On the discursive limit of 'sex'*, New York: Routledge.

Butler, J. (1997) *Excitable speech*, New York: Routledge.

Butler, J. (2004) *Undoing gender*, New York: Routledge.

Butler, J. (2005) *Giving an account of oneself*, New York: Fordham University Press.

Dahl, U. (2005) 'Scener ur ett äktenskap' [Scenes from a marriage], in D. Kulick (ed) *Queersverige* [QueerSweden], Stockholm: Natur och Kultur, pp 48–71.

de los Reyes, P. (2001) *Diversity and differentiation*, Stockholm: SALTSA, Arbetslivsinstitutet.

de los Reyes, P. (ed) (2014) *Inte bara jämställdhet* [*Not gender equality only*], Stockholm: Fritzes förlag.

de los Reyes, P., Molina, I. and Mulinari, D. (eds) (2002) *Maktens (o) lika förklädnader* [*The different (dis)guises of power*], Stockholm: Atlas.

Eriksson, M. (2013) 'Wronged white men', *NORA*, vol 21, no 4, pp 249–63.

Fahlgren, S., Johansson, A. and Mulinari, D. (2011) *Normalization and 'outsiderhood'*, UAE: Bentham eBooks.

Grip, L. (2013) *Från hel till del* [*From whole to part*] Gothenburg: University of Gothenburg.

Habel, Y. (2012) 'Challenging Swedish exceptionalism? Teaching while black', in K. Freeman and E. Johnson (eds) *Education in the black diaspora*, London: Routledge, pp 109–22.

Harrison, K. and Engdahl, U. (2013) 'Trans-health as human rights', *lambda nordica*, vol 3, no 4, pp 10–23.

Hübinette, T., Hörnfeldt, H., Farahani, F. and León Rosales, R. (eds) (2012) *Om ras och vithet i det samtida Sverige* [*On race and whiteness in the contemporary Sweden*], Botkyrka: Mångkulturellt centrum.

Johansson, E. (2015) 'Etiska praktiker, queera positioner och heterotopiska rum' [Ethical practices, queer positions and heterotopical rooms], in M. Björk and J. Wittrock (eds) *Människa, stat och utopi* [*Humans, state, utopia*], Hägersten: Tankekraft förlag, pp 95–108.

Johansson, E. and Lilja, M. (2013) 'Understanding power and performing resistance', *NORA*, vol 21, no 4, pp 264–79.

Karlsson Rixon, A. (forthcoming) *At the time of the third reading / Во время третего чтения*, Stockholm: Art and Theory.

Khamali, M. and Sawyer, L. (2006) *Utbildningens dilemma* [*The dilemma of education*], Stockholm: Fritzes förlag.

Lindeborg, A. (2013) *Om den ofeministiska jämställdheten* [*On non-feminist equality*], Gothenburg: University of Gothenburg.

Mahmood, S. (2012) *Politics of piety*, Princeton, NJ: Princeton University Press.

Martinsson, L. (2001) 'Marmorhallen' [The marble hall], in B. Lundgren and L. Martinsson (eds) *Bestämma, benämna, betvivla* [Decide, denominate, doubt], Lund: Studentlitteratur, pp 17–45.

Martinsson, L. (2006) *Jakten på konsensus* [*Striving for consensus*], Malmö: Liber.

Martinsson, L. (2014) 'Värdegrunder' [Common values], in L. Martinsson and E. Reimers, *Skola I normer* [School in norms] (2nd edn), Malmö: Gleerups, pp 111–50.

Martinsson, L. (2016) *Den aktivistiska företagaren* [*The activist entrepreneur*], Göteborg: Makadam bokförlag.

Mattsson, K. (2001) *(O)likhetens geografier* [*Spaces of (dis)similarity*], Uppsala: Uppsala universitet.

Mattsson, K. (2010) 'Genus och vithet i den intersektionella vändningen' [Gender and whiteness in the intersectional turn], *Tidskrift för genusvetenskap*, 1–vol 2, pp 7–22.

Mouffe, C. (2005) *On the political*, London: Routledge.

Mulinari, D. and Nergaard, A. (2004) *Den nya svenska arbetarklassen* [*The new Swedish working-class*], Umeå: Borea.

Probyn, E. (2010) 'Writing shame', in M. Gregg and G.J. Seigworth (eds) *The affect theory reader*, London: Duke University Press, pp 71–90.

Reimers, E. (2014) 'Asexuell heteronormativitet' [A-sexual heteronormativity], in L. Martinsson and E. Reimers (eds) *Skola i normer* [*School in norms*] (2nd edn), Malmö: Gleerups.

Rönnblom, M. (2011) 'Vad är problemet?' [What is the problem?], *Tidskrift för genusvetenskap*, vol 2–3, pp 33–5.

Spindler, F. (2013) *Deleuze*, Göteborg: Glänta production.

Stryker, S. (2013) 'Trans-health is queer (and queer health isn't normal)', *lambda nordica*, vol 3–4, pp 147–65.

Svensson, E.-M., Andersson, U., Braekhus, H. et al (2011) *På Vei: Kjönn og Rett i Norden* [*On the way: Gender and justice in the Nordic countries*], Göteborg: Makadam.

Tesfahuney, M. (1998) *Imag(in)ing the other(s)*, Uppsala: Uppsala University.

Tollin, K. (2011) *Sida vid sida* [*Side by side*], Stockholm: Atlas.

Trinh, T.M. (1989) *Women native other*, Bloomington: Indiana University Press.

Trinh, T.M. (2011) *Elsewhere within here*, New York: Routledge.

Wasshede, C. (2010) *Passionerad politik* [*Passionate politics*], Malmö: Bokbox.

Wottle, M. and Blomberg, E. (2011) 'Feminism och jämställdhet i en nyliberal context 1900–2010' [Feminism and gender equality in a neoliberal context, 1900–2010], *Tidskrift för genusvetenskap*, vol 2–3, pp 97–116.

Afterword: rethinking gender equality

Lena Martinsson, Gabriele Griffin, Katarina Giritli Nygren

> Stories matter. Many stories matter. Stories have been used to dispossess and to malign. But stories can also be used to empower, and to humanize. Stories can break the dignity of a people. But stories can also repair that broken dignity. /.../. When we reject the single story, when we realize that there is never a single story about any place, we regain a kind of paradise. (Adichie, 2009)

In her lecture 'The danger of a single story', author Chimamanda Ngozi Adichie discusses how there is always more to discover and understand about the world than what one single story can tell. The hegemonic position of the mantra of Swedish gender equality has contributed to the reproduction of a single story, so unitary that it has been talked about as an axiomatic example of what to strive for in inter/national equality politics and policies. That hegemonic gender-equality model makes it difficult to tell other stories, to live other kinds of lives and for other kinds of societies to be created (Butler, 2004).

In order to rethink gender equality it is necessary to challenge its modernist, nationalistic and postcolonial content, which have made it into a single story. Even if we have to abandon this idea of a national and at the same time universal model of gender equality, we do not have to give up our commitment to the many political projects of equalities that there are. On the contrary, we need a plurality of such political projects (Mouffe, 2005). To rethink gender equality, we have, in this volume, examined how it is (re)emerging in different and frequently problematic ways, and that there are many different simultaneous struggles for equality inter/nationally. The goal for these different struggles cannot be to find consensus or create a new single story. Rather, rethinking gender equality means entering an arena of political contestations, different models of equality, movements, spaces and actions. How to do that, how to recognise equality as a field of political contestations, is not an easy issue. The contributors to this book have pointed to some spaces for activists, feminist and other critical scholars, where controversies and contestations could, should and are already taking place. In the following we will summarise the most important strategies for future transformative actions that emerge from these.

To politicise but also challenge the gender-equality norm

There are multiple ways in which the struggle for gender equality, or any equality, could be understood, framed and performed (Mouffe, 2005). Gender equality as a national trait not only makes gender equality something 'Swedes' all seem to agree on, but turns it into a phenomenon that is supposed to represent all people living in Sweden. It thus conceals how it iterates and produces a dual-gender heteronormativity that makes those who live in line with this normativity more at home than the others. It also conceals the cultural racism that follows from the gender-equality norm, in which 'Swedes' as a group are considered more gender equal than others, who are less modern and less developed. The nationalistic norm that is said to represent everyone excludes many inside its frame (Trinh, 2011).

Our first suggestion for rethinking the gender-equality model is therefore to politicise it, or, rather, to recognise it as a political issue. Constructing gender equality as a neoliberal business, a typically Swedish phenomenon, a heterosexual binary gender issue, is performative and political. Contemporary narratives about Swedish gender equality produce and normalise some identities and social groupings while making others less possible. This is not a natural or neutral process, it is not a simple question of organisation, or about attitudes or misunderstandings. It is a question of hegemonising the practices associated with a specific model. Putting homogenising and hegemonising practices under pressure is one way to contribute to the emergence and imaginations of other kinds of thinking about equalities and other futures.

Intersectional awareness

In this volume we have asserted that the Swedish gender-equality model is not only unsuccessful when it comes to representing different relations of power between different women. It is also invested in producing differences through normalising the white, able-bodied heterosexual woman as the subject for gender-equality struggle. Another problem is that the focus in the Swedish debate and politics on gender equality and issues around gender equality has created a gap between different kinds of oppression and exclusion. While gender equality is highly institutionalised, work against other oppressive processes, such as anti-racism, lacks institutional support (de los Reyes, 2014). Gender equality is a norm that harbours many other norms regarding sexuality, whiteness, able-bodiedness and so on. It is therefore necessary to challenge this assemblage of norms through intersectional analyses that destabilise the hegemonic model of gender equality. This is of decisive importance for making other critical political interventions as well as other stories possible.

Don't be nostalgic: on temporality and economic subjectivity

Gender equalities emerge in different ways in different economic co-articulations. In this volume we have discussed how neoliberal interventions have co-opted the previous, social democratic gender-equality model. If the social democratic welfare state was built on modernist, linear rational processes that tended to depoliticise gender equality, neoliberal normativity has been another force for depoliticising the work for gender equality, suggesting that the market could solve the problem of inequalities. However, neither the social democratic model nor current neoliberal reality has succeeded in embracing the many different processes and struggles examined in this volume.

As we have argued, there is a need to challenge the naturalised single stories of economics and ask what these stories do for how it is possible to understand the struggle for change and for possible fantasies of the future (Laclau and Mouffe, 1985). In order to hope for new stories to be told and to understand the contingency of the gender-equality model, it is also important not to be nostalgic, not to look back to the old welfare society as a model that it might be possible to recreate. To have fantasies, visions and imaginaries about other economic futures is important when segregation and deepened class divides have become an effect of neoliberal politics. It is an ongoing struggle where there is a need for different fantasies and visions, and a need for places for these visions to develop and be enacted.

Undermining the notion of gender equality as a national trait

The most problematical area of Swedish gender equality today is that of gender equality as a national trait. If you are identified as a secular Swede and racialised as white, you are supposed to be gender equal, or at least more gender equal than others. As we have shown in this volume, the co-articulation of the nation and gender equality exemplifies that cultural racism does not only exist in the margins, nor is cultural racism specific to extremist right-wing parties. Cultural racism is (re)produced through the gender-equality norm and the way it is considered to be part of the 'Swedish core'. We therefore argue that it is necessary to challenge and deconstruct the merging of the notion of nation and gender equality.

To destabilise the Swedish gender-equality model, to show its problematic iterations and start working in an intersectional way, is not only important, it is absolutely necessary. This also means that it is necessary to undermine the story of gender equality as a product with Swedish origins. We need ways to understand these struggles as challenges that transcend nationalities and national identities. The struggle for various forms of equality must be recognised as a global product, performed by activists and others around the world. These struggles belong to no one as well as to everyone. Nationalising them is a way of delimiting that global significance, and of producing national imaginaries and identities.

On a certain level this means that it is necessary to think differently about space, and about politicised space. At present, multiple gender equalities coexist, some serving fascist or culturally racist parties, and others serving feminists and those striving for non-hierarchised and non-exclusionary forms of equality. The latter are not immune to contestation. There are spaces, circles or digital rooms where hegemonic understandings of feminism and gender equality are being challenged. To recognise these, while at the same time challenging the idea that there is a single way of doing 'gender equality' is another way to undermine the story of Swedish exceptionalism. And, as Diana Mulinari, a Swedish feminist with a migrant background who has changed the gender debate within Sweden, writes at the end of her chapter in this volume:

> Inspired by Latin American feminists, we will go for more (*vamos por mas*). From the location of our migrant communities attacked by these racist parties, from the location of those living clandestinely in the shadows of Fortress Europe, debates about gender equality must be radically transformed to name, include and even depart from our (without quotations marks) understanding of social justice. We want bread, but roses too.

References

Adichie, C.N. (2009) 'The danger of a single story', TED talk, http://www.ted.com/talks/chimamanda_adichie_the_danger_of_a_single_story?language=en (accessed 30 May 2015).

Butler, J. (2004) *Undoing gender*, New York: Routledge.

de los Reyes, P. (2014) 'Introduktion: inte bara jämställdhet' [Introduction: not gender equality only], in P. de los Reyes (ed) *Inte bara jämställdhet. Intersektionella perspektiv på hinder och möjligheter i arbetslivet* [*Not gender equality only. Intersectional perspectives in working life*], Stockholm: Fritzes förlag, pp 9–27.

Laclau, E. and Mouffe, C. (1985) *Hegemony and socialist strategy*, London: Verso.

Mouffe, C. (2005) *On the political*, London: Routledge.

Trinh, T.M. (2011) *Elsewhere within here*, New York: Routledge.

Index

Note: Page numbers in *italics* indicate tables. Page numbers followed by *n* refer to footnotes.